BEDAZZLED:

STEPHENIE MEYER
AND
THE
TWILIGHT
PHENOMENON

BEDAZZLED:

STEPHENIE MEYER AND THE TWILIGHT PHENOMENON

by

George Beahm

Underwood Books
Nevada City, California

Cover by Arnie Fenner/Spectrum Design

Book design by Flights of Imagination

PUBLISHED BY UNDERWOOD BOOKS (www.underwoodbooks.com)

ISBN softcover: 978-1-59929-041-6
ISBN hardcover: 978-1-59929-042-3

First edition: November 2009

This one is for Miles Ruby and her three dazzling daughters:
Lauren, Claire, and Grace.

CONTENTS

PART 1:
THE REAL WORLD OF STEPHENIE MEYER

PART 2:
THE UNREAL WORLD OF
TWILIGHT FICTION

PART 3: FANPIRE
TWILIGHT FANDOM

PART 4:
THE SILVER SCREAM

Twilight: the Movie

The Twilight Saga: *New Moon* movie

PART 5:
RESOURCES

The Seattle skyline as seen from a Kenmore Air flight.

Flanking the road on part of the drive on U.S. 101 from Port Angeles to Forks, Lake Crescent offers numerous scenic views.

PART 1:

THE REAL WORLD
OF
STEPHENIE MEYER

A NOTE TO THE READER

The Twilight franchise belongs to Stephenie Meyer, but the Twilight phenomenon belongs to the fans who started it by word of mouth recommendations, blogs, fan postings on message boards, fan fiction, websites, and conventions.

This book is a celebration of the Twilight phenomenon and Stephenie Meyer.

Specifically written for a general audience, for tweens to grandmothers, this book explores every aspect of the Twilight universe and presents a wealth of information for every fan.

A love story for women of all ages, the Twilight Saga has struck a responsive, universal chord among its readers who have eagerly devoured 70 million copies worldwide of the four books in the series.

For those who want to know more about Twilight creator Stephenie Meyer, the books, and their film adaptations, this book provides information that the reader can sink her teeth into: take small bites, though, as this book was intended to be read at a leisurely pace, preferably by the dying light of the setting sun, the onset of twilight, the coming of a new moon, or the breaking dawn.

Stephenie Meyer: By the Numbers

Four books: *Twilight, New Moon, Eclipse, Breaking Dawn*
$383 million worldwide gross for the *Twilight* film
16 Twilight conventions by Creation in 2010
8,996,200 DVDs of *Twilight*
39 foreign languages
70 million books
from one
writer

Chronology

1973
December 24: Stephenie Morgan born (Hartford, CT), the second of six children to Stephen and Candy.

1978
Morgan family moves to Arizona.

1992
Stephenie Morgan awarded a National Merit Scholarship. Graduates from high school (Chaparral High School, Scottsdale, AZ).

1993
Began dating Christiaan "Pancho" Meyer, who proposes nine months after their first date.

1994
Stephenie Morgan marries Christiaan Meyer.

1997
Stephenie Meyer graduates from BYU (Brigham Young University in Provo, UT) with a B.A. degree in English Literature.

2003
June 2: Inspired by a dream about a mortal girl and an immortal vampire in a meadow, she begins writing *Forks*. **September**: Submits *Forks* (working title) to literary agents and signs on with Writers House. Sells *Forks* and two sequels for six figures. The book is retitled *Twilight*.

2004
Twilight optioned as a movie for MTV and Maverick Films.

2005
October 5: *Twilight* is published in trade hardback by Little, Brown and Company under its Megan Tingley Books imprint, in a print run of 75,000 copies. Meyer designated as one of the "most promising new authors" of the year by *Publishers Weekly*.

2006

May 31: *New Moon* is published in trade hardback in a first printing of 100,000 copies. **September 30**: Meyer is a guest at the National Book Festival.

2007

April: Film option with MTV lapses. Summit picks up the option. Publishes short story, "Hell on Earth," in *Prom Nights from Hell*. **May 5**: Meyer hosts prom at Arizona State University. **August**: *Eclipse* is published in trade hardback with a first printing of one million copies.

2008

May: *The Host*, bought for six figures, is published in trade hardback in a first printing of 500,000 copies. **August**: *Breaking Dawn* is published in trade hardback in a print run of 3.2 million copies. First midnight book party held for *Breaking Dawn*. Goes on Concert Series Tour with Justin Furstenfeld (of Blue October). Posts notice on her website about the unauthorized release of *Midnight Sun* on the Internet. **November 21**: *Twilight* released as a major motion picture, directed by Catherine Hardwicke, from Summit Entertainment. **August**: *Midnight Sun*, a retelling of *Twilight* from Edward Cullen's perspective, is posted on the Internet and goes viral; Meyer self-publishes the work-in-progress as an e-book on her website.

2009

September 22: *The Host* is optioned by producers Nick Wechsler, and Steve and Paula Mae Schwartz, with Andrew Niccol to write the screenplay and direct. (No release date has been announced.) **November 20**: *New Moon* released as a major motion picture, directed by Chris Weitz.

2010

June 30: *Eclipse* to be released as a major motion picture, directed by David Slade.

Edward Cullen watches Stephenie Meyer write.

Charmed
by Megan Irwin

Written by an Arizona newspaper reporter, this profile/interview with Stephenie Meyer was conducted in May 2007, three months before Eclipse *went to press with a run of one million copies. Her previous book,* New Moon, *had a first printing of 100,000 copies.*

✳

Outside the entrance of ASU's old gym on a warm Saturday in May, hundreds of teenage girls stand in full prom get-ups, chattering, shrieking, and hugging in the way only adolescent girls should. It's a windy day and the girls fidget with their hair and poofy dresses while they wait for the doors to open. They are nervous and excited. Inside the gym, black and red crepe paper streamers and homemade centerpieces try to hide the fact that this is a room made for sports, not fancy dresses.

When the doors finally open, the girls stream in quickly, stampeding for the food and a place to stand near a stage set up on the far side of the gym. Their nervous energy finally has a place to go.

The scene is like every awkward school dance you ever went to, except for a few key things: It's the middle of the day. At this prom, the bored wallflowers are parents. There are almost no boys here. And it's not boys (not real ones, anyway) or first kisses or even dancing that have brought hundreds of girls to this prom.

It's a book. Or rather, an author: Stephenie Meyer, who, in the past two years, has caused an international sensation with her young adult vampire series Twilight.

The prom is actually a publicity event to celebrate a special edition of her second release, *New Moon,* and get readers hyped for *Eclipse,* the third book in her series.

The event, put on personally by Meyer with help from Tempe's Changing Hands Bookstore and ASU's English department, sold out in seven hours. It sold out so fast that Meyer decided to do two proms in one day. Tickets for the second one were gone in four hours.

Meyer sold out the ASU gym faster than presidential candidate Barack Obama filled the Orpheum Theater last fall. And though tickets for Meyer's event were only $8 (compared with $30 for Obama), all the girls here have purchased her books, which retail for $18.

The buzz today is that she's going to read the first chapter of *Eclipse*, which won't be released until late summer.

The Arcade Fire pumps through the loudspeakers in the gym as the girls shove around the stage. After what seems like forever to the fans, Meyer emerges in an enormous red dress and glides toward the podium.

With her dark hair and pale skin, she could almost fit in with the fictional bloodsuckers she's invented.

The crowd goes wild with an adolescent roar as soon as they see her. She looks out at her fans. She looks down at her paper.

"I'm a little nervous," she tells the prom. The resulting screams almost drown her out.

She shouldn't be worried.

Meyer's books have sold a combined million copies and both have topped the *New York Times* bestseller list for young adult fiction. *Publishers Weekly* named *Twilight* one of the best books of the year.

Amazon.com called it one of the best books of the decade. It's been translated into 20 languages, and there's talk of turning it into a movie.

It's not just the publishing industry that loves her. Her fans are rabidly loyal. Harry Potter loyal.

In fact, when the Harry Potter series wraps up this summer, industry insiders think Meyer and her vampires might just be poised as the Next Big Thing. Meyer's characters Edward Cullen and Bella Swan are positioned to become household names—teenagers across the globe already know them on a first name basis, the same way they know Harry, Hermione and Ron.

Though J.K. Rowling is still the best-known young adult writer in the world, Meyer is closing in on the title.

Not bad considering that four summers ago, she was a stay-at-home Mormon mom with three young sons and no connection to hordes of teenage girls. Four summers ago, she'd never written anything more than what she calls "really bad" poetry, and that was in college.

Yet at the prom, she will sign more than 1,000 books. And a few weeks later, she will tour Europe, visiting Spain and Italy, where hundreds of fans will travel hundreds of miles just to see her.

Meyer can't quite make sense of the past few years of her life.

"It's surreal," she says. "It's hard to think about."

June 2, 2003, should have been a normal day for Meyer. It was the first day of swim lessons for her kids. It was the first day of her new diet, a time to lose the weight that comes with having two babies nearly back-to-back. When she climbed into bed the night before, she certainly didn't have any reason to think her life was going to change overnight.

But it did. Around four in the morning, she woke up from an extremely vivid dream.

"It was very clear. I was an observer. When I woke up, I sat there with my eyes closed, thinking about it," she says. "It was like reading a great book when you don't want to put it down; you want to know what happens next. So, I just laid there imagining."

With three kids, she couldn't lie in bed imagining all day so she decided to write her dream down.

By breakfast, she was at the computer, where she typed the first line: "In the sunlight, he was shocking." It's now the first sentence of Chapter 13 in *Twilight*. Reluctantly, she got up to take her kids to the pool.

"The whole time, my mind was just churning," she says. "It was a really sleep-deprived summer, but one of the best of my life."

When she came home from swimming, she made lunch and kept writing. By the end of the day, she'd completed 10 pages. From that day forward, she wasn't able to stop.

The Meyers were coming off a depressing year. While she was pregnant with her youngest son, Eli, she'd fallen over— "I was *really* pregnant," she says—and broken her arm badly. Five weeks later, her husband, Pancho, was diagnosed with Crohn's disease.

"It wasn't a great time in my life. I'd put on so much weight with the two babies. My 30th birthday was coming up and I was so not ready to face being 30," she says. "I didn't feel I had much going for me. I had my kids, but there wasn't much I was doing."

Meyer needed a creative outlet. She'd painted in college, but with the kids, it was too hard, and the scrapbooking parties she went to with friends from church were fun but not exactly fulfilling

"When I switched to writing, it was a much fuller outlet for me," she says. "There was a whole lot of pleasure in that first writing experience. It felt like a dam bursting, there was so much that I couldn't get out, and then I could."

She's not the first writer to turn a dream into a novel and find success on her first try. Mary Shelley is rumored to have dreamed about *Frankenstein* before she wrote it. But the pace of Meyer's writing that summer and the wild success that followed are rare.

She didn't tell anyone what she was doing. She dropped out of her scrapbook club and didn't even go to the movies because the thought of three hours away from the computer was unbearable.

"I lost a lot of friends that summer," she says, laughing.

She didn't even tell her husband, though he'd started to wonder what she was up to.

"I was really protective and shy about it because it's a vampire romance. It's still embarrassing to say those words—it sounds so cheesy," she says. "It's not like I was going to tell him that I was writing this story about vampires, because he was just going to be even more perturbed."

Their marriage didn't exactly suffer, but they did get in little arguments.

"We're not either of us very docile people," she says. "We argue all the time because that's our personalities. We didn't get in mean arguments, but I'm sure we argued over it because we argue about everything—we argue about milk."

These days, Pancho is happy to play the proud husband. Because of his wife's success, he was able to go back to school to become an accountant, and while he was a little frustrated in the beginning, he beams when he talks about her.

"It's fun to watch," he says. "Before she wrote an international bestseller, she was just a creative and intelligent woman. She's extremely blessed."

The person who finally got the secret out of her was her big sister, Emily Rasmussen. The two have been extremely close since childhood, so when Meyer dropped off the face of the Earth, forgetting to make or return phone calls and ignoring e-mails, Rasmussen got worried.

"It was abnormal that she wasn't talking to me," says Rasmussen, who lives in Utah with her husband and daughter. "I called her and said, 'What's going on? Why aren't you calling me anymore?'"

Meyer took a deep breath and blurted it out.

"I don't keep secrets from Emily," she says. "I thought she'd laugh, but it turns out she's a big Buffy fan, which I didn't know. She wanted to see it, and, on the one hand, I was very shy about it, but on the other hand, I was in love with it, so I wanted her to see it."

Meyer e-mailed Rasmussen a couple of chapters. As the story took shape, Meyer's sister read, and loved, every word.

"I would call and hound her, and I was always there bugging her," she says. "I've read *Twilight* I don't know how many times."

Within three months, the book was done. That's a quick turnaround for a book almost 500 pages long, but Meyer couldn't stop herself.

"Obsession covers it pretty well," she says, describing her writing methodology.

By the time Meyer finished the first book, her sister persuaded her to try to publish it.

She sent out queries to agents, not expecting much.

A month later, she got a call from New York agent Jodi Reamer, who had fallen in love with the story and wanted to represent Meyer. Reamer sent the book to nine editors, expecting a long wait.

But one week later, Meyer got another call. Megan Tingley, a top editor at Little, Brown and Company, read the book on an airplane and wanted to sign Meyer in a preemptive $300,000 three-book deal. Reamer turned it down and asked for a million.

"I almost threw up," says Meyer.

The publisher's counteroffer was $750,000, the largest amount of money it had ever offered a first-time author.

"That was the most surreal day. Eli was with me, so he was thinking Mommy lost her mind for a little while," she says of her youngest child, then 1. "I was on the phone with Jodi trying to be all professional, 'Yes, I'd love that. That's great,' and then I called my sister and I could hardly talk. Eli was following me around on his play phone going, 'Hahahahaha,' imitating me."

Tingley was behind Meyer 100 percent from the start.

"It was the combination of desire and danger that drew me in. I could not put it down and I could not wait for the plane to land, so I could sign up the book," she says. "On a gut level, I knew I had a bestseller on my hands when I was halfway through the manuscript."

While Meyer worked on the sequel, Little, Brown was gearing up for a publicity blitz. The unusual circumstances surrounding her deal—unknown writer gets three quarters of a million dollars—were enough to generate a significant buzz among publishing insiders, and Little, Brown was anticipating a huge reader response as well.

"Stephenie's fans are rabid," says Tingley. "Stephenie has tapped into something very deep in her readers, and they respond on an emotional level. She really understands the hopes and fears of teenage girls."

Tingley was on to something, and today, a million teenagers around the world have devoured Meyer's story.

On the surface, the books may sound cheesy—her word—and as she says, vampire romance is a bit overdone. But the characters she's created resonate, especially with teenagers. The story centers on a 17-year-old girl, Bella Swan, who is uprooted from her home in Phoenix to live with her dad in the small town of Forks, Washington.

Though Bella is clumsy and shy, she quickly grabs the attention of Edward Cullen, a mysterious boy at her high school. The two fall for each other in that head-over-heels way that's believable only when you're a teenager.

Of course, the fact that Edward has a strong urge to kill his girlfriend and suck her blood complicates things. His conflicted nature and constant struggle are part of what pushes the series forward.

"There's something about overcoming the natural man," Meyer says. "Having free agency to decide what you're going to do with yourself is a gift. I think kids pick up on that—it doesn't matter if you're a vampire. You can choose what to do with your life. Conflicted heroes are the best kind. Edward really has to fight."

It's Meyer's characters, and their struggles, that fans have gone crazy over. Collette Morgan, owner of Wild Rumpus, a children's bookstore in Minneapolis that's hosted Meyer on previous tours, says teenagers related instantly to the characters in the story.

When *Twilight* came out, Morgan's book club, "We Know What You're Publishing and Here's What We Think of It," (they read only advance copies of books) was one of the first groups of teenagers to read the book.

"I was blown away by the reaction of these kids," she says. "They were so taken with that story. She makes the characters so believable you want to meet them. You want Edward to be at your school."

The characters become more developed, more real, in the second book as the story gets more complicated. Edward and Bella face a series of problems, including one in which Bella's best friend, Jacob Black, a Quileute Indian living on the La Push reservation, turns out to be a werewolf, part of a pack that is supposed to protect the area from vampires.

Part of what makes the story so compelling is that Meyer's vampires and other monsters play by their own rules.

The central vampire characters, the Cullen family (they run around as a clan —three other couples plus Edward), are "vegetarians," meaning they feed on large animals instead of humans. Other vampires in the story feed on humans —there's one particularly gruesome scene in the second novel—but Edward and his family have taken an oath not to.

Meyer's vampires don't turn into bats or sleep in coffins. They don't have fangs, and they can even go out during the day, though they prefer darkness because they are simply too beautiful in the sunlight.

Essentially, she has created an entirely new vampire myth.

"I haven't even seen *Interview With the Vampire.* I change the channel really fast when horror movies come on," she says. "I know the [traditional vampire] stories because everyone does, so I knew I was breaking the rules, but I didn't really think about it much until I started worrying. But vampire fans have been very open-minded."

Jana Reiss, religion editor at *Publishers Weekly* and author of *What Would Buffy Do? The Slayer as a Spiritual Guide*, says Meyer's vamps are a welcome change.

"I have yet to talk to anyone who is upset by it," she says. "I think most people are looking for innovative takes. Meyer really taps into that."

Though adults do relate to Meyer's books, once they give them a chance, it's teen girls who really go crazy for them. Kaitlan Harris runs a Twilight fan page on MySpace. The 18-year-old from Georgia started the page in 2006, two days after she finished the book.

"I loved the way I couldn't stop thinking about what was going to happen to Bella. I never read anything before that has left me wanting more. I always just put it on the shelf and that's it," she says. "But I can't help but look at the book and remember all the emotions I felt [reading]. I felt like I was living the story, and that has never happened to me."

Bree Painter, a teenager from San Diego, agrees that the books and the characters feel real.

"It's the way the story is written," she says. "Stephenie writes in a way that makes the entire thing completely believable, like I could have an Edward Cullen living right next door."

Faith Hochhalter, buyer of young-adult books for Changing Hands in Tempe, agrees that Meyer's fans have a dedication rarely seen among young adult readers, and it has as much to do with Meyer's personality as it does the story.

Changing Hands is the official outlet for signed copies of Meyer's books, and Hochhalter says that even three years after the original release, orders are still pouring in at the rate of 12 a day, from places as far away as Croatia.

"Her fans are so loyal. I feel at this point, Stephenie could rewrite the phone book and her fans would still buy it," she says. "She's so giving and warm and her fans see that and relate to it, even if they don't know that's what they're relating to. Aside from J.K. Rowling, I've never seen anything on this scale."

Meyer's fandom is reminiscent of Harry Potter mania, crazy fan sites and all. The biggest fan site, Twilight Lexicon, is run by fans who seem to do little else but talk about Meyer and her books.

The Web site's features range from detailed timelines to character outlines to fan fiction to a question-and-answer section where readers ask things like "Can vampires have sex?" (they can, but Meyer won't give specifics) to details about the Cullens' personal history.

The Lexicon group seems to know Meyer's books almost better than she does.

"The Lexicon scares me sometimes," she says. She worries that once things are explained on the Lexicon, they become fact in the Twilight universe. For example, she's explained the backstory for each of the vampire characters on the Lexicon, so now she can't change it in her books without dealing with thousands of disgruntled fans.

But she still answers their questions.

The fact that she'll go on a fan site at all speaks volumes about Meyer and is, perhaps, why her fans get so hysterical when they see her. Meyer says it's not unusual for little girls to shake and stutter when they meet her.

"It's almost rock-star status," says Hochhalter. "I want to start calling her fans Steph-Heads. She has people who go to every book signing."

Libby Scott, a teenager from New Brunswick, Canada, has followed Meyer all over North America. Scott has been to Utah, Washington, Tennessee, and Arizona to meet up with her favorite author. She remembers shaking and stuttering the first time she met Meyer.

"I couldn't even get coherent words out," she says. "She hugged me, and I was, like, 'Oh, my gosh! Stephenie Meyer is hugging me,'" she says.

Scott got *Twilight* as a gift from her mother in 2005 and has been hooked since she read the first page.

"I just obsessed. For a couple of months, that was all I wanted to read," she says. "I liked it because it wasn't stereotypical. The relationship wasn't what you normally get in a teenage romance novel. The boy isn't perfect, and it brought you into this world where you think that this could really happen. I like that she wrote fantasy in such a real setting."

Her mom, Barbara, says the family has traveled more than 22,000 miles and spent more than $10,000 so that Scott can travel to signings. Meyer even came to Scott's birthday dinner in Nashville, bearing Twilight-themed gifts.

"Because of Stephenie, we've seen parts of the continent we wouldn't have thought to go to. I mean, I'd never seen the desert," Barbara says. "It's been quite an investment, but a good investment. We told Stephenie we'll follow her until the last book."

The Scotts aren't the only family who's gone crazy over Meyer's books. Her following is international.

Meyer's had to learn some hard lessons as a result of her massive popularity, and she's become a lot more guarded as her fame has increased.

Before the release of *New Moon*, a librarian leaked spoilers from her advance copy onto the Internet.

"It was two days of straight crying [after the spoilers were posted]. I wouldn't have minded if she went online and said she hated the book without posting the spoilers. That wouldn't have bothered me," she says. "But somebody linked to it, everyone read it, and then started e-mailing me. I couldn't defend myself, so I had six months of e-mails in all caps saying 'WHY WOULD YOU DO THIS TO ME?' It was like being attacked."

In addition to the spoilers, some people who had access to the galley started selling it on eBay. One copy sold for over $350. It's not the fact that her book is being sold illegally that upsets Meyer (though it certainly angered the publisher)—she's just worried that whoever bought it was getting ripped off.

"There's no way they're going to be happy with that purchase," she says.

With Eclipse coming out this summer, the publisher decided to be much more careful. Absolutely no advance copies were distributed. Still, Meyer ran into a problem.

She lent a copy to her sister-in-law, who then asked if her other sister could read it. Meyer said okay, but it soon was passed on to another sister who passed it on to a 14-year-old friend, who made a copy for her friends. And so on.

"My fans are extremely loyal, and one girl e-mailed me. I flipped out. I was horrified," she says. "I found out it was through my sister-in-law's copy, and I met with the girls. I told them I can't write with this kind of nightmare. I can't deal with the stress, so if you guys can't keep your mouths shut, I'll have to stop writing."

No one wants to be the girl who killed *Twilight*, so they've kept Meyer's secrets under wraps. Still, she didn't get as angry as other writers might. Showing a dazzling understanding of the teenage female psyche, she didn't just threaten them, she also made them a promise.

"I told them, if they don't talk, when *Eclipse* comes out, we'll have a party and I'll make them shirts that say 'I kept the Eclipse secret,'" she says.

Still, because of the leaks, she won't even let her kids read book four. She used to read them her books as bedtime stories, but she now worries they may start talking.

"I never thought about it before, because who listens to them? But Gabe knows them really well," she says. "And the last thing I need is him trying to impress some girl . . ." she trails off in horror.

Her youngest son, Eli, 5, chimes in.

"Eclipse is coming out!! But I don't know, I don't know what . . ." he says before his mom cuts him off.

"You can't talk about it, Eli," she reminds him.

"Um, I don't know what comes after *Breaking Dawn*," he finishes meekly.

Meyer pauses for a second, then hugs him and laughs: "I don't know either."

Watching her at home with her kids, it's easy to glimpse what life was like before she became a famous writer. Back when she was just Mom to Gabe, Seth, and Eli, now 10, 6 and 5. Back when she was just Sister Meyer to her friends in her ward, the word for congregation in the Mormon Church.

Big families are the norm in the LDS faith—Meyer has five brothers and sisters—but she's not planning on having more kids. She said she might adopt a girl in the future. It would be fun for her to have a little girl, but for now, she lets her fans act as surrogate daughters.

"It makes me want to adopt a teenage girl," she says. "It would be so nice to have a girly-girl around. Someone to go see *Waitress* with. It's nice because I get to have a million teenage daughters."

She was born in Connecticut, and her family moved to the Valley when she was 4. Her dad had a new job as a finance manager. Meyer had what she describes as a typical Mormon upbringing. There are six kids in her family—three girls, three boys—and Meyer is the second-oldest in an incredibly close family. The world has always been a crowded place for her, something that translates into her books. No character, except for Bella, is ever really alone.

"When you grow up in a big family, there's always someone to hang out with," she says. "I babysat my brothers and changed diapers. I used to have mom nightmares about my brothers—when you're a mom you have nightmares about terrible things happening to your kids and you can't stop them. I had those about my brothers."

Those maternal tendencies have carried over into her life with her three boys. Eli explains the way his family works:

"Gabe is the boss of us [Eli and Seth] and mom is the boss of us all," he says.

"Yep, I'm the boss of everything," she says.

"Uh huh. And of dad," Eli adds.

Though a lot has changed for her family since her career took off, she still manages to stay home with the kids. During the day, she works on editing her novels—a task she can leave to intervene in a snack-time crisis—and does her fresh writing at night after the kids are in bed.

When she's on the road, Pancho becomes Mr. Mom, balancing a tight schedule of getting the kids to and from school and getting himself to work. Luckily, Stephenie's parents are willing to help out, and she's in the process of hiring a personal assistant to help with the kids and some of the chores that come with fame (updating her MySpace page, for example.)

"The more I travel, the harder it gets," she says. "My kids are complacent. They make it easy, but I do feel bad. They play a lot of video games."

At that moment, the boys, tired of hiding in the guest room while a reporter bugs Mommy, come bursting into the room.

Seth is wearing a homemade superhero costume, from back when Meyer still had time to sew. He says he's "Animal Time," a hero he invented. As he jumps on the couch, he explains that he has all the powers of every animal in the world and can talk to them, too.

Eli brings out a book about cars and starts explaining that he likes Porsche the best. "I know every car in the whole world," he brags.

They don't seem very impressed that their mom is going to be in the newspaper.

"Gabe is old enough to remember before and after, and his teachers get excited and send books home to get signed, but he's very blasé about it at home," she says. "The two little ones don't know anything else, so they think everyone's mom is the same."

One thing that hasn't changed is Meyer's commitment to her Mormon faith.

"It's not a church that's low on time commitments," she says.

That means three hours of church on Sunday in addition to teaching a class for the 14- to 18-year-old kids in her ward.

On her Amazon.com profile, when asked for a list of influential books, she included the Book of Mormon.

Though she wasn't a writer until *Twilight*, Meyer says she was always a storyteller. The family took a lot of trips to Utah to visit her grandparents, and she used to tell herself stories to stay entertained.

After she graduated from Chaparral High School in Scottsdale, she went to college at Brigham Young University in Utah, majoring in English.

"I don't know if I ever considered anything else. That's what I love. I love reading, and this was a major I could read in," she says. "I figured I'd go on and go to law school, but I wasn't super-concerned with supporting myself because I wasn't thinking beyond being a student."

During the summer break before her senior year, she started dating Pancho. They'd known each other since they were kids at church but were never friends until that summer.

"It's funny, because in 20 years of knowing each other, we never had a conversation. But we got along so well," she says. "On our second official date was when he proposed. He proposed a lot. Over 40 times. He would propose every night and I would tell him no every night. It was kind of our end-of-date thing. Mormons get married a lot faster. The no-sex thing does speed up relationships."

Though she doesn't write overtly Mormon literature, her religious upbringing filters into her stories. She won't, for example, ever write graphic sex. And the theme of free will throughout her books draws from Mormon doctrine.

Still, she thinks people make a bigger deal out of her religion than they should.

"I think it's because Mormons are rarer in other parts of the world," she says. "But I get more of, 'What's a Mormon girl doing writing about vampires?' from the Mormon community than I do the outside. I was more worried about [friends at church] thinking I was doing something cheesy and lame."

Don Evans, spokesman for the Mormon Church in Phoenix, says the church has no position on Meyer's books.

"Her works should not be judged by her religious affiliation. She could be Catholic, Baptist, or atheist," he says. "It shouldn't matter."

He adds that his wife and daughter are both fans.

Meyer isn't the first Mormon writer to go mainstream with "edgy" material. Science fiction writer Orson Scott Card is another well-known Mormon who's vocal about his religion but has found success in both the secular world and among his faith. He's also one of Meyer's favorite authors.

Jana Reiss from *Publishers Weekly* says it's become a point of interest because Meyer isn't afraid to mention her faith.

"Why does this keep coming up? There are a couple of reasons," she says. "She brings it up. She outs herself as a Mormon writer in a way other writers don't. The other reason is Mormonism is an exoticized religious minority. We see it with Mormon politicians, too."

Meyer got to talk to Card when he called her to try to persuade her to shop a science fiction novel she's working on to his publisher. Card didn't seal the deal, but Meyer got some great advice.

"He said, as a prominent Mormon author, you're never going to please everybody. You're going to get people who will tell you your stories cross the line — how can you be a good Mormon and write this? Then there will be other people who will say that you're limiting your art because you're letting your religion control what you write," she says. "So far, I haven't gotten it bad from either."

She does remember one Mormon woman who reviewed Twilight and analyzed how it tied into the *Book of Mormon*. She was dead wrong on every tie-in, Meyer says, though there was one deliberate *Book of Mormon* reference, Meyer says, that the reviewer missed.

Growing up, Meyer's favorite Book of Mormon story was the one about the 2,000 stripling warriors, from the book of Alma. In the story, the parents of a small group of boys are under attack but have taken a blood oath never to fight again after their conversion to Christianity. They consider breaking the oath but are persuaded not to by a prophet. Their sons, who never took the oath, go to fight instead, and because of their faith, not a single one is harmed.

Meyer sees her werewolves as her stripling warriors.

"In the history of the Book of Mormon, they [the warriors] would have been dark-skinned, the ancestors of the Native Americans who are here now. So for me, the Quileute [tribesmen, the wolves in her books] are kind of these sons who have taken on the responsibility of taking care of their families."

She may write a Mormon novel someday, but for now, she's happy working with her vampires.

"I have a novel I started that would be a Mormon comedy romance," she says. "I do wonder what it would be like, because I have these girls who will read anything I write, so I know they'll read it, and I can't imagine what their reaction would be. And what parents will think about their kids reading stuff that has quite a lot of Mormon doctrine in it."

After *Eclipse* comes out August 7, there will be one book left in the series, then Meyer plans on doing a book [*Midnight Sun*] that retells *Twilight* from Edward's perspective. She's also gearing up for a 15-city tour behind *Eclipse*. In between, she's focusing on finishing her mainstream science fiction book, *The Host*, and has about 20 other story ideas in various stages of development, including one about cannibal mermaids.

Still, she's not the type to plan too far into the future.

"When the prom hadn't happened yet, I couldn't even think about (the trip to) Italy because there was nothing until prom was done. Now there's no life until I finish editing *The Host*," she says. "I just live from crisis to crisis."

Her current worry is that *Eclipse* comes out so close to the release of the final Harry Potter book. But if her previous success is any indication, she'll be fine. In June, she enjoyed a special honor: *Twilight* and *New Moon* both topped the *New York Times* bestseller list, one as a hardcover and one as a paperback, even after being on the market for so long.

That mark of success has a lot to do with how involved she stays with her readers. The *Eclipse* prom she hosted in May is a good example.

The idea actually sprang from fans in Pasadena, California, who came to a signing and told her that the next time Meyer came to town, they were going to wear prom dresses and have a party for one of the characters, just like the prom Edward and Bella go to at the end of Book One. Meyer and her publicist jumped on the idea.

The publisher turned the prom into a PR event for the release of the *New Moon* special edition and to promote the release of Book Three. But, in the end, it really was all about the fans. Fans formed the "prom committee," a group of girls (and grown women) from around the country who helped Meyer with decorations and logistics.

At the prom in May, Meyer signed more than 1,000 books and, by night-time, had a blister on her finger. The naturally shy woman still has a hard time believing that it is all for her. She still doesn't believe she's as famous as she is and scoffs at the idea that she's approaching J.K. Rowling status. She says she's been recognized only twice, once by another author and once by two girls at an OK Go concert.

"Writer fame is like 100 percent better than any other kind of fame," she says. "Unless I'm going to an event, no one will recognize me."

But in small groups of fans, she lights up, relishing the chance to be one of the girls. At an after-party for the prom, a group of about 30 girls, and a few boys, are gathered in their pajamas, playing Meyer-themed games like Twilight Cranium. They're divided into teams: humans, vampires, and werewolves. Excitement erupts when Meyer walks into the room in her PJs, her hair still done up for the prom.

Meyer plops down in a chair and is immediately surrounded by girls. She pulls one onto her lap while another plays with her hair.

Through the cheers, one fan whispers to a friend, "See, I *knew* she'd come."

Driving north-south on Route 101, entering Forks, Washington.

Frequently Asked Questions

Disclaimer: Obviously, I cannot and do not presume to speak for Stephenie Meyer, but since bestselling authors share similar concerns, the following addresses the most common questions they are asked.

✳

When will her next book be published?

When a new book is scheduled for publication, the publisher will post information on its web site. Meyer will then repost that information on her web site, which will then be picked up by fan websites. Additionally, the major online booksellers will post advance notification of books; just type in "Stephenie Meyer" and forthcoming books, along with previously published books, will be posted.

How can I get an ARC (advance reading copy)?

Because of concerns of inadvertent release of major plot points and story elements, the publisher no longer sends these out en masse to reviewers. As a rule, most readers will not be able to get an ARC because they are intended for review purposes to mainstream media, not for fans wanting an early look.

The reader's only hope in getting an ARC is to work at a bookstore when one shows up or buy one from a bookseller, usually online.

Where can I send a personal letter to Meyer?

Send fan mail in care of her publisher. Keep in mind that a personal response is unlikely, but rest assured she will receive it. Her publisher's address:

Stephenie Meyer c/o Author Mail
Little, Brown and Company
237 Park Avenue
New York NY 10017

How can I get her autograph?

The best way is at a public event. The second best way is to bid on an auction item for a charity that has personally arranged to get books/memorabilia signed. The third alternative is to bid on eBay, but given the lack of authentication and the possibility of forgeries, it's no guarantee that you are buying an authentic signature.

When will she be coming to my town?

Meyer's public appearances are determined by her publisher, which means big cities are more likely to be selected as tour destinations; that way, she can see as many people as possible. Though she does occasionally make local appearances to benefit charity projects (notably Book Babe in Phoenix, Arizona), those are rare.

Book tours are normally scheduled in conjunction with a new book release, so when a forthcoming book is announced, look for follow-up announcements on fan websites.

Can we be pen pals?

Unfortunately, this just isn't possible because the math works heavily against her: one reader and 70 million copies of her books in print means that there's far too many people who'd like to ask her questions than she'd have time to answer. Rightly so, she preserves her time, personally and professionally, for her family and her book projects. Otherwise, the books would never get written.

Even before she became famous, her writing time was restricted to brief snatches throughout the day but mostly at night after the kids were in bed.

Can she get me a part in one of her movies?

Meyer has nothing to do with the casting. That's the job of the casting director, who is looking for SAG (Screen Actor Guild) members for all the major roles. Being an extra in a movie, however, is a possibility; information can usually be found on fan websites, as soon as they get the word from the casting company.

Can she give me information about how to get published?

There's really no mystery, secret handshake, or buddy system that will help you get published. It's all to do with having a book you feel passionately about and worrying about publication afterward. Do your own homework; there's dozens of excellent books on this subject. As a writer, you are expected to do your own research, starting with how to get published. (See "So You Want to Be a Paperback Writer" starting on page 124.)

Can she recommend a literary agent?

There are several directories available in bookstores and libraries, which an aspiring writer should consult. Again, do your homework; Meyer (or any other author) can't do it for you.

Can she read my story and comment on it?

Unfortunately, no. In these litigious times, authors cannot read unpublished work because of plagiarism concerns. Currently fighting a lawsuit that Meyer's publishers have termed "completely without merit and simply a publicity stunt…", it simply underscores the point: bestselling authors are convenient targets for frivolous lawsuits and, therefore, must err on the side of caution especially when dealing with unpublished or little known authors who are quick to claim the theft of literary property. That some amateurs really think their ideas are so priceless that pros have to steal them strains credulity.

What is Meyer's e-mail address?

In the beginning of her career, Meyer naively posted her e-mail address (probably retired by now) on her website, on the grounds that she wanted to interact with fans and respond to their questions. In the beginning, that was possible, but it soon became obvious that the collective readership wrote more e-mails than she could possibly read or answer. So she deleted it from her website and probably changed it afterward to insure a semblance of privacy.

What is Meyer's home address?

Every author has to draw a line between public interaction and the need for privacy. They want to live as normal a life as possible and do not want unsolicited letters or packages sent to their personal residence. They especially don't want fans to show up at their doorstep, usually with books in hand and a request to get them signed. Stephen King, for instance, was constantly interrupted by tourists carrying bags of books for his signature; he was forced to put up a sign saying that he works at home and cannot be interrupted. Later, he was forced to put up a fence surrounding the property, complete with video cameras, to keep the fans at bay after a man came in through the kitchen window when he and his sons were out of town and his wife, home with the flu, was in her bath robe and saw a stranger with a cigar box bristling with wires that he claimed was a bomb.

Soon afterward, King duly employed enhanced security measures with great reluctance, but it was necessary to insure his family's safety and what little privacy he enjoys.

Like King, Stephenie Meyer is a bestselling author who, unfortunately, may have to deal with unwanted people drawn to her. This is why she, too, has to distance herself from the public, which she does reluctantly. It's a price one necessarily pays for fame and success.

Don't be surprised if Meyer moves her family into a gated community in Phoenix, since fan drive-bys on a regular basis are understandably unnerving. One can't help but wonder about their motives.

The Story of Stephenie Meyer and the "Book Babe"

"The plan was for me to go entirely hermit this year (or decade), but there are always
those things important enough to pull me out of my burrow."
from Stephenie Meyer's website (March 16, 2009)

✳

What could have turned out to be a horror story turned into a fairy tale with a happy ending, thanks principally to Stephenie Meyer.

It all began with faith in a book and ended with faith in people to benefit Faith Hochhalter, a book buyer at Changing Hands, an independent bookstore in Tempe, Arizona.

Meyer, a longtime local resident, had no plans to emerge from her self-imposed hermit status, but as she explained on her website in early 2009, "One of my dear friends and mentors, Faith Hochhalter—a truly gifted book buyer who put together some of my most successful events—was recently diagnosed with breast cancer. I am not the only author who was helped along by her talent and enthusiasm, and all of us who enjoyed her influence in our lives and careers are eager to help her through this rough time."

Hochhalter became an early cheerleader for Meyer when she received an advance reading copy of *Twilight* from its publisher, Little, Brown and Company. Hochhalter, informally known as the "Book Babe," devoured *Twilight* and became an early advocate. As Hochhalter told the local newspaper, the *Phoenix New Times*, "It was the first time since buying at Changing Hands that I read an ARC that I knew was going to be a huge hit."

As she told the local paper, she immediately requested more copies for pass-around, which found eager hands. Given that the book and its first-time author were unknown, Hochalter's handselling—a time-honored practice of independent booksellers—helped build excitement for the winsome author.

On October 5, 2005, *Twilight* was published as a trade hardback. Designed by Gail Doobinin, the dust jacket sported a symbolic cover: Kimbra Hickey's hands cup a red apple, redolent with religious, romantic and philosophical meanings. The cupped apple, an iconic symbol for the Twilight Saga, can frequently be found on homemade tee-shirts and posters.

In contrast to most first authors' book signings, Stephenie Meyer's was a resounding success that, by Hochhalter's estimate, drew eighty people (mostly females) anxious to meet a hometown girl who had made the giant leap from housewife to published author: an elusive dream shared by others in Meyer's writing group, none of whom had dreamed that within their midst was a born storyteller whose books heralded the arrival of a major new talent—the biggest since Joanne Rowling, stuck on a train, conjured up a young wizard named Harry Potter.

In the years that followed, as Changing Hands became known as *the* place to go for signed copies of Meyer's thick novels, Faith Hochhalter never flagged in her enthusiasm for the Twilight saga or its local author, who stopped by the bookstore on a regular basis.

In early 2009, after leaving Changing Hands and in between jobs, Hochhalter, who lacked medical insurance, discovered a lump in her breast that she rightly feared to be an early sign of breast cancer. Unfortunately, a diagnosis of breast cancer, a pre-existing condition, would make it all but impossible to get insurance, so Hochhalter had few options.

What she did have was a community of friends in the book community, especially local authors, who rallied around her just as she had rallied support for their fledgling books.

A website (http://projectbookbabe.com) quickly went up and authors signed up for a public event to raise money to help cover some of the medical expenses. From the website: "When the publishing community heard that the Book Babe had been diagnosed with breast cancer, the response to help her out was overwhelming. A collection of items to auction has been steadily growing. So far over 50 authors from the U.S. and Europe are contributing."

One of them, of course, was Stephenie Meyer, whose participation was crucial to the auction's success, scheduled for April 4, 2009, at a high school in Tempe, Arizona.

Revenue would be generated by the sale of tickets (from $25 to $300), books, and related memorabilia donated by authors.

Tickets quickly sold out. Twilighters came in from all over the U.S. not only to see Meyer at one of her increasingly rare public events but to bid on some of the treasures she had promised to bring for its live auction.

Daanon DeCock, an operation director for the event, recalled in an interview with Michael Jung, that "We had no idea the lengths Stephenie would go to. The manuscripts, the lunch, the epilogue—she was amazing."

As is often the case, when Meyer lends her support, it's wholehearted.

Shannon Hale and the Bunny Suit Scare

After a heartfelt statement read by Faith Hotchhalter, in which she gave thanks to all of those who had taken up her cause, YA (young adult) author Shannon Hale, serving as the emcee, took center stage and devilishly gave the assembled crowd a frisson of fright. "I'm really sorry about this," Hale said. "This was really unforeseeable, but Stephenie Meyer will not be appearing today..." as the crowd collectively gasped, "...*in her bunny suit*," added Hale.

The audience laughed in relief. The show would go on with its headliner, whose participation guaranteed the event would be successful.

In addition to signing 600 books, Meyer also signed 1000 event posters with all the guests' head shots.

Going, Going, Gone!

Predictably, the Twilighters opened their hearts and purse strings to make the event successful. The evening's event raised $28,900 toward medical treatment for Faith Hochchalter, while raising awareness of breast cancer. It also launched the Project Book Babe website that continues to raise money for worthy causes.

A red velvet prom dress, worn by Meyer in 2007 at a Prom for *New Moon*, proved to be a big ticket item. The bidding started at $500 and quickly escalated to $5,500. Not surprisingly, an ardent fan bought the dress—Alison Genet of Gilbert, Arizona; she's known by Twilighters for her website, www.Twifans.com.

Book memorabilia included an epilogue to *Forever Dawn* (*Twilight*'s original title) for $5,100; two manuscripts (*Eclipse*, $2,600; *The Host*, $1,200), an ARC of *Twilight* ($1,500), and a signed one-of-a-kind *The Host* skateboard ($1,500).

The most fevered bidding of the evening proved not to be for celebrity clothing or book-related artifacts but an experience: lunch with Stephenie Meyer. Two women fiercely bid it up to $6,000 and showed no signs of giving quarter, so Meyer wisely intervened and volunteered to host two separate lunches, each for $6,500, insuring both bidders went away happy.

The Book Babe's Blog

In a blog entry published July 17, 2009, the Book Babe writes that "I had my last chemo treatment on Wednesday. ...The chemo seems to be kicking my ass more than usual.... Now that I am done, other than the next three weeks of side effects, the rest of the year will be this: wisdom teeth extraction—all of them, due to chemo wreaking havoc and creating chaos; radiation every day for six weeks, starting sometime after the wisdom teeth thing; I get a blissful few weeks off to heal from radiation and then meet the surgeon to determine whether or not I have healed enough to start [breast] reconstruction.

"I have a question for any cancer survivors who read this: Does it ever get any easier? I keep thinking that dealing with all the blood draws, the needle sticks, the poking, the appointments, the medication, the nausea, the exhaustion, etc., will get easier. ... I am finally starting to feel like a human being after the last treatment."

Web resources

http://projectbookbabe.com
http://projectbookbabe.com/faith

The Compulsively Quotable
Stephenie Meyer

On her older fans at public events: "It's the 50-year-old women who are screaming the loudest!" (EW.com, "Stephenie Meyer: Inside the 'Twilight' Saga.")

On the intended audience for Twilight: "I wrote *Twilight* for me. It's exactly what I want to read, so I'm hooked on it." (MTV Movie News, Larry Carroll, November 14, 2008.)

On writing long books: "I tried once to write a short story, and it was horrible. I don't think in short terms; I have to explore every tiny detail of things." (MTV Movie News, Larry Carroll, November 14, 2008.)

On her being a vampire writer: "See, here's the thing: I'm not a vampire person. Before I started writing about them, I'd never seen a vampire movie. I'd seen pieces of them, but I'd never been to a vampire movie. I've never read a book about vampires. I'm really not into horror, so I don't know the genre." (Reelz Channel, Jeff Otto, not dated.)

On Robert Pattinson: "He's a very mesmerizing person to be around. He's got such a compelling personality. I don't think you'd want him for a boyfriend. And you couldn't just be his friend because he's terribly sexy!" (EW.com, Karen Valby, no given date.)

On Eclipse film director David Slade: "I am thrilled that David Slade will be directing *Eclipse*. He's a visionary filmmaker who has so much to offer this franchise. From the beginning, we've been blessed with wonderful directorial talent for the Twilight Saga, and I'm so happy that *Eclipse* will be carrying on with that tradition." (http://eclipse-movie-trailer.blogspot.com.)

On closure when finishing the series: "You know, it was funny because I was expecting this sense of closure when I finished the rough draft, and I was expecting it again when I finished my editing and I knew it was going to print. But it wasn't until the books were out on the shelves that it was done, and I had that sense of crossing the finish line, like 'I've done it! I've gotten it all done!'" (*Los Angeles Times*, "*Twilight* Countdown," November 17, 2008.)

On comparisons between her and J.K. Rowling: "We can compare a lake to an ocean: They are both filled with water, but they are not the same thing. I am a fan of her books. Even if mine are sold in a phenomenal way, there will not be another J.K. Rowling. Of course, I am flattered when it is mentioned, but that's it." (Translated from an interview published in ParisMatch.com.)

On the appeal of her books: "It's hard for me to answer that because for me it's an absolute mystery. I read a lot of books and some of them that I love are really popular and there are just others that I just think, 'Why isn't everybody in the world reading this book? It's so amazing.' So when one book takes off, it's 'Why? Why does it ever happen?' I don't know why people respond to these books the way they do." (About.com, Rebecca Murray, not dated.)

On her training as writer: "Reading was really my only training in fiction writing. I never took a class or read a book on how to write. I just absorbed the basics from reading thousands of other people's stories." (allthingsgirl. net, Deb Smouse, July-August 2009.)

On finding time to write: "The greatest challenge was finding time away from my already full life. I became somewhat of a hermit that summer, neglecting friends, family, and my normal hobbies. I'm still trying to find the right balance." (A blog by Cynthia Leitich Smith, March 27, 2006.)

On the importance of choice: "They ended up being vampires in the way they are because I have strong opinions on free will. No matter what position you're in, you always have a choice. So I had these characters who were in a position where traditionally they would have been the bad guys; but, instead, they chose to be something different—a theme that has always been important to me." (*School Library Journal*, Rick Margolis, October 1, 2005.)

On her "dream" cast for Twilight: "I have great hopes for *Twilight*, however, and I have certain actors who would be my first choices for certain roles, including Henry Cavill for Edward, Emily Browning for Bella, Charlie Hunnam for Carlisle, Rachel Leigh Cook for Alice, Graham Greene for Billy, Cillian Murphy for James, Daniel Cudmore for Emmett." ("Books for Adolescents," James Blasingame, from a talk Meyer gave at the Arizona State University on November 29, 2005.)

On her young teenage fans: "I have all these teenage adopted daughters. They're impossible not to adore." (*The Arizona Republic*, Jaimee Rose, November 21, 2008.)

On pleasing all her fans with *Breaking Dawn*: "There's no way to please everyone. The email messages I get say, 'If Bella doesn't end up with Edward forever, I'm going to burn this book,' and the next one I get will say, 'If Bella doesn't end up with Jacob forever, I'll burn this book.' So that's a problem, but this is the ending I wanted all along. That's the important thing. I think people will be happy, though." (*USA Today*, "Meyer unfazed as fame dawns," Carol Memmot, August 1, 2008.)

On her relative anonymity in high school: "I was practically Cousin Itt in high school. You know, hair in the face, hide from everyone." (*The Arizona Republic*, Jaimee Rose, November 9, 2007.)

On her writing vampire books: "It was a weird thing for me, because I don't read vampire books. I don't watch vampire movies. I'm not into the horror genre. I'm a wuss; I'm a scaredy cat." (*The Arizona Republic*, Geri Koeppel, May 8, 2007.)

On the importance of characters, not plots: "I don't write for plot. Plot happens around interesting characters. Some people are completely plot-specific, some people are all about the setting, some people use words like they're dancing. For me, it's always about the people and everything that's happening to them because of who they are, what's inside." (*Publishers Weekly*, Melissa Mia Hall, May 13, 2008.)

Question posed to her in an interview: *"We'd like to name a burger in your honor. What kind of fixings should it have?"* Stephenie Meyer's answer: "The 'Stephenie' should be the name for the plainest burger you have. I'm anti-condiments." (Bookburger blog, September 8, 2006).

On her involvement with the movies: "About 90% of my suggestions were taken in. They'd come to me to consider the actors. But I was open to their interpretation. (RTE Entertainment, December 12, 2008.)

When asked if there was ever an Edward in her life: "No, no, I wish. I've had very typical, normal, human relationships all my life." (*Newsweek*, Susan Elgin, July 26, 2008.)

On the writers she'd like to talk to: "I'd love to listen in on a panel discussion featuring Jane Austen, William Shakespeare, and Orson Scott Card." (Yabookscentral.com, December 2005.)

On her fear of facing her first large audience: "On that first tour, when I had to go to school events, I was throwing up before all of them. I was so scared—I was terrified of everything I had to do." (*Seattle Post Intelligencer*, Cecelia Goodnow, August 6, 2007.)

On her musical muses: "Actually, growing up, I didn't listen to a ton. My parents were pretty strict. I only discovered music as an inspiration later in life." (*Time*, "10 Questions for Stephenie Meyer," August 21, 2008.)

Describing herself in high school: "She was a quiet girl, kept to herself. We never would have suspected her of ____, and book-obsessed." (Squeetusblog, Shannon Hale, September 8, 2007.)

On her formidable success: "I am continually shocked by the success of my books. I never take it for granted, and I do not count on it in my expectations of my future. It's a very enjoyable thing, and I'll have fun with it while it lasts. I've always considered myself first and foremost a mother, so being a writer hasn't changed my life too much—except I do travel a lot more and have less free time." (Loveitlikeithateit.com, no date.)

On getting published: "I had the easiest publishing experience in the entire world. I sent out 15 query letters to agents. I got five 'no replies,' nine rejections, and one who wanted to see it. A month later I had agents. Another month and I had a deal with Little, Brown. And it does not happen that way. If you expect that going in, get ready for heartbreak." (morningsun.net, Ed Symkus, November 17, 2008.)

On her secrecy in not telling her husband that she was writing a novel: "I didn't tell him what I was doing. So he was mystified. And a little irritated that I was hogging the computer all the time. I had as hard a time telling him I was writing a story about vampires as Edward did telling Bella he was one." (Supplemental material on the Australian DVD of *Twilight*.)

On finding time to write as a full-time mom: "I lost sleep to write. I mean you had to give something up and I wasn't giving up my time with my kids and I couldn't give up the things I had to do, so it was sleep." (Collider.com, screen name Frosty, November 11, 2008.)

On her writing habits: "I mostly write at night, from eight p.m., when my kids go to bed, until whenever I'm close to passing out from exhaustion. I edit sometimes during the day, but the words never really flow the same when I'm being constantly interrupted." (www.darkhorizons, Paul Fischer, November 14, 2008.)

On the first *Charlie's Angels*-type screenplay before Summit entered the picture: "There was another script. They could have filmed it and not called it *Twilight* because it had nothing to do with the book, and that's kind of frightening. When Summit came into the picture, they were so open to letting us make rules for them, like 'Okay, Bella cannot be a track star. Bella cannot have a gun or night vision goggles. And no jet skis.'" (Media Blvd magazine, Christina Radish, September 17, 2008.)

On staying put in Phoenix, Arizona, after getting unwanted cell phone calls: "Numbers are easy to change. Moving is harder. They'll have to drag me out of this place on a plank. Before I move, I'm going to put up a fence and get shepherds. And then I'll have a button and get to say, 'Release the hounds!'" (EW.com, "Stephenie Meyer: Inside the 'Twilight' Saga, Karen Valby, November 21, 2008.)

On online criticism: "It's a bit hard for me: I'm very thin-skinned. I used to read all the reviews on Amazon.com. I could read 100 five-star glowing reviews and the one review that's one-star—'This is trash'—that's the one that sticks with me." (*Times Online*, Tony-Allen Mills, August 10, 2008.)

On her self-assessment as a writer: "I don't think I'm a writer; I think I'm a storyteller. The words aren't always perfect." (*Time* magazine, Lev Grossman, April 24, 2008.)

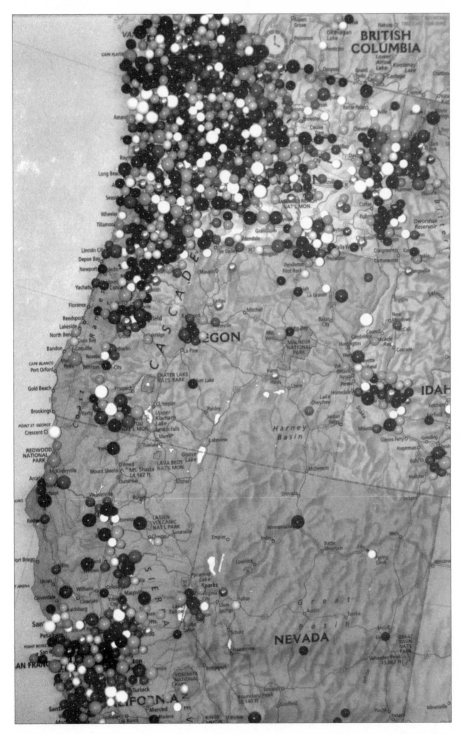

Pins posted on a wall map in the Visitor Information Center in Forks show various visitors' locales.

Stephenie Meyer
Recommends Books

Meyer recommended the following fourteen books, for which she provided anno-tations, on Amazon.com. Not surprisingly, the list includes classics of English and American literature, fantasy, mystery, and a detective book. Like most writers, she has eclectic tastes.

Pride and Prejudice by Jane Austen
Speaker for the Dead (Ender, Book 2) by Orson Scott Card
Rebecca by Daphne Du Maurier
The Complete Anne of Green Gables boxed set
The Glass Lake by Maeve Binchy
Romeo and Juliet (Folger Shakespeare Library)
Death on the Nile (a Hercule Poirot mystery) by Agatha Christie
A Company of Swans by Eva Ibbotson
Dragonflight by Anne McCaffrey
The Chronicles of Narnia boxed set
Jane Eyre by Charlotte Brontë
The Princess Bride by William Goldman
One for the Money by Janet Evanovich
To Kill a Mockingbird by Harper Lee

A Stephenie Meyer Concordance:
People, Places and Things

In news stories, profiles, and interviews, Meyer often alludes to the people, places, and important things in her life, which require some explanation.

For readers desiring more information, I have provided web addresses when available. (Surprisingly, some people you'd think would have websites do not, including Chris Weitz, David Slade, et al.)

*

Arizona, Phoenix. Stephenie Meyer's current home, where she lives with her family (husband Christiaan and three sons). "Phoenix is Arizona's capitol and the fifth largest city in the United States, with more than 1.5 million residents and growing. The city takes up more than 500 square miles, geographically exceeding Los Angeles." In Meyer's fiction, it's where Isabella (Bella) Swan called home, just before she reluctantly moved to Forks, Washington. As Bella explains in *Twilight* (chapter 1, page 4), "I loved Phoenix. I loved the sun and the blistering heat. I loved the vigorous, sprawling city." Rightly earning its nickname of "Valley of the Sun," Phoenix, notes Wikipedia, "has the hottest climate of any major city in the U.S. The average high temperatures are over 100 degrees Fahrenheit for three months out of the year, and have spiked over 120 degrees on occasion. ... With only 40 rainy days annually, it's the third-ranked sunniest places in the continental U.S., exceeded only by Yuma, Arizona, and Redding, California. (http://phoenix.gov)

Breaking Dawn. The fourth book in the Twilight saga, published in 2008, its first printing was 3.2 million copies in hardback.

Brigham Young University. Stephenie Meyer graduated in 1997 from this college that takes justifiable pride in being called by *The Princeton Review* "the country's most stone-cold sober university year after year." In other words, students go to BYU are not only serious about their studies but their religion, as well: 98% are members of the Church of Jesus Christ of Latter-day Saints. (One of Meyer's favorite authors, fantasist Orson Scott Card, is an alumnus (B.A. degree, 1975), cited as a "Trailblazer" by its alumni association. As Meyer pointed out in numerous interviews, in rankings of party colleges BYU is proudly and consistently dead last. (www.byu.edu)

Catherine Hardwicke. Film director of *Twilight*, she declined to helm *New Moon* because of scheduling and budgetary concerns. Best known for directing *Thirteen*, which featured Nikki Reed who played Rosalie in *Twilight*. (www.catherinehardwicke.com)

Changing Hands Bookstore. An independent bookstore in Tempe, Arizona, that championed Meyer's books early on, it became famous in the Twilight community for being *the* place to get signed copies of her books.

Chaparral High School. Stephenie Morgan graduated from here in 1991. Located in Scottsdale, Arizona, her experiences helped in writing about the school setting of Forks High School in the Twilight saga. (http://susd. schoolfusion.us)

Chris Weitz. Best known for directing Philip Pullman's *The Golden Compass*, he directed *New Moon*.

David Slade. The director of *Eclipse*, due out in June 2010.

Eclipse. The third of four books in the Twilight saga, published in 2007, its first printing was one million copies in hardback. (By this time, Meyer's literary career had reached critical mass, as the sales numbers of her books demonstrates.)

Elizabeth Eulberg. Formerly a publicist for Little, Brown, she was promoted to Director of Global Publicity for Stephenie Meyer, a full-time job tailor-made for her. Eulberg has fielded, by her count, up to 100 requests a week from the media for interviews and appearances.

Emily Rasmussen. Stephenie Meyer's older sister, who was the first reader of *Forks*. Encouraged by her sister, Stephenie completed the first draft of 130,000 words (498 pages). The dedication for *Twilight* reads: "For my big sister, Emily, without whose enthusiasm this story might still be unpublished." In 2004, Stephenie made her first trip to Forks, accompanied by her sister, then seven months pregnant.

Forks. The original title to the book that would be published in 2005 as *Twilight*. (*Forks* is a confusing book title. One had to wonder whether it is a book about "cullenary" delights?) Meyer wisely agreed with her agent that the original title, for which she still harbors a lingering fondness, needed to be changed for marketing reasons.

Forks, Washington. Its population is a little over 3,000 people. The principal setting for the Twilight saga, it was specifically chosen by Meyer because the storyline for her novels required a remote, small town near the coastline with a preponderance of rainy/overcast weather (119 inches annually). Meyer's search on www.google.com turned up Forks, Washington. In *Twilight*, a gloomy Bella Swan writes, "In the Olympic Peninsula of northwest Washington State, a small town named Forks exists under a near-constant cover of clouds. It rains on this inconsequential town more than any other place in the United States of America. It was from this town and its gloomy, omnipresent shade that my mother escaped with me when I was only a few months old."(www.forkswa. com)

Hartford, CT. The city in which Stephenie Morgan was born, on December 24, 1973, to Stephen (whom she is named after) and Candy. The family left Hartford when Stephenie was four years old. (www.hartford.gov)

Infiniti G35 coupe. Wanting something else to drive other than the family van, Meyer bought this luxury sports car: finally, a car of her own.

Jodi Reamer. She is Stephenie Meyer's agent. "I'm an agent and an attorney and have been at Writers House for 14 years. I handle both children's books, from young-adult to picture books, and adult books. My focus is commercial fiction. I would love to represent a legal thriller," she wrote on a website for the publishing community (www.publishersmarketplace.com).

Little, Brown and Company. Stephenie Meyer's book publisher, the firm has issued the four novels, *The Host* (a science fiction novel), two movie tie-in companion books, and *The Twilight Saga: The Official Guide*, originally scheduled for publication on December 30, 2008, but now indefinitely postponed. My guess is that it will be published sometime in 2010 or 2011 (www.hatchette-bookgroup.com)

Megan Tingley Books. Megan Tingley is Stephenie Meyer's editor at Little, Brown and Company. The Twilight books are published under her imprint.

Midnight Sun. Intended as a fifth book to the Twilight saga, it's a retelling of *Twilight* from the perspective of Edward Cullen. After it was virally spread on the Internet, the distraught author temporarily stopped work on it.

MySpace (www.myspace.com). Stephenie Meyer no longer maintains a page on this or any other social networking site. Before she closed her MySpace page, it had attracted over 150,000 friends. (Her Facebook page is run by fans.) She currently posts only on her official website.

Muse. Cited in the acknowledgments of the second, third, and fourth novels in the Twilight saga, this band is one of Meyer's favorites; in fact, she cites it as a major musical inspiration for *New Moon*. (http://muse.mu/)

National Book Festival (Washington, D.C.). Sponsored by the Library of Congress, this festival hosted (among others) Stephenie Meyer in 2006. She gave a talk at the Teens & Children Pavilion and also signed books. Held annually in September on the National Mall, the festival draws an estimated 85,000 people who cherish the written word. (www.loc.gov/bookfest/)

National Merit Scholarship. Stephenie Meyer was a recipient of this scholarship, which allowed her to attend Brigham Young University (Provo, Utah). The scholarship, established in 1955, cites her on its website as one of the "scholars you may know." The purpose of the NMSC is "to identify and honor academically talented U.S. high school students, to stimulate increased support for their education, and to provide efficient and effective scholarship program management for organizations that wish to sponsor college undergraduate scholarships." (www.nationalmerit.org)

New Moon. The second of four books in the Twilight saga, published in 2006, its first printing was 100,000 copies in hardback. It is the basis of the film adaptation of the same name, released on November 20, 2009.

Port Angeles, Washington. Located in the Olympic Peninsula, this town is a favorite tourist destination for native Washingtonians. It's also a gateway to nearby Victoria, Canada. In *Twilight*, Bella Swan flies from Seattle to this town on a "small plane" and is picked up at its airport by her father. The location of a fictional restaurant named La Bella Italia, its real-world counterpart is Bella Italia. In September 2009, the town celebrated TwilightFest, its first Twilight celebration, borrowing a page from Forks' annual celebrations that started in 2006. (www.portangeles.org)

San Diego Comic-Con. Held annually in San Diego, California, this started out as a convention for comic book fans but morphed into a major media opportunity for nearby Hollywood. Film studios show trailers and brings its movie stars to help build early buzz on the Internet. In 2008 Comic-Con hosted *Twilight* film director Catherine Hardwicke and its cast, drawing a record crowd of over 6,000 predominantly female fans, some of whom had camped out in order to get a seat in the auditorium where the panel was held and a film clip shown. In 2009, history repeated itself as a record crowd gathered to scream its approval of *New Moon*, at which its three main cast members appeared: Robert Pattinson, Kristen Stewart, and Taylor Lautner.

Scrapbooking. An activity Meyer enjoyed prior to taking up the pen and writing phone book-sized novels, this is, states Wikipedia, "a method for preserving personal and family history in the form of photographs, printed media, and memorabilia contained in decorated albums or scrapbooks." (www.scrapbook.com)

Seth Morgan. Stephenie Meyer's youngest brother, he is the webmaster of her official website, her exclusive web presence. (www.stepheniemeyer.com)

Twilight. The first of four books in the Twilight saga, this is the book that launched Meyer's literary career. A rising star, Meyer, some felt, would eclipse that of another stay-at-home mother whose first novel went on to extraordinary success—Joanne Rowling, who wrote a series about a young boy at a wizarding school. *Twilight* was published in 2005 by Little, Brown and Company under its Megan Tingley Books imprint. It is also the basis of the film adaptation of the same name, starring Robert Pattinson in the role of Edward Cullen and Kristen Stewart in the role of Bella Swan. Its first printing was 75,000 copies in hardback.

Twilight Lexicon. A website that Meyer has termed "the brightest star in the Twilight universe," she specifically cited its staffers (Lori Joffs, Laura Cristiano, Michaela Child, and Ted Joffs) in the acknowledgments of *Eclipse*. (www.twilightlexicon.com)

Writers House. A major literary agency based in New York City that represents Stephenie Meyer. She termed it her dream agency when she initially sought literary representation. From its website: "Writers House was founded in 1973 with a vision for a new kind of literary agency, one that would combine a passion for managing a writer's career with an integrated understanding of how storytelling works.

An employee at Dazzled by Twilight in Port Angeles, Taylor Moore strikes an iconic pose.

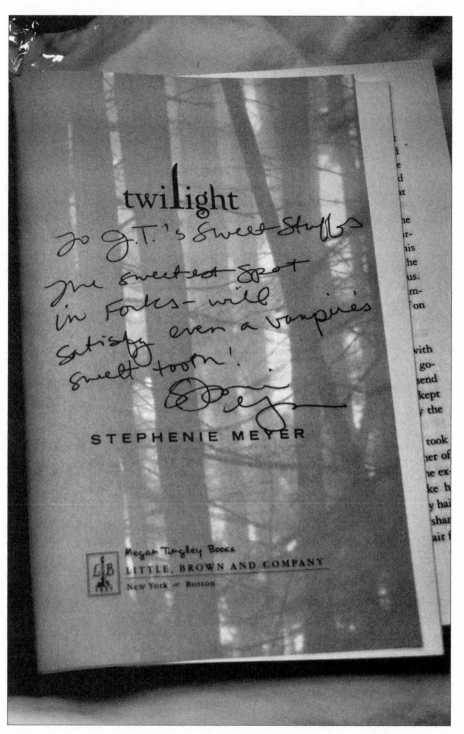

An inscribed copy of *Twilight* on display at JT's Sweet Stuff in Forks.

Changing Hands:
The Official Stephenie Meyer Bookstore

Perfected by independent booksellers, it's called "hand-selling." It's the art of putting a book in a customer's hands and personally recommending it. It's at the heart of the independent bookselling experience.

Independents are also where local authors can form deep and lasting ties to their mutual benefit: a symbiotic relationship between writer and bookseller, who work in concert to put books in the hands of readers.

All of which explains the success of an indie bookseller in Arizona, where for 34 years they've done just that: put books into the hands of readers. Actually, they do a lot more than that; they hold book signings, of course, but also a wide range of other events and activities of community interest. They do it so well that in 2007 Publishers Weekly *voted the store as the "Bookseller of the Year."*

Their key to success, of course, is to have employees who are passionate about books. This is so critical that, even before you walk in the door and fill out an application, they encourage you to read what they've posted online to insure you're a good "fit" with the store. "We are seeking employees who are book lovers and customer-oriented. ... Bringing books and people together is personally rewarding, yet working in a bookstore is not for everyone. ... We see teamwork, book knowledge, flexibility and, above all, customer service as critical elements to the success of this store."

∗

Stephenie Meyer fans have always had a special place in their hearts for the Changing Hands bookstore because their employees were early advocates of her books long before she became a global phenomenon. Given that forgeries of signatures are commonplace from unscrupulous online sellers, it's reassuring that there's a place where one need not worry: The books stocked are indisputably signed by Meyer—good to know before shelling out a couple hundred bucks for a copy.

A full service bookstore, their employees championed Meyer's books long before she became a bestselling author. Consequently, Meyer repays that show of faith by selecting using the star power of her name as necessary to help out the bookstore, especially its charity events.

The availability of book stock varies. Currently available:
Twilight for $300.
New Moon for $200.
Eclipse for $200.
Breaking Dawn for $250.
The Host for $100.

Store Address

6428 S McClintock Drive
Tempe AZ 85283
Phone: (480) 730-0205
www.changinghands.com

Stephenie Meyer at the National Book Festival

An annual event, the National Book Festival on the National Mall in Washington, D.C., plays host for one Saturday in September to dozens of high-profile authors and book lovers that number up to 100,000. With pavilions set up by category ("Children, Teens & Children, History & Biography, Fiction & Fantasy Mysteries & Thrillers, and Poetry & Prose") and by state, the National Book Festival offers something for everyone's literary tastes.

Those with a taste for Stephenie Meyer's books slaked their thirst at its 2006 event at which she addressed a predominantly young crowd and signed books for an hour afterward.

Given that Meyer had just published her first book the previous year, it speaks to her popularity that she would be asked to attend as a guest, when countless other writers with more books and more writing experience have not been proferred an invitation to this august gathering of booklovers in September.

✳

After a brief introduction, Meyer took the stage, with a copy of *New Moon* in hand, as young girls screamed their approval. Speaking extemporaneously, Meyer let the applause die down and admitted, "I'm just a little bit terrified right now, so bear with me if I start talking too fast."

Meyer, who is articulate and showed no signs of stage fright, spoke at a rapid clip and covered a lot of ground. Before reading from chapter one of *New Moon*, she explained that she had "no intention of being an author" and admitted she'd feel more comfortable among the audience, since she's still very much the reader and somewhat uncomfortable in her new role, but the enthusiastic crowd allayed her fears and helped put her at ease.

After the reading, she spoke of herself as an example of someone who got atypically published, comparing it to a lightning strike: It can happen but it's very rare. She took the opportunity to explain that she is a symbol for all the aspiring young girls out there who want to be writers, especially the quiet ones who are going to write no matter if they get published or not. "I represent them," she explained. "You can put yourself out there and sometimes it turns into magical things."

With the prefatory remarks out of the way, she went directly into fielding questions. "Hop up to the microphone, brave girls," she urged, and lines began forming. All the questions, save one, were from young girls who had obviously read the books and knew them by heart. Among them: What was her favorite book? Where did she get the idea for Bella? What's Edward Cullen's favorite color? Will *Midnight Sun* be published? How many books will be in the Twilight series? What did she draw on for her vampire and werewolf myths? Will she ever rewrite—outside of *Twilight*—the remaining three books in the saga from Edward's point of view? What was her inspiration for the title *Twilight*? What changed her mind about publishing it? Did she base any of the characters from people in her real life? What's it like writing about a character so perfect as Edward? Was she happy with the artwork for the *Twilight* cover? Who's her favorite character from *Twilight* and *New Moon*? What's it like writing about Forks, which is so different from Arizona? How did she get the idea for the Volturi? And did she plan on writing a second book after *Twilight*?

Meyer fielded all the questions and answered them with authority. "When you create a world like that, it's all yours. ... There's nothing better than living in a world you've created."

Meyer knows every aspect of that world, which explains her confidence in responding quickly to all the questions posed that day. It's also one of the secrets as to why the series is so popular: The Twilight Saga is a fully realized world, set in our time, and female readers love to lose themselves in it and step into what she's called a storyteller's dream.

Web resource (www.loc.gov/bookfest/2006/authors/meyer.html)

Meyer's talk is available as streaming video. That address will take you to her page with a photo and brief biography. Under her name, click on the word "webcast" to begin playing it. The running time is approximately 30 minutes.

Stephenie Meyer addresses a crowd at the National Book Festival in Washington, D.C., in 2006.

PART 2

THE UNREAL WORLD
OF TWILIGHT:

FICTION

Bella Swan's Song
and her Immortal Beloved

"The Man by Vaughn Bode is very sad and very touching and full of the loneliness that must have been beast/man's long before we knew more of love and what it could do to save us from the uncaring universe, and, often, ourselves."
—Ray Bradbury in a letter to George Beahm

✳

Love is unquestionably worth living for, but is it worth *dying* for?

Bella Swan must forsake her mortality in order to be with her immortal beloved, Edward Cullen, who worries incessantly about the consequences, including possibly losing her immortal soul. Bella would have to forsake her mortal world and leave it permanently behind, and watch those whom she loves grow old and eventually die; she, however, would remain preternaturally young and beautiful, as if frozen in time. Forever young.

Forever young is the state that Edward Cullen surprisingly and reluctantly found himself in after being saved from certain death by Dr. Carlisle Cullen. Born in 1901, Edward's lived over a century without a soulmate. It feels like a commuted life sentence as he watches those around him—Carlisle and Esme, Jasper and Alice, Emmett and Rosalie—bond and grow closer with every passing year. Edward, however, remains alone.

✳

Some years ago, I sent the celebrated writer Ray Bradbury a copy of a comic book, *The Man* by the late Vaughn Bodé. It's the story of a caveman who knows no other humans but bonds with a small creature, his sole companion. One day, the caveman goes out to hunt and bring back food for himself and the little creature whom he has named Erg, left behind unprotected. During his short absence, another caveman sees Erg, kills the trusting creature, and cooks its remains over an open fire. Once again, the caveman with no name is alone. He talks aloud to his hunting stick and opines, "Stick, we are empty. We will sit and be quiet. Erg will come back."

Sitting on an outcropping of rock, as the wind blows leaves around him, the caveman stands up, discards his hunting stick away, and shouts, "I am alone."

The last cartoon panel shows the tiny figure of the caveman at a distance, leaves swirling around in the foreground.

Bradbury, moved to comment, wrote back to me. So many years later, it made me think of Edward Cullen, who also had never known love but only loneliness ... until Bella Swan stumbled into his life. Suddenly, his life had a renewed meaning as he experienced for the first time the regenerative and redemptive power of love. He realized what he was living for and, if necessary, would die for—a realization soon shared by Bella: They are destined to become soulmates for all eternity.

When Bella and Edward finally meet, we realize the evolving, increasingly intimate nature of their relationship: initially strangers, they are fellow students, become friends, then confidants, and eventually lovers. Discovering each other in the most unlikeliest place—a small town called Forks in the Pacific Northwest—they show us an eternal love that will conquer time itself, because of its enduring power: They are immortal and immune from time's corrosive touch.

It is love with one's immortal beloved—forever.

That is at the heart of the Twilight Saga and that is why women all over the world, of all ages, have taken the book and its timeless message to heart: a tween reads the book and imagines a breaking dawn as she looks forward to the first time she falls in love; the teenager, struck with the full power of adolescent love, lives in agony, wondering how she can even manage to get through another painful day, as time slows to a painful crawl, eclipsing everything else in her life; the twenty-to-forty-year-old who has lived enough of life to know that some relationships work out while others fail, some realizing it's time to seek a new relationship; and the grandmothers who wistfully look back at a lifetime of relationships to fondly remember their first, unforgettable love at a time when they are in the twilight of their lives.

✳

Without pain, how can we know joy when we find it?

It is Bella's and Edward's and Jacob's pain in which we commiserate; it is their joy and triumphs that we ultimately share and celebrate.

This is a lesson that can be retold to every generation. Ray Bradbury's eloquent observation offers an explanation to baffled critics as to why the Twilight Saga has struck a responsive chord, plucking at millions of heartstrings worldwide: It reaffirms the miracle and wonder that is love.

the **robert**

pattinson album

paul stenning

Paul Stenning biography on Robert Pattinson.

New Blood:
The Cullens as a new breed of vampires

"I'm the world's most wussiest vampire writer."
— Stephenie Meyer in a talk given at the Library of Congress
National Book Fair in September 2006

*

Wussy or not, Stephenie Meyer's coven of vampires, the Cullens, have won their way into the dark hearts of fans everywhere. "Vegetarian" vampires, they cull animal blood instead of slaking their thirst on traditional fare: human blood.

In contrast to the Cullens, traditional vampires also populate her novels: in *Twilight*, we are introduced to Laurent, Victoria, and James; in *New Moon*, we meet the Volturi, the ruling family of vampires who live in Volterra, Italy.

But even at that, Meyer's vampires fail to satisfy the bloodthirsty fans who have been raised on *Dracula*, Vlad the Impaler, the infamous Hungarian "Blood Countess" (Elizabeth Báthory), countless horror movies, and the Vampire Lestat, among others.

The hoary traditions about vampires have no place in the Twilight Saga, a contemporary retelling of the vampire legend: The Cullens, Meyer's good vampires, have a sense of fashion, an ethos of political correctness (no drinking human blood), and a taste for expensive, fast cars.

Some reviewers of the books and film adaptations complain that Meyer's books fall short as vampire novels and films, which is somewhat misguided. For those seeking traditional vampire fare, Meyer's offerings are relatively blood-less: violence, for the most part, is offstage. In the books, there are no lingering scenes of bloodletting, no blow-by-blow descriptions of wholesale slaughter, no pages covered in blood. But the books were never intended to be primarily about vampires per se; the Twilight Saga is principally Bella's story and her life-changing encounter with Edward Cullen. At heart, the Twilight Saga is a romance with a supernatural twist: an old-fashioned boy meets girl, boy falls in love with girl (and vice versa), but boy turns out to be a vampire, which is what the girl wants to be, too.

The romance element is more Jane Austen than Kathleen Woodiwiss: Bella is the blossoming flower and Edward is the cold flame. From the website of Romance Writers of America: "Two basic elements comprise every romance novel: a central love story and an emotionally-satisfying and optimistic ending. A central love story: The main plot centers around two individuals falling in love and struggling to make the relationship work. ... An emotionally-satisfying and optimistic ending: In a romance, the lovers who risk and struggle for each other and their relationship are rewarded with emotional justice and unconditional love."

More specifically, the Twilight Saga falls into a subcategory called "paranormal romance" which the Romance Writers of America define as one "in which the future, a fantasy world, or paranormal happenings are an integral part of the plot."

The novels, however, aren't *only* about falling in love. They're about responsibility, choice, commitment, virtue, and conservative values like abstinence until marriage, which is why the Book of Mormon goes a long way toward explaining the understructure of Meyer's novels: They have the trappings of the supernatural and romance world, but they are, in the end, ultimately conservative, reflecting Meyer's personal worldview tempered by the tenets of her religion.

Interestingly, the Cullens don't strike me as being anything like a traditional coven; if anything, they can be likened to comic book superheroes like the Fantastic Four or the X-men, of whom Meyer is particularly fond.

Most of the original X-Men, in particular, seem to share much in common with the Cullens: a leader who brings them together, with a shared sense of values (Professor Xavier = Dr. Cullen), the Iceman (all the Cullens are ice-cold to the touch), the Beast (think Emmett Cullen), the Angel (think Edward Cullen), Cyclops, and Marvel Girl with her telepathic and telekinetic powers (think Alice Cullen or Marvel's Sue Storm from The Fantastic Four).

In short, Meyer has popularized a new breed of vampires: young, hip, beautiful, and immortal. The baroque vampires of Anne Rice are history, as is Rice's interest in writing about them: She has forsaken the Vampire Lestat to write about Jesus Christ in a series of novels that draws heavily on her Catholic faith. No question: Stephenie Meyer is the reigning Queen of the Vampire Writers.

Currently, this template is all the rage: the old-world vampires have largely been banished to the past, destroyed by sunlight, nailed up in their coffins and buried forever under the light of a new moon.

In a cover story for *Entertainment Weekly* (July 31, 2009), the pop-cult magazine provides its "ultimate guide" to our favorite bloodsuckers over the years, noting that "With *Twilight* a phenomenon, *True Blood* attracting converts by the millions, and hordes of new vampire projects looming in the shadows, bloodsuckers are haunting every corner of our lives: bookstores, televisions, movies, and more."

Obviously, the Meyer "mix" of vampires, romance, and conservative values has served up an intoxicating brew that today's readers find irresistible. With millions of copies of the Twilight Saga in print worldwide, the series tapped a rich vein and continues to draw new blood.

Meyer did not bind herself to the conventions of the past because, for the most part, she grew up without the background that horror writers have battened on: vampire lore from literature, cinema, and popular culture. In Jeff Otto's interview with the vampire writer, from www.reelzchannel.com, Meyer confessed, "See, here's the thing. I'm not a vampire person. Before I started writing about them, I'd never seen a vampire movie. I'd seen pieces of them, but I'd never been to a vampire movie. I've never read a book about vampires. I'm really not into horror, so I don't know the genre. I think it's why [my books are] different. It's not a genre where I know what the walls are. I break through them because I don't know that they are there."

The differences between the traditional and new breed of vampires:

Traditional: *Nosferatu*
- fugly (Coppola's Count Dracula)
- allergic to garlic, holy water, and the crucifix
- killed by a wooden stake through the heart
- long fangs
- drinks human blood
- sleeps in coffins lined with their burial earth
- burns up in sunlight
- relatively easy to destroy
- shape-shifts into creatures of the night like wolves or bats
- dresses in long gowns, wears chokers, and looks very old world
- can only enter a house by invitation
- not worried about their damnation or salvation
- presumably cannot have inhuman relations (i.e., sex)

Contemporary: The Cullens
- supernaturally handsome and beautiful
- not allergic to garlic, holy water, or the crucifix
- cannot be killed with a stake through the heart
- razor-sharp, normal-looking teeth

- weaned from human blood and drinks animal blood
- doesn't sleep at all
- sparkles in sunlight
- very difficult to destroy
- cannot shape shift
- dresses fashionably in today's styles
- has a predilection for entering a house by stealth (a la Edward)
- worried about their souls, or lack thereof (a la Edward)
- can be quite lusty when aroused and violently so (a la Edward)

Cardboard stand-ups of Bella and Edward.

On the Dark Side of the Moon: Edward Cullen

by Tessa Cox

Think back to the first time you read *Twilight*. A love story between two "star-crossed lovers" unfolds and along the way they encounter some problems, some danger, and even some near-death experiences. In the end, though, all is well and as we read the epilogue we are privy to one final moment where our heroine feels the cold lips of her beloved brush against her throat once more. We close the book, sigh, and realize at that very moment, and probably for many yet to come, Bella Swan is not the only one who is smitten and dazzled by Edward Cullen.

As a manager for a major book chain for over ten years, I have the privilege of being around a variety of books daily. Occasionally, I read a book that really hooks me and I feel compelled to pass it along to my customers. Once I've made *Twilight* my recommendation, some take me at my word, while others need a little more convincing. I can't tell you how often these skeptics come back into the store only days later anxious for the next book.

Certainly, we could attribute the success of the series to our fascination with the supernatural world of vampires and werewolves, or Bella's accessibility. Bella is our voice and constant companion. We love her, get upset with her on occasion, and feel her embarrassment and pain. Because her presence in the book often feels like our own, we have little choice but to see Edward as she sees him. Like Bella, we need to know where he is, what he is doing, what he is thinking, and how he feels in every situation.

After sweeping statements such as these, I acknowledge that there is a small contingency of fans who disagree with me. These fans probably hold to a belief that Bella should have been with Jacob Black in the end; they no doubt could argue their points quite convincingly. Knowing, of course, that it would be impossible to dissuade them, I offer this simple observation: Jacob Black is not the reason you first became enraptured with *Twilight*, nor is he the reason you couldn't wait to begin reading the next book. Your infatuation with Jacob began sometime during the course of reading *New Moon*. While you were falling for Jacob's sunny smile, the rest of us were aching for our tortured Edward to return.

So why are we so addicted to Edward Cullen? It's not as if we haven't seen echoes of his character in some of his literary cousins. Edward could effortlessly challenge Romeo's romantic proclamations, and no doubt his upstanding moral code and chivalrous conduct would win the approval of even Mr. Darcy. Perhaps it is Edward's beauty, his strength, his intensity, his wit, or a combination of all these things, but regardless of what the reasons are for our fascination, he undoubtedly leaves an imprint on the reader.

Consider his physical presence. Bella is struck by Edward's beauty when she spies him in the lunchroom that first day at school. Later, when they have their first conversation in biology and she gets a chance to make a better observation, she notes his "musical voice," "dazzling face," "flawless lips," and "a crooked smile so beautiful that I could only stare at him like an idiot" (*Twilight*, pp. 43-44). She compares the first time he accidentally brushes her hand to an electric current passing through her body (p. 45), and in almost every subsequent meeting she is absolutely entranced by his face, his scent, his clothes and his manner of speaking. Long before the casting of Robert Pattinson in his role as Edward Cullen, part of the reader's fascination was the piecing together in our own minds what this creature of perfection might look like.

In our postmodern, idealistic world we could argue that superficial factors like physical beauty have no impact, but we would most definitely be lying to ourselves. Culturally, we are obsessed with the concept of "ideal beauty," so why wouldn't our perfect fantasy portray our hero as the most physically attractive man imaginable? We should also note that, although Edward is irrefutably gorgeous, Bella as our first-person storyteller undoubtedly affects how we see Edward; we are witnesses to her ever-increasing crush, and inevitably begin to develop one of our own. In fact, Bella's fascination with Edward's appearance is ceaseless. Even on the eve of their wedding in *Breaking Dawn*, she can't get enough of looking at him, touching his skin, and his chest. Furthermore, in the wake of her transformation she discovers that her vampire senses have only served to feed her obsession. She observes:

> The greater part of my senses and my mind were still focused on Edward's face.
>
> I had never seen it before this second.
>
> How many times had I stared at Edward and marveled over his beauty? ....

> I'd thought this was the one sure physical thing in my whole
> world: the flawlessness of Edward's face.
> I may as well have been blind.
> For the first time, with the dimming shadows and limiting weak-
> ness of humanity taken off my eyes, I saw his face. I gasped and
> then struggled with my vocabulary, unable to find the right words. I
> needed better words (*Breaking Dawn*, p. 390).

One of Edward's most likable qualities is his apparent nonchalance, his complete lack of awareness about his own beauty. His hair is perfectly coiffed, and he obviously cares what clothes he wears lest he incur the wrath of his sister Alice. But he is in no way self-absorbed about his appearance. His crooked smile that drives Bella wild is a natural, easy response, and the intense gazes that leave her shivering are to him just the way he looks. He is so unaware, in fact, of how much he affects people that Bella actually has to bring it to his attention in *Twilight* when he interacts with their hostess on their impromptu date at a Port Angeles restaurant, La Bella Italia:

> He flashed his gleaming smile, dazing her momentarily. . .
> "You really shouldn't do that to people," I criticized. "It's hardly
> fair."
> "Do what?"
> "Dazzle them like that—she's probably hyperventilating in the
> kitchen right now."
> He seemed confused.
> "Oh, come on," I said dubiously. "You have to know the effect
> you have on people."
> He tilted his head to one side, and his eyes were curious. "I dazzle
> people?"
> "You haven't noticed?". . .
> "Do I dazzle you?"
> "Frequently," I admitted (*Twilight*, pp. 167-168).

Bella's constant observations about Edward's attractiveness and her ordinariness make her far more concerned about physical appearances then he ever appears to be. He has thought her beautiful all along, while she has never been able to see herself as beautiful—until, of course, the last book.

Like Bella, so many aspects of Edward's outward appearance dazzle many of us, while for others, Edward's magnetism is due to his actual physicality—his vampire self. Not unlike the hero of other romances, Edward possesses not only beauty but skill. In many of these romances the hero's skills are often physical, while in others, their skills may be more introspective and cerebral. Stephenie Meyer chose to bestow on her hero a combination of these attributes: beauty, strength, speed, fighting skills, intelligence. Traditionally and in modern times, vampires have always possessed a dangerous, enigmatic, and often, a sexual quality. Having evolved from the cape-wearing, fang-bearing creatures of the night, to a more modern depiction of immortality and power, it is easy to see why we are compelled to be in their company. Edward and his family defy the very essence of what they are. In making Edward's thirst controllable and secondary to the action of the story, Meyer has allowed the reader to see him as an extraordinary creature, instead of a monster.

Edward is also a distinctive vampire hero from other literary vampires because of his sensuality, not sexuality. As previously stated, traditional and modern depictions of vampires are often very sexual. In fact, it is the rare vampire novel (geared toward adults or young adult readers) that doesn't include at times graphic sexuality of bloodlust and physical lust competing on equal terms. What's fascinating about the Twilight series is that Meyer succeeds in making abstinence erotic, which she primarily achieves through Edward's character. As the vampire hero in another story he would no doubt be able to slake his thirst and desire as he pleases, but as Meyer's hero, he cultivates a sensuality based on restraint: the more he resists Bella—her scent, her kisses, her embraces, and her coaxing him for more—the more we want the same. We anxiously anticipate the union of Edward and Bella in the last book, but in our reading of the first three we have the opportunity to slowly discover, or rediscover, romance and sensuality in simple gestures, glances, or spoken words. Constantly and acutely aware of Bella's scent, his desire is a natural by-product of being near her. It's clear that his desire for her blood is powerful, but he also admits, " 'I may not be a human, but I am a man' " (*Twilight*, p. 311), assuring her that he also wants her as a human man would desire a woman. In Bella's case, Edward's very presence or his faintest touch is an assault on her senses:

> With deliberate slowness, his hands slid down the sides of my neck. I shivered, and I heard him catch his breath. But his hands didn't pause as they softly moved to my shoulders, and then stopped. His face drifted to the side, his nose skimming across my collarbone. He came to rest with the side of his face pressed tenderly against my chest. Listening to my heart . . . I don't know how long we sat without moving . . . I knew at any moment it could be too much and my life could end . . . I couldn't make myself be afraid. I couldn't think of anything, except that he was touching me (*Twilight*, p. 276).

It isn't until Bella's transformation that Edward finally surrenders his tightly reined restraint insofar as she's concerned. Until then, he continually dazzles us with unprecedented moments of sensuality, whether it's as simple as their first delicate touches shared in the meadow or moments infinitely more intimate.

The singular package of perfection that is Edward Cullen might seem unrealistic, and indeed it is "unreal." Once again, I reiterate that Edward exists in a world of fantasy—a world where immortality is possible. If one possessed countless years to study, read, travel, and experience life, wouldn't it be inevitable that one would be more intelligent than most, more adept at smiting down one's enemies, and more eloquent a conversationalist? Wouldn't it be possible to acquire skills and abilities such as composing music, playing an instrument, or speaking several languages? Until Bella came into Edward's life, there was nothing but these pastimes to keep him occupied. In *Breaking Dawn*, he explains this to Bella:

> "There's a tremendous amount of time left over when you don't have to sleep. It makes balancing your ... interests quite easy. There's a reason why I'm the best musician in the family, why—besides Carlisle—I've read the most books, studied the most sciences, become fluent in the most languages ... Emmett would have you believe that I'm such a know-it-all because of the mind reading, but the truth is that I've just had a lot of free time" (*Breaking Dawn*, p. 485).

While we can easily attribute Edward's talent and intelligence to years of living the immortal life without distraction or sleep, is it possible to say the same of his wit and charm? Since Bella is Edward's first love, or even the first to ever spark his interest, we must assume his charm is unpracticed, unrehearsed. Before her, Edward's social interactions were mostly limited to his family. He voluntarily positions himself as the outcast to such an extent that when he actually speaks to Bella in front of their fellow students in the lunchroom, they all seem fascinated.

Like his charm, Edward's wit shines around Bella because he not only finds her amusing, he also finds it amusing to quip and tease with her. Though he often views it as frustrating that he can't read Bella's mind, it is perhaps why we are more able to see his humor when they are together. For the first time in his vampire life, he is unencumbered by the excess of thought and emotion crashing in upon him. He has the privilege of experiencing only his thoughts and feelings and therefore has the freedom to make his own witty observations, find the humor in a situation, or simply just laugh. We see examples of this side of Edward in statements like, "Friends don't let friends drive drunk ... you're intoxicated by my very presence" (*Twilight*, p. 284), or "You should probably know that I'm breaking the rules right now. Well, not technically, since [Charlie] said I was never to walk through his door again, and I came in the window . . . But, still, the intent was clear" (*New Moon*, p. 503). If a comment leaves Bella embarrassed, blushing, or casting him a frustrated glance, he seems to find it worth the effort. It is Bella who draws out his lighter side, just as she touches his mysterious darker side. This dichotomy of character is undoubtedly one of the strongest elements of his attraction—the humorous, witty, good-mannered Edward versus the darker, dangerous, more intense version of himself. He is the immortal "bad boy" with the conscience and heart of a gentleman.

We don't often see the darker side of Edward because even in the most extreme of moments he is able to retain a certain level of control. One of the greatest examples of this is when Victoria finally meets her demise at Edward's hand. Even while he is intensely focused on Bella's safety, Edward more than matches Victoria's skill with calm, quickly, practiced movements during their fight. Bella compares his attack on Victoria to the movements of a dance, and describes the scene to leave us believing that Edward's instinct to take her life is natural and without reservation. She observes, "[Victoria] began to back away from Edward . . . She wheeled and flew toward the refuge of the forest like an arrow from a bow. But Edward was faster—a bullet from a gun. He caught her unprotected back at the edge of the trees and, with one last, simple step, the dance was over. Edward's mouth brushed once across her neck . . . And then the fiery tangle of hair was no longer connected to the rest of her body" (*Eclipse*, p. 553).

As if killing Victoria was simply on his list of things to do, he quickly composes himself and his only immediate concern in the aftermath is whether or not Bella is afraid. For Bella, who appears at this moment more fascinated than fearful of him, it is not her first encounter with Edward's darker, more dangerous side. In *Twilight*, Edward warns her, " 'Never forget I am more dangerous to you than I am to anyone else . . . The fragrance coming off your skin . . . I thought it would make me deranged that first day. In that one hour, I thought of a hundred different ways to lure you from the room with me, to get you alone . . . You would have come'" (p. 270).

It is perhaps the reality of knowing that this darker side of Edward exists that makes Bella, and the reader, even more drawn to him. We are mystified by his almost limitless self-control. Whether from a natural cautiousness, or from years of practice and study, Edward's actions are very calculated. While the rest of the Cullen family can empathize with the struggle he endures to control his thirst, no one in the series is tested to Edward's limits. Having thrown caution to the wind by choosing to follow his heart and be with Bella, Edward has subjected himself not only to an unpredictable life but one of constant restraint and self-control. He confesses to Bella, "[Y]ou are exactly my brand of heroin" (p. 268); later in *New Moon* as they meet with the Volturi, Aro refers to Bella's blood as "La tua cantante," meaning that she is Edward's "singer," that her blood sings to him. Privy to Edward's memories through his own unique gift, Aro is astonished by Edward's restraint and even questions how it is possible for him to be in close proximity to Bella when the call of her blood is so strong (p. 471). Since there isn't a single individual in the series as demanding on Edward as he is on himself, he would never be able to live with himself if he were to ever lose an ounce of control where Bella is concerned. Until her transformation occurs, Edward doesn't allow for his concern over Bella's well being to cease. Every moment they are together, whether intimate or social, he is forced to take steps to restrain himself whether it's as simple as not holding her hand too hard, or as complex as not slaking his constant thirst for her blood. He is, as he terms himself, a "sick, masochistic lion" (p. 274).

There is no argument that Edward's self-control where Bella is concerned is uncanny, but it's more than a compulsion to do the right thing that forces him daily to exert what he refers to as "mind over matter" (*Twilight*, p. 300). He does it because he loves her with everything within him, and her safety and happiness is more important to him than anything else. Arguably, this is the greatest contributing factor for our own love affair with Edward Cullen. With every meaningful look, every crooked smile, every intimate conversation, and with every gentle caress, we long to be cherished the way Edward cherishes his Bella. She has awakened something deep within him, and for the first time in his long life he is finally living.

Ever the romantic, Edward has no reservations about sharing how he feels with Bella: a brief comment like, " 'You are my life now' " (*Twilight*, p. 314); a passing statement such as, " 'Look after my heart—I've left it with you' " (*Eclipse*, p. 94); or a sweeping confession the likes of, " 'Before you, Bella, my life was like a moonless night. Very dark, but there were stars—points of light and reason . . . And then you shot across my sky like a meteor. Suddenly everything was on fire; there was brilliancy, there was beauty' " (*New Moon*, p. 514). Edward Cullen has a talent for leaving us breathless and weak in the knees. Our near bouts of swooning can most likely be attributed to the fact that, unlike Bella, most of us have never experienced such devoted attention, especially expressed in such poetic terms. In truth, we have dreamt about having that kind of romance in our own lives. We want to be the object of one's desire, the center of one's fascination, and the focus of one's obsession. Like Bella, we wouldn't necessarily mind finding out that Edward has been watching us sleep at night. Because there is nothing in Edward's life more important than Bella, that intensity of desire keeps us turning the pages. Edward Cullen is exactly our brand of heroin.

In our modern world, chivalry isn't something we often think about or expect to find in our everyday lives. No doubt, some may even view the idea of chivalry as archaic or insulting to the sensibilities of the modern woman, for the time of knights riding up on their white steeds to rescue the damsel in distress is long gone. We'll avoid the feminism debate as it concerns the Twilight Saga, but let me offer a simple observation: if we women have moved on from wanting chivalry in our lives in some capacity, why is this series so successful? The millions of copies sold of Meyer's books serve as a social testimony, perhaps suggesting that we are not as removed from the knight and steed as we might profess: chivalry may not be dead but merely lay dormant, as we wait for our shining knights. We are Bella waiting for our Edward.

Edward not only puts his own needs and desires as secondary to Bella's, but also does so with determination, grace, style, and chivalry. Born in 1901, he is an old-fashioned gentleman who opens doors for ladies, lends his jacket when Bella is chilled, and steadfastly adheres to certain sexual boundaries. How often—in literature or in life—do we find a man who prefers to wait until marriage to have sex? Again, part of his concern is for Bella's safety, because he's not certain he would be able to control his thirst, his incredible strength, and his sexual desire for her, held only in check by his own moral compass. In fact, he is so adamant that they wait that Bella tells him that she feels as if their roles are reversed. She remarks, "'You make me feel like a villain in a melodrama—twirling my mustache while I try to steal some poor girl's virtue'" (*Eclipse*, p. 453). Nor is this the only instance of role reversal between Edward and Bella. In *Twilight*, it's actually Edward who insists that he be introduced to Charlie before they continue "dating," while Bella was content to put it off as long as possible.

Edward always sees to Bella's needs before his own, and therefore it's important for him to know at all times that she is well and safe. Whether that means she is resting when she's tired, eating when she's hungry, or not being chased by bloodthirsty "evil" vampires, it is all the same to him. Though the label isn't always attractive, it's not unfounded to say that for most of the series, Bella is our "damsel in distress." She is a trouble magnet. Even when she seems to be doing something completely harmless and innocent, she has a knack for getting herself into a predicament or a dangerous situation. For someone like Bella, it's in her best interest to have a supernatural boyfriend who can use his mind-reading powers to often pinpoint her location, use his super speed to get to her quickly, and use his super strength to ward off her enemies. Bella has survived a van that almost crushes her, strange men nearly attacking her in Port Angeles, and surviving several encounters with vindictive, non-vegetarian vampires. She has survived it all only because Edward was there to protect her.

Throughout the series, Edward proves to be Bella's angel, but in many ways she is also his, as in *Breaking Dawn* when she becomes such a powerful vampire, but there are many ways to be saved. As he so often expresses, his life without Bella is empty. She sees the good in him, and her absolute trust in his character and his soul allows him to think of himself as more than a monster. In *Twilight*, Edward spends a great deal of time focusing on why they shouldn't be together. In *New Moon*, he attempts to defy the odds of any harm ever coming to her by leaving. In *Eclipse*, he begins to realize that whatever the consequences may be he doesn't want to be without her. And by *Breaking Dawn*, because she is the most integral part of his existence, he has finally found, in their eternal life together, true happiness.

As Stephenie Meyer commented in an interview in a supplementary disc to *Twilight*, by the end of the series Edward is an optimist. Whether an optimist or pessimist, it makes little difference to me. I am dazzled.

A cardboard stand-up of Bella Swan.

On the Light Side of the Moon: Bella Swan

by

Tessa Cox

I did not attend my high school prom. That simple confession probably has many people feeling sorry for me, but the reality is that I was actually asked to prom by three different guys and politely declined each invitation. While all the girls at my high school were piecing together their perfect ensembles of dress, accessories, hair, and make-up, I was only pretending to care about it when they would bring it up in conversation. It was really not my thing. I was the friendly, intelligent girl who was editor of the school paper, took Shakespeare courses as electives, and was incredibly bad at sports. Remind you of someone? Okay, so Isabella Swan did actually go to her prom (coerced every step of the way), and she wasn't the editor of the school paper. Nevertheless, there are many similarities between this odd but lovely girl who exists in a world of fantasy, and the flesh-and-blood person I see in the mirror everyday (including the fair skin). The amazing truth is that I am not alone in sharing this bond with her. There are millions of us Bellas out there.

When Stephenie Meyer chose to make Bella the central figure in the Twilight series, the one telling the story, she created an almost instant connection between reader and protagonist. Countless literary masterpieces are written in first person. It is, however, for me and so many others the first time we have felt such a strong connection to the voice on the page. Bella is not a world traveler exploring exotic locations, a rich noble living in a castle, or a no-nonsense businesswoman in Manolos. She is an ordinary girl learning to live with extraordinary circumstances. We may never find out for ourselves what it's like to have a vampire for a boyfriend, but all of us who read these books have had to deal with tough situations and reap the consequences that follow.

There are many qualities about Bella that make her an exceptional character; one of the strongest is her accessibility. She may be your fictional twin as she is for me, or you may only see parts of yourself within her. She's not incredibly beautiful or graceful, and she doesn't always do or say the right thing. She actually prefers the jeans and tee-shirt look to any fancy dress or outfit Alice tries to put on her. She isn't overly concerned about her hair or make-up, she doesn't initially have a lot of money or obsess about having more, and she drives a worn-out, old truck. She has moments of awkwardness and feeling out of place, moments of strength and courage, and moments of being afraid. In giving us Bella, Stephenie Meyer has seamlessly constructed an accessible character so identifiable that even when her transformation into a vampire occurs, we still feel at ease with her. We still recognize her humanity, even in her new superhuman form.

Take, for instance, a moment she describes in *Breaking Dawn* when the final confrontation with the Volturi occurs.

> I could feel [my shield] flex like just another muscle, obedient to my will. I pushed it, shaped it to a long, pointed oval. Everything underneath the flexible iron shield was suddenly a part of me—I could feel the life force of everything it covered like points of bright heat, dazzling sparks of light surrounding me. I thrust the shield forward the length of the clearing, and exhaled in relief when I felt Edward's brilliant light within my protection . . . I focused totally on Edward, ready to shield him instantly if something went wrong (*Breaking Dawn*, 691).

We have no possible way of knowing what it's like to have a supernatural gift like Bella's, but because we have journeyed with her along the way, we understand every single emotion she is feeling at this moment. Edward has become an integral part of her happiness, as well as our own. We know how it feels to want to protect those we love most, and when we see them in danger our natural instinct is to "shield." Her physical body, strength, and abilities may have changed from human to vampire, but her mind has remained the same; we still know her as intimately as we did before her transformation.

Bella is not a character on a journey to discover who she is, because she already knows exactly who she is, even if she's not entirely comfortable in her own skin. Like all of us, she's critical of her looks and her shortcomings on a regular basis. She's extremely self-deprecating, even to the point of frustration, but she doesn't try to be someone she is not. A marvelous example of this quality is the way she behaves when she first develops her crush on Edward. The stereotypical actions of a girl infatuated with a boy usually motivates that girl dressing differently to catch his eye, making a concentrated effort to see him, and generally being very flirtatious whenever she's around the object of her affection. We have seen these countless times throughout our lives, and in truth, we are probably guilty of behaving exactly the same way. Most of us probably would, but not Bella. Bella actually seems the polar opposite of this behavior. She dresses the same and even hopes at times that she will not see Edward, because she feels so incredibly awkward around him and confused about his odd behavior. She admits to her infatuation, but it never occurs to her to put on a show for his benefit.

For one accustomed to the role of the adult—taking care of Renee, taking care of Charlie, buying the groceries, cooking the dinner, doing the laundry, —it's not surprising that often Bella's emotional maturity seems far beyond that of her peers. She's still a teenager who occasionally makes impulsive, nonsensical decisions, but most of the time she takes time to ponder the weight of every situation. When she admits that she is "unconditionally and irrevocably" (*Twilight*, p. 195) in love with Edward, it isn't a whimsical revelation or fancy. She's thought about it, considered the insanity and impossibility of the situation, and then makes a conscious decision to be with him. She accepts the danger, the unknown, the unconventionality, and doesn't count herself a martyr for loving a vampire because it's her choice to have this life.

Bella is a young woman who leaves the impression that she knows exactly what she wants, yet she is still willing to compromise if it doesn't cost her what's truly important. Consider Bella's apprehensions about marriage. For obvious reasons relating to her parents and some of her own reservations, she has a problem with the concept of marriage and has never imagined she would be the marrying type. In contrast, Edward's old-fashioned ideals seem to set marriage on a pedestal. It's extremely important to Edward that they marry. Bella concedes not only because she desperately wants to sleep with him and he won't otherwise, but also because she realizes they both essentially want the same thing: to be together as long as time allows them to be so. She can't rationalize her willingness to be committed to him forever in an immortal life, yet not be willing to say vows and wear his ring. In choosing to make Edward happy, she has compromised nothing of what she really wants.

However, when it comes to those decisions that to her are the most important, not even Edward can change her mind. In his desperate attempt to save Bella's soul and spare her a life as a monster, which is how he sees himself, Edward passionately opposes Bella's fervent wish to become a vampire. Though she is moved by his love and concern, she will not be dissuaded. For Bella, the most important reason is that it will allow her to be with Edward forever, but there are other factors as well. She explains to Edward, " 'I'll be the first to admit that I have no experience with relationships . . . [b]ut it just seems logical . . . a man and woman have to be somewhat equal . . . as in, one of them can't always be swooping in and saving the other one. They have to save each other equally'" (*Twilight*, pp. 473-474). Another reason she is determined is for the safety of others in her life, notably Charlie and Jacob, and her fear that her relationship with Edward has put them in danger. She alleges, "I wished there was some way that I could be the only one to suffer, but I knew that was impossible. At the same time, I was hurting them more by staying human . . . I was a danger magnet; I'd accepted that about myself. Accepting this, I knew I needed to be able to take care of myself, and protect the ones I love. . ." (*New Moon*, pp. 536-537).

Later in the series we find Bella in a situation where she is once again forced to make another important decision and stand firm on her own: Bella's pregnancy, which eventually costs her the price of her human life, is a major contention in the Cullen family. Edward, who has never been very good at seeing himself as anything less than a monster, is absolutely convinced that the "baby" growing inside Bella is dangerous. Bella, however, sees it as the child Edward created with her, and it is impossible for her to see it as anything less than miraculous. "This child, Edward's child . . . I wanted [this baby] like I wanted air to breathe. Not a choice—a necessity" (*Breaking Dawn*, p. 132).

Some readers have criticized Bella's decision to keep her hybrid baby as reckless, spinning it as nothing more than pro-life propaganda. Readers are free to interpret a work as they see fit, but I think this argument misses the point entirely. Reckless or not, Bella chooses to keep the baby because it's what she wants, even if means opposing the will of her husband and Carlisle's medical advice. She is neither trying to set an example by keeping this baby nor feels morally or ethically obligated to do so. She wants it because it's part of her, and part of the man she loves. She is willing to make the ultimate sacrifice because her compulsion to love this baby is so strong.

It's fascinating that a character with Bella's insecurities can demonstrate the acts of courage and strength that she so often does: the same girl that typically feels ordinary and vulnerable can run off alone in an attempt to save her mother from James. She holds her own in the Cullen family, even before she becomes one of them; she socializes with a wolf pack; she faces the likes of Victoria and the Volturi; and there is no limit to what she would do for Edward or Renesmee. Bella is made strong by her immense capacity to love and care for others. Her constant concern for the safety and well being of those she loves is always apparent, whether it's worrying about Charlie having dinner, or Edward avoiding self-destruction in the Volturi city. Carlisle theorizes that some of the enhanced abilities, or gifts, vampires possess are often a result of who they were in their human life. In Bella's case, this is certainly true. Her ceaseless love and concern for those in her human life is translated into her vampire life by her ability to produce an invisible, protective shield at will. Her shield is so powerful, in fact, that it conjures fear in the Volturi. In many ways, this is a

David-and-Goliath-type ending where we suspected all along that Bella was exceptional in her own way, but we didn't imagine just how exceptional.

Edward, with his self-restraint and constant battle not to hate himself, is the Twilight Saga's broody, dark hero. The sparks of life and bright points in his darkness are Bella's unconditional love and trust. She determines, "The bond forged between us was not one that could be broken . . . he was irreversibly altered as I was. As I would always belong to him, so would he always be mine" (*New Moon*, p. 527). She sees his goodness. She has never thought of him as the soulless monster he perceives himself to be. For Bella, he is no monster but her angel. She reflects:

> I could never for a second forget that I was holding someone more angel than man in my arms . . . Our gazes locked for a moment; his golden eyes were so deep that I imagined I could see all the way into his soul. It seemed silly that this fact—the existence of his soul—had ever been in question, even if he was a vampire. He had the most beautiful soul, more beautiful than his brilliant mind or his incomparable face or his glorious body (*Breaking Dawn*, pp. 23-24).

With her absolute trust in who he is, not what he is, Bella teaches Edward how to love. In a small, insignificant town called Forks, Edward Cullen finds his ideal balance in the quiet, uncoordinated girl from Phoenix who fills his dark with light. As we slip into and inhabit the "shell" Bella creates for us as she tells the story, we imagine that our Edward is waiting for us somewhere out there, too; and, like Bella, we don't have to be incredibly beautiful, popular or eloquent in order to deserve him.

In the infinite, and sometimes vacuous, labyrinth that is young adult literature these days, it's incredibly hard to find something distinctive. When we read this series, we recognize that Bella is distinctive. We could discuss whether or not she is representative of the ideal feminist, or whether her uncanny need to be saved represents female regression, but at the end of the day it is all moot. The bottom line is that Bella is something different, and in a literary world for teens saturated with the importance of being popular and "hooking up," I will always take the bookworm with a crush on a vampire. Bella is intelligent, hopeful, and certain of her choices. She loves and takes care of others, and doesn't pretend to be something she is not. In the end, even as an exceptionally powerful vampire, she's still just a young woman continuously learning how to be herself. Remind you of someone?

The Twilight Saga:
Kindling Interest in eBooks

Twilighters who want to keep all 2,444 pages of the Twilight Saga with them know that their bulk presents a formidable carrying problem—in hardback, that's an eight inches tall stack of books!

The answer, especially for younger readers who have grown up in the wired universe, is the e-book capable of allowing bibliophiles to carry entire libraries, so they can always satisfy their print fix.

The Twilight series is readily available in e-book format. Here's a recap of what's available, where, and the current prices.

Amazon's Kindle

A proprietary format that allows books to be downloaded through a wireless connection, the Kindle platform offers more than 300,000 books. Available in two configurations ($299 for a 6-inch diagonal screen, $489 for a 9.7-inch diagonal screen), the Twilight Saga in eBook format is less expensive than the print equivalent: *Twilight* and *New Moon* for $6.59 each, *Eclipse* for $7.79, and *Breaking Dawn* for $9.99.

The Kindle's advantages: its portability, its easy-to-read "E Ink" display, its ability to increase the font size to enhance readability, and its "try it before you buy it" feature.

Go to www.amazon.com and type "Kindle" in the search engine for more information.

Adobe Digital Editions

Book Group, which publishes the Twilight Saga, has adopted the Adobe ePub/Digital Edition as its preferred format; the books are "read only," printable (for a specified time period), and temporarily transferable (libraries can loan them out).

The Amazon Kindle (screen size, six inches diagonal).

Once the Digital Editions software is installed on your computer, you can download the Twilight Saga for $80.94 (a discounted price) from www.booksonboard.com. (The individual books cost from $10.99 to $22.42).

Audio downloads of all four books are also available.

Though one can read ebooks on a laptop or a netbook, their backlit screens are admittedly hard on the eyes for prolonged periods.

Apple's iTunes store

For the ultimate in portability, Apple Computer sells both audio and text versions of the Twilight Saga for the iPod and iPhone.

Savvy customers are waiting until spring 2010 to see if the rumors are correct: Will Apple finally issue a portable tablet-sized iPod? That's what it'd take to make e-books really take off for Apple. But when asked about Amazon's Kindle, Apple cofounder Steve Jobs told the *New York Times*, "It doesn't matter how good or bad the product is. The fact is that people don't read anymore. Forty percent of the people in the U.S. read one book or less last year."

Given Jobs' penchant for tossing red herrings to the media on a regular basis, his fishy comments should be taken with a grain of salt.

Interestingly, the Twilight Saga is available on Apple's iPod and iPhone, in plain text form using a proprietary format, the Iceberg Reader, which simulates a printed page. All but *Breaking Dawn* are priced at $9.99 (*Breaking Dawn* is $19.99).

Of course, the Twilight Saga is also available in audio, as well.

What makes the iPod/iPhone such a great platform for Twilighters is its versatility: you can easily download the soundtracks and freely download film trailers and Twilight-related podcasts (check out "Imprint: The #1 Twilight Podcast").

I have an iPod and enjoy watching the film clips, listening to downloadable music and podcasts, and surfing websites, but reading a book on such a tiny screen is an unacceptable trade-off in exchange for portability.

I'll wait until Apple comes out with the tablet-sized iPod with a diagonal screen of up to ten diagonal inches. (When Apple rolls this out, it may dampen sales for the Kindle, which lacks color, a true web browsing experience, downloadable film clips, and music downloads.)

For more information, go to the iTunes Store and, type "Twilight Stephenie Meyer" in the search engine. Click "See All" to pull up the varied Twilight offerings. You'll be surprised at what pops up: fan fiction, trivia quiz books, studies guides, and other fan-generated ebooks.

Prefatory Note:
an Overview of the Twilight Saga

Since this book is principally intended as a resource and reference guide, and as a supplementary source of information about the novels, I have deliberately avoided a detailed discussion of the characters and a detailed plot synopsis of each book for several reasons.

First, a detailed look at each of these would in itself be book-length—far beyond the scope of this book, which focuses on the Twilight phenomenon.

Second, a detailed book look has already been excellently done by Twilight experts at www.twilightlexicon.com, which has the added benefit of having access to Meyer for fact-checking.

Third, this kind of material is exactly what Meyer will be discussing at length in her own *Twilight Saga: The Official Guide*; thus, anything I write would be redundant and, obviously, incomplete.

Fourth, a detailed plot synopsis gives away the plot. As this book will be read by new and old readers, spoilers are kept to a minimum by reprinting what the publisher has said about each title and what reviewers have noted.

The U.S. editions are the bases for my discussions, since they are the true first editions published worldwide.

✳

Twilight: 498 pages

1. original title: *Forks*. The original title was discarded because Meyer's editor and publisher felt it lacked impact. After discussing other options, they wisely chose "Twilight," an atmospheric word that opened the door to other properly suggestive book titles.

2. publication date: October 5, 2005.

3. dedication: for her older sister, Emily Rasmussen. Concerned that she hadn't heard from Stephenie, Emily finally called to ask why. When Stephenie admitted she was writing a novel, Emily soon became its first reader. It was Emily's encouragement that got Stephenie to take the next step and do the research necessary to get the book on the road to publication.

4. editions available: in print form, advance reading copy, hardback, trade paperback, paperback; e-book (various formats); audiobook; and a Collector's

Edition (slipcased with enhanced production values). A graphic novel from Yen Press (an imprint of Hachette) has been announced but no publication date has been set.

5. first U.S. printing: 75,000 copies in trade hardback.

6. cover art explained: Choice is at the heart of this novel. Rich in symbolism, especially in myth and popular culture, the apple beckons: to bite or not bite? Meyer's biblical allusion—the fruit of the tree of knowledge of good and evil in the Garden of Eden—makes it clear that Bella Swan made her choice and, as a result, would come to know both: knowledge of the light and dark side of human, and inhuman, existence. The book's dedication, from Genesis: 2:17, reads: "But of the tree of the knowledge of good and evil, thou shalt not eat of it: for in the day that thou eatest thereof thou shalt surely die."

7. literary inspiration: *Pride and Prejudice* by Jane Austen.

8. back story: Visited by a nocturnal muse, Stephenie Meyer had gotten the original idea for the story in a dream on June 2, 2003. She had never published anything before tackling a novel, completing a 130,000 word manuscript in three months. She typed on the family desktop computer in an open hallway with one baby on her lap and another at her feet.

9. The publisher's copy: "Isabella Swan's move to Forks, a small, perpetually rainy town in Washington, could have been the most boring move she ever made. But once she meets the mysterious and alluring Edward Cullen, Isabella's life takes a thrilling and terrifying turn. Up until now, Edward has managed to keep his vampire identity a secret in the small community he lives in, but now nobody is safe, especially Isabella, the person Edward holds most dear. The lovers find themselves balanced precariously on the point of a knife—between desire and danger. Deeply romantic and extraordinarily suspenseful, *Twilight* captures the struggle between defying our instincts and satisfying our desires. This is a love story with bite."

10. Citations and Awards

New York Times Editor's Choice

Publishers Weekly, "Best Children's Book of 2005"

Publishers Weekly, "Best Book of the Year"

American Library Association (ALA), "Top Ten Best Book for Young Adults"

American Library Association (ALA), "Top Ten Books for Reluctant Readers"

School Library Journal, "Best Books of 2005"

Amazon.com, "Best Book of the Decade...So Far"

11. *Perspectives:*
Stephenie Meyer

On Bella's appeal: "I didn't realize the books would appeal to people so broadly. I think some of it's because Bella is an everygirl. She's not a hero, and she doesn't know the difference between Prada and whatever else is out there. She doesn't always have to be cool, or wear the coolest clothes ever. She's normal. And there aren't a lot of girls in literature that are normal. Another thing is that Bella's a good girl, which is just sort of how I imagine teenagers, because that's how my teenage years were." (Gregory Kirschling, EW.com.)

On dealing with the publishing world on *Twilight*: "When I first started with *Twilight*, I didn't have any experience. I didn't know what I was doing. So I was pretty intimidated by the editors and the publishers, and I felt like I was a kid in school with the principal telling me what to do! It was hard for me. There were things I changed in the story that I sometimes think maybe would have been better [if I hadn't], but I found what really unleashed the lioness waiting inside was when they tried to mess with who my characters were. When they said, 'This is how we would like this to go,' I was like, 'Edward would never do that! That's impossible!' It always got back to that. If it was something [threatening] the characters, I could hold my own. And that taught me the confidence I needed to continue with a career in writing." (Larry Carroll, Kim Stolz, MTV, August 6, 2008.)

On writing from a female perspective: "It was for me a very natural thing to write from the female perspective, because I wasn't thinking about what I was doing. I wasn't thinking, 'Wow! I want to promote girl power.' This was just for me. It was just a real natural thing and I'm glad that it's in the hands of a woman because I think you see things differently. I'm also glad that the male fan base is building because we ladies grew up reading books through school that were written by men. We were assigned to read them, and you get the male perspective down pretty well. But boys don't always have to read books written by girls or see movies from that point of view, and I think it's just good for communication to have that interchange of ideas." (Sara Castillo, Fearnet.com, August 8, 2008.)

Meyer's Inner Circle

Book editor Megan Tingley, under whose book imprint, the Twilight books are published: "Stephenie's fans are rabid. Stephenie has tapped into something very deep in her readers, and they respond on an emotional level." (Megan Irwin, "Charmed," *Phoenix New Times*.) • "Maybe it sounds trite, but I've been in this business for 20 years and it's rare when you read something and just know.... These books have every element of a totally satisfying blockbuster."

(Rachel Deahl, *Publishers Weekly*, July 23, 2007.) • "I know I'm on to something big when I respond to something that is outside my favorite genres. I'm not a vampire fan. And I'm not a romance fan either. But this book has vampires, romance and suspense. Also, the heroine is appealing because she's every girl. She's not rich, she's not gorgeous, but she's strong." (Jeffrey A. Trachtenberg, *The Wall Street Journal*, August 10, 2007.)

Stephenie's big sister Emily, to whom she dedicated the book: "It would be me and my five little friends, because of course I loaned out my books and got my whole neighborhood reading, and we'd go to the ice cream store, and she'd read some of the *Midnight Sun* manuscript to us. Those were the gatherings that Stephenie really loved." (Karen Valby, "Stephenie Meyer: Inside the 'Twilight' Saga," *Entertainment Weekly*, November 21, 2008.)

Media

From Amazon.com's editorial staff: "Deeply romantic and extraordinarily suspenseful, *Twilight* captures the struggle between defying our instincts and satisfying our desires. This is a love story with bite."

From *Booklist* (Ilene Cooper): "There are some flaws here—a plot that could have been tightened, an over reliance on adjectives and adverbs to bolster dialogue—but this dark romance seeps into the soul."

From *Kirkus Reviews*: "This is far from perfect: Edward's portrayal as monstrous tragic hero is overly Byronic, and Bella's appeal is based on magic rather than character. Nonetheless, the portrayal of dangerous lovers hits the spot; fans of dark romance will find it hard to resist."

From the *New York Times* (Elizabeth Spires): "The premise of *Twilight* is attractive and compelling...but the book suffers at times from over earnest, amateurish writing. A little more 'showing' and a lot less 'telling' might have been a good thing, especially some pruning to eliminate the constant references to Edward's shattering beauty and Bella's undying love."

From *Publishers Weekly*: "The main draw here is Bella's infatuation with outsider Edward, the sense of danger inherent in their love, and Edward's inner struggle—a perfect metaphor for the sexual tension that accompanies adolescence. These will be familiar to nearly every teen, and will keep readers madly flipping the pages of Meyer's tantalizing debut."

From R.J. Julia Booksellers (Karen Rosenthal, Children's Department Manager): "I'm not usually a vampire book reader, but I haven't read a book in a long time that had as much sexual tension and creepy terror throughout as *Twilight* by Stephenie Meyer [Little, Brown]. The main character is extremely compelling. The protagonist is so consumed with her crush on him that she blocks everything else, and the fact that he's a vampire adds a whole other level.

It really is the perfect crossover book. It will appeal to kids who read fantasy and darker books, but also kids who like more realistic fiction like *Sisterhood of the Traveling Pants*, and all those kids who read *Gossip Girl*... It's a riveting action book but thoughtful as well. Sometimes teen books can be plot-driven and the quality of the writing goes out the window, but this one has both."

James Blasingame, Department of English, Arizona State University: "Although this is a vampire tale, it is just as much a sweet and innocent love story. The two lovers are drawn to each other for reasons over which they have no control, they are unsure of how to manage their relationships amid friends and family who will surely not understand, and the depth and devotion of their love is never under question. Their love is as spiritual as physical although they never have intimate relations (you'll have to read the book to find out why not.) ... This is a fantastic first novel, and Meyer is developing quite a following. The sequels...will be hard for bookstores to keep on the shelves."

Readers

From www.lovevampires.com: "Twilight is simply and yet beautifully written. The descriptions of Forks leave you feeling like you can almost smell the damp air and hear the rain falling on the roof.

"The romance between Edward and Bella is both touching and compelling. There is a melancholic feel to their impossible love, yet at the same time they both are unwilling to give up hope that their relationship is not doomed. The book reaches a fever pitch of excitement as the romance between Bella and Edward turns into a frantic race to stay alive.

"I have heard *Twilight* described as 'a vampire story for people who don't like vampire stories' and I think I would agree with that. This book really has something for everyone. Young adult readers, vampire fans or romance readers will all find *Twilight* to be an appealing story."

An 11-year-old girl who saw Meyer at a book signing at Salt Lake City: "You're like my favorite author ever! I'm a person who judges authors a lot, and I don't have anything bad to say about you. I mean, I'm really tough; I didn't even like *Harry Potter*." (Karen Valby, "Stephenie Meyer: Inside the 'Twilight' Saga," *Entertainment Weekly*, November 21, 2008.)

Booksellers

Rene Kirkpatrick, book buyer for All for Kids: "In teen circles, she's bigger than 'Harry Potter.' Teenage girls, 12 and up—you mention Stephenie Meyer, and they all know her. I don't think it's going to be long before everybody knows who she is." (Cecelia Goodnow, *Seattle Post-Intelligencer*, August 6, 2007.)

Cheryl McKeon of Third Place Books: "On a scale of 1 to 10, she'd be about a 12—in enthusiasm among our readers and in sales."

Scholastic book editor Cheryl Klein: "It's a fascinating book. I also felt strongly reading it that it was not a *good* book, though when I asked myself why, my reasons were all political and aesthetic and not emotional.... Still, when I thought about the book from a sheerly emotional perspective—which can and often does matter more than anything else in a reading experience—then I totally understood why so many readers love this book so passionately, why they would call it not only a *good book* but one of the best ever: because more than any book I've read in a long time, it captured the exhilaration and fear of falling and being in love." (Cheryl Klein's blog, Brooklyn Arden, January 8, 2009).

New Moon: 563 pages

    1. original title: *New Moon*

    2. publication date: September 6, 2006

    3. dedication: her father, Stephen Morgan, after whom she was named

    4. editions available: in print form, advance reading copy, hardback, trade paperback, paperback; e-book (various formats); audiobook; and a Collector's Edition (slipcased and with enhanced production values).

    5. first U.S. printing: 100,000 copies in trade hardback

    6. cover art explained: Not suggested by Stephenie Meyer, the cover design/ photo was the publisher's idea. The flower in question is a ruffled tulip. On her website, Meyer states "I don't know what the tulip means—I didn't have anything to do with this one." Meyer's original idea incorporated a clock image, perhaps to suggest the Palazzo dei Priori, the clock tower in Volterra, Italy.

    7. literary inspiration: Shakespeare's play, "Romeo and Juliet."

    8. Book title symbolism: A "new moon" is "the moon either when in conjunction with the sun or soon after, being either invisible or visible only as a slender crescent." With Edward Cullen deliberately forsaking Bella for her own safety, she's plunged into a world of personal darkness: one with no light, symbolically suggested by the lack of luminance of a new moon.

    9. Publisher's copy: "The 'star-crossed' lovers theme continues as Bella and Edward find themselves facing new obstacles, including a devastating separation, the mysterious appearance of dangerous wolves roaming the forest in Forks, a terrifying threat of revenge from a female vampire, and a deliciously sinister encounter with Italy's reigning royal family of vampires, the Volturi."

Perspectives:

Stephenie Meyer

"With *New Moon* and *Eclipse*, I had fairly detailed outlines, and I wrote out of order. I focused first on the scenes that excited me, and then did the transitions between them after most of the story was written. ... Usually my mom, dad, and a few of my siblings are my first readers, and then I give it to my agent." (Deb Smouse, allthingsgirl.net, May/June 2008.)

Media

Cindy Dobrez, *Booklist*: "The writing is a bit melodramatic, but readers won't care. Bella's dismay as being ordinary (after all, she's only human) will strike a chord even among girls who have no desire to be immortal, and like the vampires who watch Bella bleed with 'fevered eyes,' teens will relish this new adventure and hunger for more."

Hillias J. Martin, *School Library Journal*: "Less streamlined than *Twilight* yet just as exciting, *New Moon* will more than feed the bloodthirsty hankerings of fans of the first volume and leave them breathless for the third."

VOYA (Voice of Young Adults): "Vampire aficionados will voraciously consume this mighty tome in one sitting, then flip back and read it once more. It maintains a brisk pace and near-genius balance of breathtaking romance and action."

Eclipse: 629 pages
1. original title: *Eclipse*
2. publication date: August 7, 2007
3. dedication: to her husband and three sons
4. editions available: in print form, hardback, trade paperback, paperback; e-book (various formats); and audiobook.
5. first U.S. printing: one million copies in trade hardback
6. cover art explained: The symbolism of a frayed, torn ribbon suggests how Bella's life became frayed, then torn, as it fell apart. She is torn in her decision between choosing between Edward or Jacob, and between the vampires and the werewolves.
7. literary inspirations: *Wuthering Heights* by Emily Brontë
8. Publisher's summary: "As Seattle is ravaged by a string of mysterious killings and a malicious vampire continues her quest for revenge, Bella once again finds herself surrounded by danger. In the midst of it all, she is forced to choose between her love for Edward and her friendship with Jacob—knowing that her decision has the potential to ignite the ageless struggle between vampire and werewolf. With her graduation quickly approaching, Bella has one more decision to make: life or death. But which is which?"

Perspectives:

Stephenie Meyer: "In *Twilight* and *New Moon*, Bella commits to becoming a vampire without once really examining what price she'll pay. In *Eclipse*, Bella fully comprehends that price. And then she chooses to pay it. Every aspect of the novel revolves around this point, every back story, every relationship, every moment of action." (In a FAQ about *Eclipse* from her website.)

Media

Publishers Weekly: "The legions of readers who are hooked on the romantic struggles of Bella and the vampire Edward will ecstatically devour this third installment of the story begun in *Twilight*, but it's unlikely to win over any newcomers. ... Once again the author presents teenage love as an almost inhuman force." (2007.)

Liesl Schillinger, *New York Times*: "What subversive creature could dream up a universe in which vampires and werewolves put marriage ahead of carnage on their to-do lists? The answer, of course, is a writer of steamy occult romantic thrillers who happens to be a wholesome Mormon mother of three—a category of one, solely occupied by Stephenie Meyer. The author is well aware of the jarring contradiction between her real and imaginary lives." (August 12, 2007.)

Breaking Dawn: 754 pages

1. original title: *Breaking Dawn*
2. publication date: August 2, 2008
3. dedication: to her literary agent, Jodi Reamer, and her "favorite band," aptly named Muse.
4. editions available: hardback; e-book (various formats); audiobook; and a Special Edition (supplementary text in the book and a bound-in DVD of the August 2008 *Breaking Dawn* concert series with Stephenie Meyer and Justin Furstenfeld (of the band Blue October).
5. first U.S. printing: 3.2 million copies in trade hardback
6. cover art explained: Stephenie Meyer's idea, the chessboard symbolizes the game of life with the transformation of Bella, once a powerless pawn, she is now a queen, the most powerful piece on the board.
7. literary inspirations: Shakespeare's "The Merchant of Venice" and "A Midsummer Night's Dream."
8. back story: Aware of the leaks that spoiled the release of J.K. Rowling's *Harry Potter and the Deathly Hallows*, Meyer urged her readers to avoid spoilers online and to report any postings to the publisher.
9. Publisher's summary: "Her imminent choice to either join the dark but seductive world of immortals or pursue a fully human life has become the thread from which the fate of two tribes hangs. Now that Bella has made her

decision, a startling chain of unprecedented events is about to unfold with potentially devastating and unfathomable consequences. Just when the frayed strands of Bella's life...seem ready to heal and knit together, could they be destroyed ... forever?"

10. Awards:

British Book Award for "Children's Book of the Year"

The series as a whole won "2009 Kids' Choice Award for Favorite Book"

Perspectives:

Stephenie Meyer: "The Twilight Saga is really Bella's story, and this was the natural place for her story to wind up. She overcame the major obstacles in her path and fought her way to the place she wanted to be. I suppose I could try to prolong her story unnaturally, but it wouldn't be interesting enough to keep me writing. Stories need conflict, and the conflicts that are Bella-centric are resolved." (From Meyer's website's *Breaking Dawn* FAQ.)

Meyer's Inner Circle

Megan Tingley: "Stephenie Meyer has written a dazzling grand finale to an epic love story." (Press release, February 7, 2008).

David Young, Chairman and CEO of Hatchette Book Group USA: "Stephenie Meyer has already achieved so much in her young career and this year further establishes her as a major force in the publishing industry. Given her remarkable talent and her passionate, ever-growing fan base, there is no limit to Stephenie Meyer's success." (Hatchette Book Group press release, February 7, 2008, "*Breaking Dawn* will release on August 2, 2008.)

Major Media

Publishers Weekly (August 4, 2008): "Flaws and all, however, Meyer's first three novels touched on something powerful in their weird refraction of our culture's paradoxical messages about sex and sexuality. The conclusion is much thinner, despite its interminable length. ... This isn't about happy endings; it's about gratification. A sign of the times?"

Bidisha: *The Guardian* (August 7, 2008): "Just like her vampire idol, Meyer remains an enigma. She is an imaginative storyteller, a prolific author and a newly powerful figure in the publishing market. She is able to successfully cross genres and audiences, as her recent and excellent adult science fiction novel, *The Host*, has proved. But her kudos among young female readers have been achieved through a series that drapes Dracula's cape around Barbara Cartland's shoulders."

"The themes in the books, in Tingley's view, are ageless. At its core, the story is about choice. The Cullens choose not to prey on humans; Bella must choose whether to become immortal. Though the Twilight series is marketed in the industry's young-adult category (age 12 to 18), Meyer tackles issues of identity and relationships in a way that appeals to 50-year-olds and 10-year-olds alike." (Laura Yao, *The Washington Post*, August 1, 2008).

Midnight Sun: 264 manuscript pages
    1. original title: *Midnight Sun*
    2. publication date: August 28, 2008
    3. editions available: an ebook in Adobe PDF with security measures enabled: no exporting or printing. According to the file's name, this is the fourth draft of the partial manuscript. There are 12 chapters, the last titled "Complications."
    5. first official publication: online on the Web on Stephenie Meyer's website
    6. literary inspirations: After reading fan fiction written from Edward Cullen's perspective, it became clear to Meyer that a large number of fans simply misunderstood Edward. By rewriting *Twilight* from his perspective, she hoped to clear up their misunderstandings of his character and motivations.
    8. back story: Meyer had no intention of releasing it prematurely until circumstances forced her hand. She gave a copy to someone who passed it along. It was soon reproduced virally on the Web. As Twilight fans wrestled with a dilemma—to download and read what the author had never intended for public consumption, or wait patiently until the book was eventually published—Meyer stepped in and cut the Gordian knot by posting it on her website, to spare her readers the dilemma.

The book's premature release has resulted in an indefinite delay in publication.

Little, Brown's press release: "A partial draft containing chapters of *Midnight Sun* by Stephenie Meyer has been leaked on the Internet without the knowledge or permission of either Stephenie Meyer or Little, Brown. Although these early chapters were never intended to be published in their current form, Stephenie Meyer has decided to authorize the posting of these rough, initial chapters on her website in fairness to her true, loyal fans. While no decisions have been made at this time regarding the publication of *Midnight Sun*, Stephenie Meyer is currently at work on other writing projects. Little, Brown looks forward to our continued publishing relationship with Stephenie Meyer and, like her many fans, we are eager to experience her next literary creation."

As Meyer explained on her website, "I feel too sad about what has happened to continue working on *Midnight Sun*, and so it is on hold indefinitely." She elaborated in an interview for *Entertainment Weekly* (November 6, 2008) that "It's really complicated, because everyone now is in the driver's seat, where they can make judgment calls. 'Well, I think this should happen, I think she should do this.' I do not feel alone with the manuscript. And I cannot write when I don't feel alone. So my goal is to go for, like, I don't know, two years without ever hearing the words *Midnight Sun*. And once I'm pretty sure that everyone's forgotten about it, I think I'll be able to get to the place where I'm alone with it again. Then I'll be able to sneak in and work on it again."

Her fans are divided on this issue. They are either willing to wait patiently until Meyer decides to complete it, or they are disappointed and angry at the proceedings, which can be seen by the various petitions posted at www.thepetitionsite.com.

Insider's Tip:
Where to Find Meyer's private correspondence, extras, outtakes, and remixes on the Web

Lest anyone begin howling in outrage, let me be clear: these are works that were published online by Stephenie Meyer on her website.

Using film and music terminology, fictional outtakes and remixes are available from Meyer's website. Go to the "file folder tab" for "Twilight Series" and, for each book, you'll find text not available elsewhere. Some of this material will undoubtedly see print in *The Twilight Saga: The Official Guide*, so readers will eventually have a copy in permanent form.

Book by book, here's a listing of what's available, in Adobe PDF form, for *Twilight* and *New Moon*. (There are no entries on her site for *Eclipse* or *Breaking Dawn*.)

Twilight
• "Badminton"
• "Flight" a.k.a. "Shopping with Alice" (the original chapter 20)
• "Emmett and the Bear"
• "Extended Prom Remix"

New Moon outtakes and extras
• "Narcotics"
• "The Scholarship"
• "If Jacob Didn't Break the Rules"
• "Rosalie's News"
• "Miscalculation"
• "Being Jacob Black"

The Twilight Lexicon

A treasure trove of information about Stephenie Meyer and her work, this website greatly benefited from an early affiliation with Meyer, who became fast friends with the web mistress and other staffers. As a result, long before the hundreds of websites on *Twilight* materialized, this early relationship forged at the beginning of her career, soon after the publication of *Twilight*, makes this the premiere Twilight fan website in terms of proprietary material. It's little wonder that Meyer said that this one is "the brightest star in the Twilight online universe."

The result is that Twilight Lexicon includes twelve, lengthy personal letters from Meyer that shed considerable light on her work, in addition to a missing *Twilight* scene; there's also transcribed questions-and-answers from several public talks.

The Meyer material can be accessed from the home page. On the left side, under its four main headings (**Twilight Lexicon, The Author, Twilight Saga,** and **Twilight Movies**), note that under **The Author** heading, there's a link titled "Correspondence with Stephenie." Click on that to bring up a drop-down menu of all the original material.

The Lexicon portion is fascinating reading. In terms of its coverage (character biographies, places, cars, clothing, timeline, vampire mythology, werewolf mythology), this is authoritative and remarkably complete. Stephenie Meyer's official guide will likely cover the same ground and incorporate some, if not all, of this material.

PART 3 - FANPIRE:
TWILIGHT FANDOM

In Tillicum Park, on Stephenie Meyer Day, Twilighters wait to buy a special postmarked envelope from the postmaster in Forks.

Telltale Signs that You've Been Smitten by Twilight

You've adopted a Twilight character name for your online identity.

You spend your free time obsessively searching websites for every morsel of information about Stephenie Meyer, the Twilight books, the film adaptations, and the Twilight actors. And you really can't help yourself!

You name your newborn son Edward or your newborn daughter Isabella. (If you name your daughter Renessme, she'll never forgive you, and your husband is well within his rights to divorce you.)

You Google "vampires" because you want proof they are real. You know they are.

You buy a silver Volvo SR60 R, the same one Edward Cullen drives. So what if it costs $38,500?

Sadly, you are familiar with the term "restraining order" as it relates to you and Robert Pattinson.

You are convinced that you, like Edward, can read minds, so you drive recklessly and speed, until you get pulled over for the first time and given a summons to appear in court to explain yourself. (Don't use the "Edward" defense; it *won't* work.)

When in Forks, you deliberately speed in order to get a souvenir—a speeding ticket from the local police. (This souvenir will cost you up to $200.)

It's *way* past your bedtime, you've got to get up at the breaking dawn to get to work, and you're up long past midnight surfing online because You Can't Help It: You suffer from OCD (Obsessive Cullen Disorder). Even your family doctor can't help you.

You dragged your girlfriends, your reluctant boyfriend, your parents, and anyone else you could lasso to go to see the movies ... and lost count of how many times you've done so. And you don't care what others think.

You have memorized entire paragraphs from the Twilight novels or film dialogue. Backwards.

You have both cardboard cut-outs of Edward Cullen and like to pose and have pictures taken with them.

You've bought more than one version of the movie DVD and have watched it more times than you can remember.

When someone you know criticizes *Twilight*, you leap passionately into the breech and defend it.

The only time of the year when you go out "dressed to the nines" is at a Volturi-themed costume ball at a Twilight convention.

You haven't read Stephen King but you really hate him because he needlessly dissed Stephenie Meyer, saying she can't write belles-lettres. "The real difference is that Jo Rowling is a terrific writer and Stephenie Meyer can't write worth a darn. She's not very good," the king of horror told *USA Today*. You are excused from wanting to go to Bangor, Maine, and storm his bat-decorated, welded iron fence that surrounds his home.

You're with your boyfriend and accidentally call him Edward even though that's not his name. He returns the favor by "accidentally" calling you Bella, which distresses you.

Your copies of *Twilight* have fallen apart due to prolonged rereading. You go to the hardware store and buy glue to repair your damaged copies.

The dishes go unwashed, the rugs go unvacuumed, the dirty clothes pile up and go unwashed, and the microwave is your best friend. You think this is *normal*.

You save up for a vacation ... and go to a Twilight convention. You spend way too much money. And you don't *care*.

You've been to Forks, Washington more than once. The Forks Coffee Shop waitresses know you by name. And you always get a Twilight-themed room when checking into a local motel.

You're on a first-name basis with Mike Gurling and Marcia Bingham at the Forks Visitor Center because you're always in contact with them. By phone. By e-mail. By fax. Not to mention the personal visits.

Glitter is your best friend because you like to sparkle like a vampire.

The Nike executive who owns the home in Portland, Oregon that served as the Cullen house in the film version of *Twilight* is not surprised to see you "accidentally" on his property, asking about the whereabouts of the "Cullen family."

When in Port Angeles, Washington around dinnertime, you will only eat at

Bella Italia restaurant and always order the mushroom ravioli.

You sigh deeply when you see promotional movie stills of Ashley Greene in the role of Alice Cullen because you love her fashion sense and want to buy knock-offs.

You've written a paper that you're presenting at a Twilight conference. It's about Edward. *Big* surprise.

You have a Twilight bumper sticker on your car. More than one, actually.

Your boyfriend has become increasingly concerned about your mental health because he thinks you spend *way* too much time being obsessed by Twilight. You tell him to deal with it or find someone else.

You carry the Twilight books on your family vacation. And, worse, quote favorite lines to your beleaguered family, who now know them by heart.

You've bookmarked all your favorite Twilight websites, which you visit several times daily. Okay, um, hourly. Oh, heck, every minute, okay, so stop *bothering* me!

When there was a possibility that Taylor Lautner was going to be dumped from the cast of *New Moon*, you sent angry e-mails to Summit Entertainment executives because they're, like, so retarded.

Money is no object where travel is concerned: If Stephenie Meyer is making a public appearance, holding a charity auction, or hitting the road for a book tour, YOU'RE THERE. What else *matters*?

The number-one sign that you're obsessed with Twilight: You believe that reality is for people who can't handle fantasy—like Twilight.

A Typical Comic-Con Press Conference with Robert Pattinson, Taylor Lautner, and Kristen Stewart: *A Parody*

Ladies, please welcome Robert—"

Screaming ensues, mimicking the sound of a jumbo jet starting to take off.

"—Pattinson, Taylor Lautner...."

More screaming ensues, mimicking the sound of a second jumbo jet taking off.

"And Kristen...."

More screaming. Third jumbo jet.

"Stewart...."

The few men in the audience have wisely covered their ears; the more experienced boyfriends and husbands insert custom-fitted earplugs and clap on sound-suppressing headphones.

The crowd finally quiets down to a low murmur. Robert Pattinson taps the microphone and smiles broadly.

Screaming ensues, mimicking the sound of The Beatles' arrival in New York City in the sixties. It sounds like a squadron of fighter jets just roared overhead.

"Sorry about that!" Pattinson adds, grinning again.

More screaming ensues. Sounds like a space shuttle has just lifted off from Cape Canaveral in Florida. RPATTZ exchanges wondering looks with fellow panelists.

"Ladies, *please*, let the panelists answer their questions!" begs the moderator. "We only have a half hour!"

The screaming subsides.

"So, panelists, what's a typical day like for you on the movie set?"

Quoting a line from page 315, chapter 15 of the hardback edition of *Twilight* ("The Cullens"), Robert Pattinson says, "Breakfast time for the human."

Twilighters who have memorized the book instantly recognize the line from the book, but because Pattinson also knows the book cold, the resultant shrill screaming is so loud that it sounds like a large truck with a full load of frightened pigs has locked brakes at 60 miles per hour while taking a hairpin curve: in other words, it's unbelievably loud screaming. Comic-Con security guards peer nervously inside the cavernous hall, wondering if an atomic bomb just detonated. Nearby fan boys dressed as Stormtroopers shake their heads in dismay. "There goes the neighborhood," they mutter.

"Please, ladies, I don't want to rob—"

More screaming. They *thought* he was going to say "Robert."

"—you of what little time we have left, so please keep it down to a dull roar!"

"We've got to be good stewards—"

More screaming. Very loud. Sounds too much like "Stewart." As in Kristen. Who kissed Robert Pattinson in *Twilight*.

"—of the time we have left, which we're rapidly running out of."

Taylor Lautner leans forward in his chair and growls into the microphone, imitating a wolf.

Unbelievable screaming. Fans are certain to be deaf after today. Audiologists all over the U.S. are going to be busy for months afterward, selling hearing aids.

"Sorry!" he says, waving his hand. "Had to *clear my throat!*"

Collective laughter. Kristen and Robert are cracking up and wiping tears from their faces. This is just too much.

A girl from the audience in the front row holds up a sign. "RPATTZ BITE ME." The jumbotron monitors show the excitable teen bouncing up and down with her hand-decorated sign.

Robert Pattinson sees the sign, points to her, leans into the microphone, and makes a biting sound, clacking teeth together. It's displayed twenty feet high on the jumbotron monitor.

More screaming. Sounds like three jumbo jets have just lifted off from Seattle's Seatac airport. Maybe four.

Not to be upstaged, Kristen Stewart interjects, "And then Rob fell off the bed with me at Catherine Hardwicke's Malibu house during his audition!" Pandemonium erupts.

The moderator throws away the microphone and walks off the stage, at which point the panel mercifully concludes, perhaps saving a few eardrums in the process. The boyfriends and husbands in tow appear to be happy beyond relief and sprint out, headed for the nearest liquor bar in search of a restorative—Jack Daniels or Jim Beam.

Quileute elder Chris Morganroth III holds a crowd of over 200 spellbound at a campfire storytelling session on First Beach at La Push on Stephenie Meyer Day in 2009.

Stephenie Meyer Day Celebration in Forks, Washington

Up to 1,500 people showed up to celebrate Stephenie Meyer Day 2009 in Forks, Washington, but she was nowhere in sight. At home and writing new fiction, Stephenie Meyer chose to sit out the weekend's festivities, but her presence was very much felt: the whole town, lead by the Forks Chamber of Commerce, got behind the celebratory event and threw a party that drew fans from all over the U.S. and from overseas destinations, including Germany and Australia. (Note: Meyer's actual birthday is December 24, which is obviously impractical for any celebration, so the date of Bella Swan's birthday was used instead—a reasonable substitute.)

Meyer, who had attended the town's celebration in her honor in July 2006, has not returned because the event has mushroomed in size from a few hundred to a capacity crowd that would make it impossible for her to enjoy any privacy: She routinely draws several thousand people and requires a larger venue than what Forks can provide. In other words, it'd be a mob scene: Imagine the Twilight crowd at Comic-Con suddenly placed in Forks. It'd strain the infrastructure of Forks to the breaking point: too few restaurants, insufficient lodging, and a traffic nightmare on its main street, Forks Avenue.

As it was, the attendance would have been even greater if the city simply had more lodging. Every motel, cottage, and inn within a half hour's drive of Forks had sold out months ago. During the event weekend, the local motels fielded countless calls asking about room availability. Sorry, but we're booked solid, they said. (Twilight Traveler's Tip: Book a room for next year's event as early as possible.)

For many of the attendees, this was a return trip to Forks. They had, on their own or through the local tour companies, seen all the key sights in town, but the line-up of events and the opportunity to hobnob with fellow fans is more than sufficient justification for a return trip.

As was the case the previous year, the busiest days were Friday and Saturday, since most people spent Sunday to head back home for the upcoming work week.

September 12 schedule of events

8:00 a.m., directly across from the high school, Congregational Church raised money to help repair its church by holding "Bella's Birthday Breakfast." For $10, attendees got their choice of any two crepes (strawberry, apple, or blackberry) and two links of sausage and a beverage.

9:00 a.m., a book sale ("Bella Loves Books") was held at the Forks Public Library.

10:00 a.m., a tour of Forks High School ($3 admission to benefit the school's rebuilding efforts); vendors in Tillicum Park sold food, jewelry, souvenirs, books, clothing, and other Twilight-themed merchandise to a capacity crowd; Forks' mayor Nedra Reed cut the ribbon at Dazzled By Twilight, officially opening the town's latest retail establishment. Author George Beahm (*Twilight Tours*) and artist Tim Kirk respectively signed and sketched at Tillicum Park and, later, at Dazzled by Twilight.

11:00 a.m. and 12:00 noon, additional tours of the Forks High School were conducted.

12:30 p.m., in Tillicum Park, Spradlee and Josh Swerin gave a concert.

2:00 p.m., Twilight fans met in Tillicum Park for their annual group portrait.

2:30 p.m., in Tillicum Park, a Twilight look-a-like contest was held.

3:30 p.m., at the Forks Memorial Library, decorated cars were judged and prizes awarded.

4:00 p.m., at the Forks High School, clips from a new documentary, *Twilight in Forks: Saga of a Real Town*, were shown.

6:00 p.m., at the Twilight lounge at Vagabond Restaurant, the Mitch Hansen Band put on the first of two concerts.

6:30 p.m., at First Beach in La Push, a traditional campfire storytelling by a Quileute elder (Chris Morganroth III) drew a crowd of approximately 200 people. Also present: actress Tinsel Korey, who appears as Emily Young in *New Moon*.

10:00 p.m., at Business Park Round House, the Twilight Music Girls gave a concert. Sponsored by Leppell's, the show cost $20.

September 13 schedule of events

10:00 a.m., vendors set up for a second day of sales.

11:00 a.m., the second performance of Spradlee and Josh Swerin.

1:00 p.m., at Tillicum Park, the town's mayor made a formal proclamation that this weekend was officially designated Stephenie Meyer Day. Also, sponsored by Leppell's, a Twilight scavenger hunt was held.

1:15 p.m., at Tillicum Park, Forks Chamber of Commerce Executive Director Marcia Bingham cut slices from four large cakes, which were quickly devoured.

2:00 p.m., at Tillicum Park, a second group photo of Twilighters was taken.

2:15 p.m., at Tillicum Park, a Twilight trivia contest was held.

Dazzled by Twilight's Grand Opening

In terms of retail, the success story in town is unquestionably Dazzled by Twilight. Starting from a small retail store in the downtown district, the store soon outgrew its initial location and leased a second location in the same city block. At the same time, Dazzled by Twilight also set up a satellite store in nearby Port Angeles, principally to serve Canadian visitors, weekenders from Seattle and Tacoma, and locals.

The new Forks store, designed to be an immersive, Disney-like experience, is replete with a wall-sized mural of First Beach, a babbling brook, freestanding trees, display cases of Twilight memorabilia, a gazebo decorated with lights (recalling the prom scene in the *Twilight* movie), cardboard cut-outs of Bella and Edward, and an homage to the local timber industry.

The Twilight inventory is, as you'd expect, extensive; a full line of licensed product is on hand, along with an impressive offering of locally produced jewelry. The product lines include books, audio books, music on CDs, the DVD of the *Twilight* movie, clothing, jewelry, collectibles, gifts, mugs, glassware, branded coffee and tea, and odds 'n ends (calendars, posters, magnets, stickers, book-markers etc).

My personal favorites: the jewelry, the etched red wine glass, the "Twilight series" coffees from the Vashon Island Coffee Roasterie, and the similarly branded teas.

Web Resources

www.forkswa.com

www.dazzledbytwilight.com

Dressed to kill, Twilighters vamp it up for the Volturi Ball at TwiCon 2009.

Twilight Conventions

Insofar as fandoms are concerned, the guys have laid claim to Star Wars and Star Trek. At the San Diego Comic-Con, which has traditionally been a male gathering of the geek tribe, some muttered darkly about the influx of Twilighters—thousands of girls who showed up to fill a convention hall to scream their approval when the principal cast of Twilight showed up to promote the film.

To paraphrase Bob Dylan, the times are changing.

TwiCon, a Twilight convention held in Texas in the summer of 2009, played host to an estimated 3,000 fans, mostly female. Men, though, were welcome at the Volturi Ball. A formal event in which a personable, young man dressed in a tux would have found his dance card quickly filled, it was an occasion for women to dress up to be the belles of the ball.

A sold-out event, TwiCon proved to be a challenge to its newbie con organizers, who acknowledged online after the event that, at times, their staff was overwhelmed. Comments posted on a TwiCon message board made it clear that some fans, after spending thousands of dollars, were disappointed.

A potentially bigger problem looms on the horizon for unauthorized Twilight-themed conventions: Summit Entertainment has recently teamed up with veteran convention organizers Creation Entertainment, which means independent events may find the availability of the film stars restricted, many of whom are already booked through the end of 2010 for Creation's conventions.

Creation Entertainment (www.creationent.com/calendar.htm)
After its Twilight convention in February 2009, they reported:

> Wow! That's all we can say about the very first Twi/Tour Convention and the launch of Creation Entertainment's Twi/Tour that took place on February 20-22, 2009. A giant sold-out crowd (thanks to all!) came ready to have the time of their lives and boy, did they! The atmosphere was electric as fans from around the world were on hand to celebrate the amazing success of Twilight and to cheer on their favorite stars!

All of the guests from the film were sensational in person, on-stage, answering audience questions, autographing, partying with fans and doing photo ops. Our special thanks to Kellan Lutz, Ashley Greene, Jackson Rathbone, Peter Facinelli, Billy Burke, Michael Welch, Christian Serratos, and Rachelle Lefevre for making the weekend so incredibly memorable.

A special shout-out to Jackson and 100 Monkeys for rocking the house like Elvis on Saturday night, and our appreciation also to our other musical performers The Bella Cullen Project (awesome job, ladies!), Goodnight Juliet, and the fantastic Michael Welch who also danced with the Vampire Court winners, an experience they won't soon forget! Thanks also to the super-talented Hillywood Show cast for hosting the weekend and being such a major part of its success. And, of course, we couldn't have done it all without the support of the generous Twilight fan community including panel participants from TwilightMoms, Twilighters.org, and Twilight20Somethings.

The official tie-in offers attendees more bang for their buck in terms of exclusive offerings. As Creation Entertainment explained on its website, "The weekend gatherings will feature on-stage appearances by Twilight celebrities, exclusive footage screenings, panel discussions, Twilight-themed parties, musical performances, costume and trivia competitions, auctions, autographing, merchandising, and photo opportunities."

The big advantage is that Creation's experience factor in running hundreds of cons over the years means that the events are typically trouble-free of logistical and scheduling nightmares that plague enthusiastic but inexperienced con organizers, who must cope with unexpected emergencies: a movie star cancels at the last minute, or catered food doesn't show up as guests get hungry.

Judging from all accounts posted online at its website, the Creation conventions catering to Twilighters are popular. One satisfied customer wrote,

First of all, I have to say that my daughter and I had never been to a convention or any event of this nature. That being said, we had a blast. The Q & A sessions were fun and the guests were so easygoing and seemed to really be happy to be there. The autograph sessions were orderly and timely. The photo sessions were quick (even with the long lines) and the photos were high quality. The welcome night was a perfect way to kick off the night and the concert with 100 Monkeys was crazy fun. The ball was a change of pace from the weekend since it was a little slowed down. It was the perfect way to end the busy day. Also having the guests come stop by each table gave us the opportunity to feel special.

I've been to several Creation conventions, both as a featured guest and as an attendee, and can say without fear of contradiction that they are smoothly run and thoroughly professional in every regard. So if you want to attend an official Twilight convention, you can't go wrong with one of Creation's events, scheduled in major U.S. and Canadian cities.

Fantasy Twi-Life Tour (www.twi-life.com)

Not officially linked to Summit Entertainment, this organization has the requisite depth of experience required to put on major fan conventions. Its Twilight-themed conventions have, or will, include Orlando, Florida; Nashville, Tennessee; Miami, Florida; Baltimore, Maryland; Norfolk, Virginia; Parsippany, New Jersey; Denver, Colorado; San Diego, California; Seattle, Washington; and Cincinnati, Ohio.

The major draw are the celebrity guests—the film stars. Scheduled movie stars include Ashley Greene, Alex Meraz, Edi Gathegi, Justin Chon, Gil Birmingham, Chaske Spencer, Tyson Houseman, Tinsel Korey, Bronson Pelletier, and Kellen Lutz. Musical guests and others (including Kimbra Hickey, the hand model for the *Twilight* book cover) are also scheduled for appearances.

A three day weekend pass is $70, but individual day passes are also available. Premium passes that allow special access cost correspondingly more ($110 to $295).

Don't Get Conned: Convention Tips

Culled from various websites worldwide and my own personal experience attending dozens of cons over the years, here's some time-tested tips that will make for a better convention experience:

1. Always keep your badge with you. Replacing it's a drag.

2. Wear comfortable shoes and clothing. You'll be on your feet all day, so plan accordingly. Change socks frequently.

3. Bring a small backpack to carry miscellaneous items. You aren't going to scale Mount Everest, so leave that oversized backpack at home.

4. A mailing tube of at least 20 inches is useful to store and protect movie posters. Get one with a carrying strap.

5. A schoolbook-style, three-ring notebook with plastic sleeves is essential for storing and protecting signed photographs, which are fragile.

6. Take breaks as necessary. Because a convention is a three-ring circus, think like a marathoner does: pace yourself.

7. You aren't going to be everywhere, can't see everything, can't experience every event, and can't buy all you want in the dealers' room. So decide in advance what's most important to you and plan accordingly.

8. Make reservations at nearby hotels for dinner, so you don't have to stand

in line for a table along with other conventioneers who, like you, didn't plan accordingly.

9. Get your tickets early, especially for event tickets that tend to sell out quickly.

10. Bring cash. A good rule of thumb is $50 to $100 a day. Avoid ATM machines near the con, which may run out of cash, in addition to surcharges for each transaction. (If you're staying at a hotel, ask the clerk at the front desk if they will cash a small check. Many will do so as a courtesy to guests.)

11. Have a copy of the schedule with you at all times. You'll be consulting it regularly.

12. Swag is usually limited on a first come, first serve basis, so find out who's giving away what, where, and when, and be there first. Free stuff goes quickly; the best stuff always shows up on eBay within days after the event at scalper's prices.

13. Be patient. Nobody likes standing in line, so wait your turn; bring a book or something else to occupy your time.

14. Bring some snacks. Convention food is expensive. Bottled water, hot dogs, nachos, popcorn from the food kiosks add up pretty quickly, so bring some snacks from home or buy local refreshments at a grocery store or full-service drugstore: bags of peanuts, dried fruit, fruit, or candy/energy bars.

15. If there's a nearby drugstore, get there and stock up on essentials you left at home. It's always cheaper than the hotel gift shop and convention kiosks.

16. Above all, *have fun*. Isn't that why you're attending in the first place?

Twilight Fan Trips:
A Vampire Baseball Game

by Sara Gundell

On a beautiful, sunny day in Portland, Oregon, the stars of *Twilight* returned to the city where they filmed the hit movie to play baseball and raise money for a good cause. The event was sponsored by Twilight Fan Trips.

Peter Facinelli, Edi Gathegi, Rachelle LeFevre, Michael Welch, Christian Serratos, Alex Meraz, Kiowa Gordon, Solomon Trimble, and other local actors hit the playing field at Portland's PGE Park on Saturday, July 4, 2009, for a charity baseball game. The event helped raise money for the Make-A-Wish Foundation of Oregon, gave fans a chance to see their favorite *Twilight* stars in person, and celebrate Independence Day with America's favorite pastime.

The day-long event started early in the morning, with a live podcast from several *Twilight* fan sites. During the first part of the morning, crew members and select lucky fans played a baseball game on the field; meanwhile, fans who had purchased special tickets met with some of the actors for a Q&A session over coffee. Later, the actors met with local and national media for interviews before taking to the field for the big event.

The actors—including some from the Portland area—split into two teams: led by Peter Facinelli, the Veggie Vampires Dances with Wolves played against the Portland Purple People Eaters, led by Rachelle LeFevre.

Despite the oppressive heat and cloudless sky, the "vampires" managed to keep their sparkling under control and ran the bases at normal human speed, so fans could easily follow the action. The game played was all in good fun—despite a few, occasional "disagreements" between the teams—and fans were impressed by how well the actors played.

The Veggie Vampires Dances with Wolves won the game, but the real winners were the fans and the Make-A-Wish Foundation of Oregon, which is what inspired the actors to spend their 4th of July holiday away from home.

"Anything we can do to help good causes, we're there," Facinelli said.

After the baseball game, the actors signed hundreds of autographs and posing for numerous photos with fans, some of whom had lined up for over two hours to meet their favorite actors. The *Twilight* stars were exceptionally gracious, even signing extra autographs and taking photos when they weren't legally obligated to do so. Most actors even took the time, if only for a minute, to talk one-on-one with fans.

Michael Welch, who plays Mike Newton in the *Twilight* movies, said participating in the Make-A-Wish fundraiser was a no-brainer for him. "I know that I'm not that big a deal," Welch said. "I know that I was just lucky, and somebody gave me an opportunity. But at the same time, I do realize that perception is reality, and if I can contribute to the magic in a kid's life, and all I have to do is show up and say 'hi,' take a picture, or sign something, it's the least I can do."

Web resource
> www.fantrips.travel

Robert Pattinson at the U.K. premiere of *Twilight*.

Maggie Parkes

150 Reasons Why We Love Edward *freaking* Cullen!

by Rachel Heaton

Rachel Heaton lives in the U.K. and is an ardent Twilight fan who could just as easily have come up with more reasons to love Edward without repeating herself.

✳

He's a true gentleman.
He'd rather hurt himself than you.
He'd love you for all eternity.
His love is as strong as imprinting.
He wishes he could dream of you.
He admits he wishes he could dream of you.
He isn't ashamed of it.
He sparkles.
He dazzles us.
He wants to protect his virtue.
He wants to protect yours, too.
He doesn't want you to go to hell.
He doesn't think he's good enough for you.
He can read minds—it's just cool.
He can pick you up with one hand.
He's super-fast.
He drives insanely fast.
He doesn't crash when he drives insanely fast.
He slows down when it bothers you.
He wants to marry you A.S.A.P.
He's a vegetarian.
He loves baseball.
He prefers brunettes.

He plays the piano.
He gets emotional.
He watches you sleep.
He has an extensive vocabulary.
He's got his own style.
He's unique.
He's really smart.
He's old-fashioned.
He's a pessimist, but we love him for it.
He had green eyes.
He drives an awesome car.
He has pretty colour-changing eyes.
He loves his family.
He's loyal.
He could save you from being hit by a car or van.
He's unselfish even if he thinks he is selfish.
He tells hilarious jokes.
He can't take a joke when it's about you being eaten.
He has a car for every special occasion.
He'd rather be ripped and burnt to death than be without you.
You can practically smell his testosterone.
He's very persuasive.
He's definitely a superhero.
Kryptonite doesn't bother him.
He wasn't bitten by a radioactive spider.
He could take on any super hero any day—and win.
He would die for you.
He would do anything to keep you safe.
He would do anything to keep you happy.
He would buy you whatever you want.
He buys cool cars for people he loves.
He makes being a hostage fun.
He makes other girls melt.
He makes other girls want to kill you because he loves you.
He is the modern-day Romeo.
He makes girls' heartbeats go crazy.
He promises forever—and means it.
He has amazing self-restraint.

He holds you in your sleep.

He sings you to sleep.

He sings your nightmares away.

He says the word "sexy" on occasion.

He can look totally bewildered even after a century.

His body is rock hard.

Only a vampire can love you forever.

His mood swings are hot.

He may not be human, but he is a man.

He's a vampire who just wants to be good.

He would happily break Jacob's jaw.

He will never leave you, even if you kiss another guy.

He wants to save your soul.

He can climb into your room through your window.

His crooked smile makes you forget to breathe.

He smells of heaven.

He wouldn't die in a plane crash.

He wouldn't let you die in a plane crash, either.

When he smiles you can't help but smile back.

He growls.

He is your vampire angel.

He has morals.

He's romantic.

He's passionate.

He isn't afraid to admit how much he loves you.

He isn't afraid to tell you what he's thinking.

He has a melodic chuckle.

He has perfect handwriting.

He makes sarcasm sexy.

He makes jealousy sexy.

He makes angry sexy.

He makes Volvo's sexy.

He makes Aston Martins sexy.

He makes being emotional sexy.

He makes old Chevy pickup trucks sexy, even if he doesn't own one.

Aww hell, he makes *everything* sexy!

He doesn't eat but still watches the food network.

He can cook.

Only he can pull off driving a Volvo.

He never sleeps.

He isn't human.

He isn't a werewolf.

He doesn't want you to ever get hurt.

He bites.

He uses words like "unequivocally" in everyday conversation.

He will never have morning breath.

He will buy a bed for you, even though he doesn't need it.

He kisses well when you're a human.

He kisses insanely good when you're a vampire (finally).

He'll never let you go.

He's charming.

He won't fight fair.

He gives you hand-me-downs.

He'll stay with you and miss all the fun.

His family loves you.

He can quote Romeo.

He's got an amazing body.

He's rich.

He has awesome taste in music.

He appears out of nowhere and kisses you.

He says you are beautiful, not only that you *look* beautiful.

He can enter your room without anyone noticing.

He can run downstairs without parents knowing.

He gives you his jacket when you're cold.

He only has eyes for you, even when surrounded by hot girls.

He will stand in front to protect you when you're in danger.

He will stay young, gorgeous, and sexy forever.

He will pick a fight with the Volturi.

He loves you for who you are, not what you look like.

Even when you're in sweats and tee-shirt, he still says you're beautiful.

Even when you're ill, he says you're beautiful.

He looks after you when you're sick.

He's jealous of all your boy mates.

He will write you a song.

He's a virgin!

He whispers nice things in your ear.

He thinks you're cute when you're jealous.
He will kiss you in the middle of a fight.
He's able to make you immortal.
He hugs you behind your back.
He wants to be able to give you children.
He's been single since 1918.
He holds your face when kissing you.
He tries not to get carried away.
He gets carried away.
He apologizes when he gets carried away.
He doesn't lie (much).
He tells you you are his heaven.
He's Edward *freaking* Cullen!

Washington State natives Maarika Vercamer and Shayla Kieneker are obviously smitten by Edward Cullen.

So You Want To Be A Paperback Writer: Time-Tested Advice For Aspiring Authors

"The most important thing you can do is to write for yourself. Don't think about any other audience, don't worry about a demographic, and don't let the thought of publishing ever enter your mind. Enjoy the story and enjoy the creation process. If you aren't enjoying yourself, then you shouldn't be writing. After your story is all done, *then* you can worry about what comes next. But keep your storytelling pure, and focus on pleasing yourself first."

—Stephenie Meyer in an interview with Deb Smouse on allthingsgirl.net (May/June 2008)

*

An American success story, Stephenie Meyer had an idea for her first novel; a mere five months later, she had a lucrative three-book deal. Given that Meyer was an obscure housewife who had hoped to make only enough to pay off the family van but became an international franchise in her own right, aspiring writers want to know how she did it; many of them have stardust in their eyes and hope to get their first book published, some hoping to strike it rich and live the life of a bestselling author.

Here's time-tested advice on what has worked for writers from Stephen King to J.K. Rowling.

Apprenticeship

1. Read as much as possible, fiction and nonfiction, not only in the areas you are personally interested in (e.g., romance fiction or fantasy fiction) but in areas outside your normal interests. Everything you read becomes useful background information.

If you find reading a chore, don't waste your time dreaming about becoming a writer; find something else that doesn't seem like work to you. Bonafide writers can't keep their hands off books, magazines, newspapers and, when all else fails, the back of cereal boxes. They are compulsive wordaholics and cannot *not* read. It's an absolute that you must *love* reading to be a writer.

2. Sit down and write. Don't talk about writing, commiserate with others about your writer's block, or find a million ways to procrastinate and not write. If you don't make the time to write, if you can't discipline yourself to write on a regular basis, you'll never be a published writer.

3. Finish what you write, be it a poem, short story, novella, article, or novel. Dean Koontz, who in his early years shoveled asphalt on a road construction crew, said that writing is harder work than heavy manual labor. Know and accept that, and you'll be way ahead of your contemporaries who are waiting for inspiration to strike, or complaining about how they can never find the time to write.

Writers *make* the time as Meyer did: She began writing at a desktop computer with a small child on her lap and one at her feet. Because she never shortchanged time with her children, she had to find the time elsewhere. She found it after putting the kids to bed and sacrificed some of her sleep time to write. (What sacrifices are *you* willing to make?)

4. Get constructive criticism, preferably from teachers at school or experienced writers at a local group who have serious intent. Some writers' groups are merely social in nature and meet only to have a good time and ease the loneliness that's intrinsic to the writing life. Instead, seek a group that reads work aloud and offers useful advice.

5. Don't put the cart before the horse. Don't worry about contracts, agents, and publishers until *after* you've got something to sell. Make sure you've sweated blood over it and had it critiqued and then rewritten until it's the best you can do. Then, and only then, should you worry about professional publication.

Far too many amateurs spend all of their time worrying about what's down the road instead of what's in front of them: the blank page that must be filled. In other words, you don't *need* an agent—until he needs you.

6. Learn how to properly format a manuscript: double-space in a normal font (Courier is best) with your name/work on the upper left and the page number on the right. The font should be in a 12 or 14 point size. Use 20-pound white paper (*not* erasable). Make your manuscript look professional and it'll be taken seriously. Don't use an unreadable typeface in a tiny font size; use only twenty-pound white bond paper; don't wrap the package so securely that it's a battle just to open it.

After the book is written

1. Do your homework. Find out who is publishing the kind of book you want to write. Go to the bookstore and become familiar with the names on the bottom of the book's spine (Random House, Harper Collins, Ballantine Books,

et al.). These are the publishers' names to be found in industry directories.

2. Buy, borrow, or go online to access *Writer's Market*, a directory of book publishers, magazines, literary agents, etc.

3. Buy or borrow a copy of an agent's directory that lists literary agents, what they are looking for, and how to submit to them. Then follow those instructions to the letter.

An alternate source is www.publishersmarketplace.com, which also lists agents. It's a great place to explore the publishing community online.

4. Start reading the trade journal to the book publishing industry, *Publishers Weekly*, at your local library or online at www.publishersweekly.com.

5. Once you've identified likely literary agents, send a one-page query letter to see if they'd like to see more. They will usually ask for three contiguous chapters and an outline if they're interested. (Send *only* if they express an interest. They do not want, and will not accept, unsolicited manuscripts.)

6. Don't worry about pros stealing your ideas—they're commonplace; it's the *execution* of an idea that's important. Professional writers don't need to steal from unpublished, little-known writers. As Stephen King pointed out on his website, "Unless there's deliberate copying (sometimes known as 'plagiarism'), stories can no more be alike than snowflakes. The reason is simple: no two human *imaginations* are exactly alike."

7. Don't sit around in front of your mailbox and mope, waiting for a response from an agent. Get back to work and write another book—*now*.

8. And above all: *Don't quit your day job*.

Final tips:

Write *your* book, not your imitation of Stephenie Meyer's Twilight series, J.K. Rowling's Harry Potter novels, or Stephen King's suspense fiction. Write a story with its unmistakable stamp of *you* on every page. In other words, emulate and don't imitate.

Remember that Stephenie Meyer's rapid ascension to fame and riches is on par with winning the lottery, which she's quick to point out in public talks. Just because it happened to her doesn't mean it's going to happen to you.

Expect to get lots of rejections.

If you're finally published professionally, expect to make some money but not necessarily a fortune.

Your publishing experience will almost surely have nothing to do with Stephenie Meyer, except perhaps that you share a common dream: to take the words in your head and heart, put them down on paper, and have someone want to read them badly enough to pay money to do so.

That should be enough for now.

Recommended Books

• *How I Write: Secrets of a Bestselling Author* by Janet Evanovich with Ina Yalof. Stephenie Meyer credits Evanovich's website for information on how to get published.

• *On Writing: A Memoir of the Craft* by Stephen King. Yes, I know King dissed Meyer, but trust me on this one: This is the single best book ever written by a writer for aspiring writers. It not only *shows* (the first part, a memoir) but *tells* (a nuts-and-bolts construction on how to write). If you are an aspiring writer, this is essential.

• *Dan Poynter's Self-Publishing Manual: How to Write, Print and Sell Your Own Book*. Even if you aren't planning on self-publishing (which, by the way, should *not* be confused with print-on-demand, which is, as the name clearly states, *printing*), read this and learn about what goes on behind the scenes in the book industry, from manufacturing to promotion. This is the self-publishing bible that launched a thousand books, including several of my early books.

• *The Elements of Style* (50th anniversary edition). Short, pithy, authoritative. Buy it. Read it. Study it. You won't regret it.

• *The Chicago Manual of Style: The Essential Guide for Writers, Editors, and Publishers.* The gold standard, this is the definitive reference work on bookmaking, writing style, production and printing.

• *Writer's Market: Where and How to Sell What You Write.* Now up to its 88th annual edition, this is a detailed, authoritative directory of book publishers, magazines, trade journals, literary agents, and much more. Indispensable.

• *1001 Ways to Market Your Books* by John Kremer. He's the master of book marketing and offers time-tested advice that is especially useful for any author who wants to fully understand the marketing function in book publishing. As they say, writing is 1% inspiration and 99% perspiration: marketing a book is simply hard work. This book makes the process a little easier to telling you exactly what to do—a real boon to writers who, for the most part, are wired to write, not market, their books. (An oft-heard comment: "I'm a writer—marketing the book is the *publisher's* job, not mine." So not true!)

A Forks souvenir: a small road sign that notes a small but significant change in the town's population.

Dazzle Me!
Slogans on Merchandise from Café Press and Zazzle

Entrepreneurs with a flair for design and original expression find self-publishing through Café Press an inexpensive way to get into manufacturing without any upfront costs. If your idea and its execution are above the rest of the pack, you, too, can be a howling, entrepreneural success.

In what has to be a unique arrangement between a major film studio and its fans, Summit Entertainment has set up on Café Press its "Official Twilight Movie Fan Portal," which allows fans to use dialogue, characters, and places in the Twilight universe to come up with their own sanctioned product for sale on www.cafepress.com: 21,500 designs thus far that are available on 682,000 various products.

The restrictions set by Summit Entertainment:

- No use of the official Twilight movie logo
- All images must be tagged with "twilight movie"
- No use of images or depictions of the actors in the movie
- No use of profanity, vulgar or hate language
- No use of explicit sexual language or graphics
- No use of copyrighted material from the movie or its promotional materials (e.g. no use of images of the movie, movie posters or from the movie website)
- No political party associations (e.g. republican, democrat, or candidates)
- No blood
- No fangs
- No stakes through the heart
- No coffins
- No bats
- No use of Twilight book cover images

- No pictures of apples
- No journals (you cannot create Twilight journal products)
- No calendars (you cannot create Twilight calendar products)
- No Cards (you cannot create Twilight postcards, greeting cards and note cards)
- No Undergarments (you cannot create Twilight thongs or boxer shorts)

Here's a selection of some of the slogans, which make a lot of sense to Twilighters but, otherwise, will surely draw a blank stare from your husband, boyfriend, or non-Twilight friend.

✳

Jasper says relax.
Stupid lamb seeking sick, masochistic lion.
You say "clumsy" like it's a bad thing.
OCD: Obsessive Cullen Disorder.
You better hold on tight, spider monkey.
Say it out loud. Say it. Vampire.
WAIT! Did you say something? It wasn't Edward-related
and I tuned you out the first time.
I'm a sick, masochistic lion.
I'm a stupid lamb.
Mommy's little nudger.
Bite me.
Stupid, shiny Volvo owner.
Do that again and I will so give you a paper cut right
in front of Jasper.
I drive like a Cullen.
Edward can bite my pillows, break my headboard,
and bruise my body any day.
And so the lion fell in love with the lamb...then the lion left. Team Jacob.
Forget princess! I wanna be a vampire!
Jacob can imprint on me any day.
You brought a snack?
Quileute Reservation: Wolf Refuge.
Team Bella. We trip over flat surfaces.
Isle Esme: Sun, Fun and Edward.
You don't sparkle? I see no point in talking to you.

Jasper? Oh, Hale yes!

Dazzle me.

I like my men cold, dead, and sparkly. Team Edward.

It's a Twilight Thing. You wouldn't understand.

I never received my letter to join the wizards, so I am moving to Forks
to live with the vampires.

Team Jacob (because he didn't leave).

La Push Cliff Diving Association. Established 2004.

I'm no Alice. You're just predictable.

My heart belongs to my husband, but my neck belongs to Edward.

Dear Jacob, I WIN. Sincerely, Edward.

Proud fanpire. It's all about Team Edward.

Edward is the new Harry.

Christmas wish list: 1. Move to Forks, 2. Meet Edward, 3. Become a Vampire.

Bitten by Edward. I only wish...

Sorry, boys, I've already been imprinted.

Alice knows...

Bite me. Vampires only!

Team Stephenie.

Pale is the new tan.

Why am I covered in feathers?

Bitten and smitten.

A fictional vampire is ruining my marriage.

All I want is a gorgeous, immortal, cold Volvo (silver-colored) owner that
sparkles and bites me.

Edward prefers brunettes.

Air conditioner or space heater? *You* decide.

Good girl gone vampire.

Web Resources

www.cafepress.com
www.zazzle.com

First Beach at La Push.

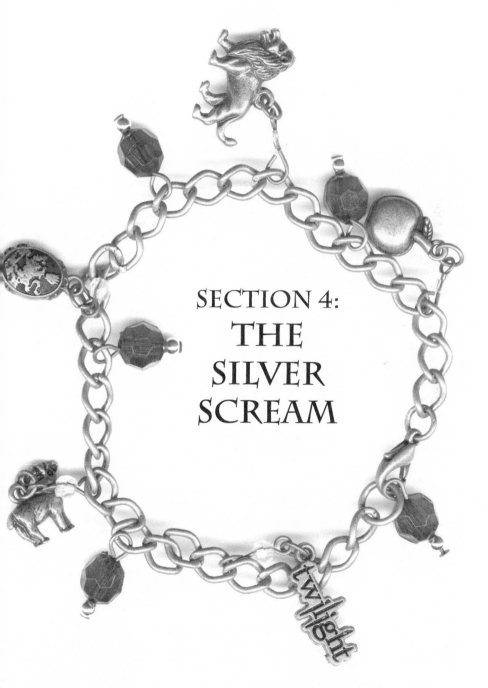

SECTION 4:
THE
SILVER
SCREAM

Twilight Charm bracelet

Twilight from Book to Screen

It sounds anecdotal, but there may be some truth in this: Worried sick about how a film will open—i.e., how well it will perform over its opening weekend, which is considered an early indicator of its possible success—film executives in Hollywood keep trash cans nearby so they can use them in case they need to vomit. An expensive film that "opens" poorly is sufficient cause for firings, studio consolidations, the potentially devastating loss of a film franchise, and other nightmares that keep worried film executives up at night. In other words, with millions of dollars invested and at risk, making a motion picture is partly an act of faith but mostly a major investment.

New Moon director Chris Weitz, who wrote and directed *The Golden Compass*, knows all too well the repercussions of a movie that doesn't meet the studio's expectations. With an impressive production budget of $180 million, New Line Cinema had hoped to follow up Peter Jackson's success with *The Lord of the Rings* ($3 billion worldwide) with a similar one for Pullman. Unfortunately, for all parties concerned, *The Golden Compass* opened at only $26 million; and when the dust settled and the smoke cleared, it had grossed only $70 million domestically, though it went on to gross $302 million in foreign sales.

According to the news agency Reuters, the studio had hoped the opening box office gross would be up to $40 million. New Line executives, said Reuters, declined to comment.

Visually stunning with an ensemble cast, *The Golden Compass* proved to be the studio's undoing; heads at New Line rolled and the studio was subsequently absorbed by Warner, which will not likely green-light a sequel.

For Chris Weitz, redemption will almost surely come in the form of *New Moon*, which *Entertainment Weekly* projects to be the biggest film of the holiday season for 2009. Industry insiders and major media agree with *EW*. In Hollywood, where sure things are the rule more than the exception, *New Moon* will eclipse everything else showing during the holiday season. Look for *New Moon* to open at $80 million.

Summit Entertainment is fortunate indeed to have bought into a winning franchise, but in the beginning, things weren't so clear-cut: Hollywood always has its eye, like Sauron in *The Lord of the Rings*, scanning the horizon in search of the Next Big Thing. One tactic Hollywood employs is to get in on the ground floor, to option books while still in manuscript form, to preempt the competition.

A book scout sent a copy of the unedited manuscript to an independent producer, Greg Mooradian, who was smitten by its timeless love story. In an MTV interview, he explained, "I'm the one who discovered the book. ... At the time I first read *Twilight*, it was well before it was published. We had no idea what it would become." He took it to Paramount. In April 2004 MTV (a division of Paramount) was tasked with developing the project.

Unfortunately for Paramount, the project never got off the ground; and when its option expired, Mooradian pitched it to Summit Entertainment, which acquired the film rights in February 2006.

Director Catherine Hardwicke was brought in to get the book adapted to the screen in a timely manner. The first priority was to create a usable script because the existing script depicted Bella Swan as an athletic, butt-kicking *Charlie's Angels*-type on jet skis with the FBI running around: a generic action-adventure film that would surely have disappointed Meyer's fans and, in the process, prematurely killed a potentially lucrative franchise. Had that script been developed into a movie, Stephenie Meyer remarked that had its title been removed, no viewer would ever have connected it with *Twilight*. The remedy was to go back to square one, take a closer look at the book itself, enlist the active aid of the author, and find a screenwriter who could faithfully translate the book to film.

Summit moved forward quickly.

Greg Mooradian signed on to be one of the film's producers, along with Wyck Godfrey and Guy Oseary.

Melissa Rosenberg, tapped to write the screenplay, turned in a tight 109-page script, approved by Meyer, who was brought in to insure the movie stayed true to the Twilight universe.

With veteran director Catherine Hardwicke at its helm, the most critical concern had to be addressed: casting. Choosing a Bella Swan would not be a monumental problem, but finding the perfect Edward Cullen, the key to the book and movie franchise proved to be a paramount challenge.

Meyer's own choice, British actor Henry Cavill, was too old to pass for seventeen, Edward Cullen's stated age, so the search was on.

Like the search for the right Harry Potter, which took months of screening thousands of young boys, finding the right Edward proved to be a challenging task. Interestingly, one of the actors who auditioned for the role, Michael Welch, would find a place in the film. He missed out on the biggest role in the fledgling film franchise. He would not be Bella's paramour but a fellow student with a crush on her—a member of the supporting cast.

After seeing thousands of head shots and winnowing them down to ten for the final cut, Hardwicke had soon found her Edward in British actor Robert Pattinson. Stephenie Meyer agreed, saying that he had the right combination of looks with a dark edge. The attraction between Pattinson and Stewart was undeniable, said Hardwicke. "When I met Kristen," said Robert Pattinson, "there was instant chemistry. She brought something out of me that I can't even explain," he said in an interview for www.theimproper.com.

As soon as Robert Pattinson was cast in the role, a firestorm erupted online. Concerned about what fans were saying about her son, his mother helpfully scoured the Web and sent emails to him to share what she had found. Among them, a petition started by outraged fans, already numbering 75,000; they adamantly opposed the casting choice. And a website in which an apoplectic fan said RPattz (as he was nicknamed by fans) looked like a gargoyle. It didn't assuage his feelings that other fans were just as vocal in championing his cause.

Stone-faced in public, Pattinson realized that no matter what the fans thought, he couldn't let them distract him from his job: to become Edward on screen. Toward that end, he wrote personal journals and consulted with Stephenie Meyer, who gave him an early copy of *Midnight Sun*—*Twilight* rewritten from Edward's point of view—to better help him understand his character.

When the principal cast finally debuted in public at the San Diego Comic-Con in July 2008, thousands of female fans roared their approval. Edi Gathegi, Cam Gigandet, Rachelle Lefevre, Taylor Lautner, Kristen Stewart, and Robert Pattinson were understandably surprised by the obviously vocal fans whose screaming shook the rafters.

When asked "what's it like dealing with all the fans," Pattinson admitted, "This is the first time I've really seen any of them, so I don't know. It just baffles me. It's nice, though."

Pattinson was gobsmacked. Previously best known for his role as a senior who competes in a tournament that turns deadly for him in *Harry Potter and the Goblet of Fire*, he sees himself as an actor, not a celebrity, and certainly not someone who should be treated as if he's a superstar.

Comic-Con, if evidenced by this crowd, proved to be an affirmative sign that *Twilight* would likely hit the screens with the overwhelming approval of its fans; they were dying to see their favorite novel on the big screen.

Robert Pattinson had no idea what lay ahead: After *Twilight*, he would literally be pursued by fans in the streets, subjected to unwanted hugs and kisses in public, and in one instance, chased down in New York City, where he ran into the street and was struck by a taxi. "People ambush me and try and find out what hotel I'm staying at, as well as wanting to touch my hair. Everyone just screams and screams. It feels surreal," he said, reported by www.starpulse. com.

For now, however, Pattinson was pleased to be on board for what promised to be a steady gig—three more films in the series, if the first one could justify its modest investment.

Coming off a major book tour to promote two back-to-back novels (*The Host* and *Breaking Dawn*), Meyer was understandably fatigued but realized the importance of promoting the film; she reluctantly found herself back on the road to give it her all. Her efforts were supplemented by the fan effort online, with hundreds of dedicated websites reporting every morsel of news, publishing every candid photo of the principal cast, and virally sharing every rumor, many of them involving Robert Pattinson, a super massive black hole of attention irresistibly drawing fans and major media.

As the witching hour approached, with 600 midnight showings of *Twilight* domestically, Summit executives were understandably nervous, but their concerns were somewhat mollified when all the midnight showings sold out.

The online speculation about the film's quality had begun in earnest.

On www.cinemablend.com, Josh Tyler put his foot firmly in mouth when he offhandedly wrote: "It's probably not any good. In fact, it looks like a direct-to-DVD castoff, but its fans are so addicted to the books that they're lining up to see it in droves. In fact, the thing is already selling out. ... The Twekkies will be out to see this thing in force on Friday. The question is: will anyone else? The trailers look terrible and I don't know anyone who hasn't read the books who's even remotely interested in seeing it."

Had Summit Entertainment read Tyler's pre-show assessment and took it to heart, they'd have reason to worry. Among Twihards and Twilighters (as they term themselves—*not* "Twekkies"), their intense approbation drowned out Tyler's isolated voice in the wilderness. The true fans would make up their minds after seeing the movie.

Summit Entertainment wisely downplayed expectations. Better to expect the worst and hope for the best than to celebrate prematurely.

On November 21, 2008, *Twilight* hit screens nationwide and, by late Sunday, the resounding numbers spoke for themselves: the Twilight franchise was suddenly the hottest property in town. An admittedly stunned Summit executive, Richie Fay, president of domestic distribution, admitted that "This certainly exceeded our expectations by a great deal. The fan base was huge."

As was the case with *Titanic*, the biggest grossing film of all time, *Twilight*'s audience base, comprised mostly of young women, went to repeated viewings, just as their male counterparts turned out in full force for repeated viewings when *Star Wars* originally debuted.

Though some fans complained that the computer-generated imagery for the sparkling effect for Robert Pattinson was unconvincing—a criticism Meyer voiced herself—they had not only shown up in droves but drove its box office take to the top of the charts in record time.

The modestly budgeted film of $37 million "opened" at nearly $70 million. After 19 weeks in release to 3,649 theaters nationwide, it would close with a domestic gross of $191 million, supplanted by a foreign gross of $192 million.

Summit executives wasted no time in immediately announcing that the second book in the series, *New Moon*, was green-lit and would go into production as soon as possible. Summit immediately began negotiations for Hardwicke to helm the second film, with an increased (but not substantial) budget and a truncated production schedule.

Catherine Hardwicke was having dinner in Paris with Pattinson and Stewart when she took the job offer call from Summit on her cell phone. She later reported, in *Twilight: Director's Notebook*, that they had offered her "more money than I or anyone in my family has ever seen." The downside was that they wanted it fast and on a budget only slightly more than the original: $37 million upped to $50 million.

With great regret Hardwicke turned down the offer, citing two concerns: the time allotted to shoot the film, which she felt was rushed, and a budget that, while an improvement over her *Twilight* budget, was not commensurate to what she felt she needed to bring *New Moon* to the screen with fidelity, noting the considerable expense of CGI that the film would require.

Hardwicke made it clear that she'd consider other films, so she wasn't burning bridges; she just couldn't commit to *New Moon*. (Summit later hired her to helm *If I Stay*.)

Afterward, Summit contacted Chris Weitz to serve as the pinch-hitter; he stepped up to the plate, knowing that he was almost certain to achieve with *New Moon* what he had not with *The Golden Compass*: a healthy domestic gross that might exceed *Twilight's* $191 million gross.

Weitz, who gladly took the job, can thank Hardwicke for finding the perfect cast: the principal and supporting actors are all well cast.

Fueled by the same Twilight phenomenon that drove *Twilight* to the top—Web buzz from fans, mainstream media coverage about the film stars, and a triumphant return to Comic-Con in 2009—*New Moon* is poised to repeat, if not best, history. (In Hollywood, there's no such thing as a sure bet, but this is as close as it gets to a no-risk major motion picture.)

Fans, though, raised concerns about the CGI after seeing the second trailer from the film, in which Jacob Black transforms into a wolf. The CGI-generated image of Jacob-turned-wolf was all bark but no bite. Weitz was wise to surf the Net and gauge the fans' reactions. In the third trailer, released in September 2009, the wolves look significantly better.

✳

To promote *New* Moon, in a joint statement released through Summit Entertainment by Kristen Stewart and Robert Pattinson, addressed to "all of our wonderful, loyal and fantastic fans," the two stars thanked the collective members of Twilight fandom. "Without your passion, interaction and support, this film would not be where it is today—the #1 movie in America! From every city, every stop, every interview we have done, you've made this an unbelievable, nearly surreal experience...and so cool that we were all in this together."

Their joint statement recalled Peter Jackson's address to the fan website www.theonering.net, which threw a big party the night *Return of the King* took Oscars in every category in which it was nominated. Stewart and Pattinson's statement affirmed to Twilighters that their collective support is viewed by Summit and the cast and crew of *New Moon* as instrumental to its eventual success.

What film executives took away from the theonering.net experience was that fans *must* be part of the marketing and promotion efforts, that their early support is crucial. The studios, after all, own the films but the Twilight phenomenon is owned by the fans.

Eclipse is scheduled for release on June 30, 2010. The film will be directed by David Slade. Because of the tight back-to-back film schedules, Weitz would be involved in post-production and unable to take on the responsibility of filming *Eclipse* simultaneously.

At this writing, no release date has been officially announced for *Breaking Dawn*, the fourth film in the series.

From Deep Space to Vampires: Twilight Invades Comic-Con

by Tessa Cox

The annual Comic-Con in San Diego, California is not an event I've ever had a desire to attend. Don't get me wrong: I love science fiction and fantasy, but I just never saw myself there among the droves of hardcore fans that dress up as Stormtroopers and know the exact distance in light years from Tatooine to Endor (*Ed. note: less than 12 parsecs.*). Honestly, who could possibly love a series of films or books that much?

Well, fast forward to a picture of me in spring of 2008. I had just finished reading the first three books in Stephenie Meyer's Twilight Saga and was anxiously anticipating the fourth and final installment in August. On top of that, the first movie in the series was not only scheduled to be released later that year, but they had just announced that Summit Entertainment's panel at the San Diego Comic-Con that summer was going to feature some actors from the film, the director, and Stephenie Meyer herself. Though a late bloomer to the series, I had definitely made up for lost time by this point. I got my hands on any merchandise available and was sporting t-shirts, buttons, talking non-stop about anything Twilight-related and making new converts along the way. It seemed only the next practical step that I attend Comic-Con to feed my obsession.

Having convinced some of my friends to tag along, we arrived at the convention center a little after 5:00 a.m. We assumed that only a handful of people would be in line at that ungodly hour, and our extremely early attendance would certainly result in getting seats very close to the front for the panel discussion beginning at 1:30 p.m. How foolish! It's really my own fault for not putting together the big picture: book sales were soaring, merchandise was popping up everywhere, and there was a growing number of hits on the Web for Twilight. I should have realized that even my noble gesture of arriving at the break of dawn was not going to secure me a seat up front.

After parking, we soon noticed a line forming at the front of the building. Almost immediately, we realized that many of the people standing in this line were either wearing a Twilight tee-shirt, holding a Twilight poster, or reading a Twilight book to pass the time—definitely not a good sign for securing my seat in the front. But once we actually reached the line I started to think it wasn't too bad after all. There were about 120 people in line before us, and I know the information I read about the hall where the panel discussion was taking place said that it can seat at least 6,000. No problem. Well, this is when it would have been beneficial to be a seasoned Comic-Con attendee because while I was celebrating my assumed victory, on the other side of the convention center was a line that had been formed the previous night with people camping out to get the best possible seat for *my* panel. I was presently standing in the line for *registration*.

At about 7 a.m. they let us enter the main building and register. Having figured out where we needed to go at this point, we quickly made our way over to the notorious Hall "H" only to find that the line was already wrapped around the building, and was now circling the entire convention center. Again, there was no doubt about why these people were here—the evidence of *Twilight* was everywhere. For some, they only wore subtle pieces like a button that simply stated Edward's famous "Be Safe," while others went the distance to show their devotion—twin girls with homemade tee-shirts full of quotes from the books, belonging to Team Edward or Team Jacob; a twenty-something girl with thick glasses, a ponytail, and a tiara with a shirt proclaiming, "Mrs. Pattinson;" and the forty-something mom in the crowd with a vest she had sewn together herself with the only available online stills from the movie in full color. There were lawn chairs, blankets and picnics, and the occasional outburst of squeals and laughter all around. By now, we had been standing or sitting in line for nearly four hours. The sun was starting to make us sweat and we were applying sunscreen and using our program books to fan ourselves.

People showed up with all their Twilight books and their Twilight posters and magazines because Stephenie Meyer and the rest of the panel were also scheduled to do a signing. Once we arrived and registered, we discovered that there was going to be a raffle for about 200. Leaving the others to stand in line, my best friend and I went inside to make an attempt at getting selected. I can honestly say that I've never been so close to getting trampled to death in my entire life. It was exactly like a herd of cattle had been let loose at the instant they announced that the raffle was going to begin. The idea was that we would all stand in two lines, and at the front of these lines were Comic-Con volunteers holding bags with tickets inside. If you reach inside the bag and find that the ticket you select has a mark on the back, you are a lucky winner. That is, of course, if you could survive the lines forming in the first place.

Sadly, I didn't select a ticket with a marking. I was undoubtedly upset because I would have loved nothing better than to meet Ms. Meyer and the cast, but I then decided that being at the panel was going to be amazing and I should make the best of it. My own equanimity didn't seem to resonate with many of the agonized girls who were crying real tears at not being selected, while others among us were jumping up and down with unabashed joy at having picked the right ticket. Truth be told, I even saw a girl who pulled a ticket with a mark and then proceeded to dance in place and run to a man I assumed was her father who, while he was holding hardcover copies of Meyer's books, twirled her around in celebration like a scene from a movie.

We made our way back to our spot in line to wait with our friends. By that time the line had moved forward incrementally because they needed to accommodate the hoards of people who were continuing to line up. After waiting almost another hour in line, we were let into the building to begin seating for the panel. Although we arrived at 5 a.m. with only a slight detour through registration, we were still toward the back of the hall. As I considered the incredible number of people still standing in line outside and likely not to make it in, I was grateful for any seat. Within a short amount of time the hall was at maximum capacity—6,500 people were in attendance for a glimpse of the film, the actors, the author, and to hear what they had to say. At that moment, it was obvious that *Twilight* had gone from being bestselling books to a genuine phenomenon.

Hall "H" was not solely to be used for the purposes of *Twilight*, though. First, there were several panels for other films coming out later in the year, including some from Summit Entertainment. The seats were too close together for comfort, and you could tell people were starting to get restless. The Comic-Con staffers were doing their best to keep order, but it was clear that they had not expected all those people to show up, so they were a bit unprepared. The whole room was reminiscent of a volcano waiting to erupt if it didn't get what it wanted very soon. Then, almost two hours from the time we entered the hall, it finally happened: the screens at the front lit up with the logo from the *Twilight* film, and the crowd exploded with cheers, screaming, and applause. As I looked around me, I began to realize that there were young girls (maybe between 8 and 12), teenagers, twenty-somethings, thirty-somethings (like myself), forty-somethings, moms, grandmas, and even a few guys in attendance. It was as if I had not really seen them all day, and that this series, though largely embraced by females, had something for everyone, regardless of age. The moms were clapping and yelling just as loud as their daughters, and there I sat, a 30-year-old woman with an obsession for a series largely written for teens with a gigantic crush on a teenage vampire. My heartbeat elevated at the prospect of seeing the woman who created this magic, and the actor who would portray my vampire on film.

The panel's host came out, roused the crowd, and began to introduce the attendees: Rachelle Lefevre (Victoria), Cam Gigandet (James), Edi Gathegi (Laurent), Taylor Lautner (Jacob), Kristen Stewart (Bella), Robert Pattinson (Edward), Catherine Hardwicke (director), and Stephenie Meyer. Though everyone in attendance was welcomed warmly by the crowd, it was Rob Pattinson and Stephenie Meyer who inspired squeals and screams the auditorium for what seemed like several minutes. After the noise died down and everyone was seated, the panel discussion began with the host asking the panel a series of generic questions about why they joined the project, what was the most challenging part about the project, what was their favorite scene, etc. When asked what was her favorite Edward/Bella moment, Stephenie Meyer literally almost made the crowd salivate when she said that her favorite Edward/Bella moment was in *Breaking Dawn,* so she couldn't talk about it because the book had not been released yet. (I'm *still* trying to figure out as to which Edward/Bella moment in *Breaking Dawn* she referred to.) Another entertaining element of the panel was watching Rob Pattinson as he squirmed in his chair, played with his hair, and drank glasses of water. He was obviously uncomfortable with the open adoration he was receiving from the crowd (cat-calls each time he would speak), and in no way was he prepared for his instant popularity.

They showed the audience an exclusive clip of the film (the climactic fight scene between James and Edward in the ballet studio), making the crowd go wild. Eventually the time came for the audience to line up and ask questions to the panelists. Some questions were dignified and relevant (e.g., "Can you tell us anything about the soundtrack?"), while others were embarrassing: a forty-something-year-old woman asked Pattinson and Lautner, "Can you tell us if you guys wear boxers or briefs?"

After numerous questions from the audience, the panel ended with another rousing round of applause. I can honestly say that I was glad to have been in attendance, but just as glad to leave the hall because my ears were ringing from all the screaming. There was no doubt that those in attendance were adoring fans, and although I also let out a few shouts, it would have been nice to actually hear what was being said. Later that night, I went online to read a transcript of the panel because there was so much of it that I wasn't able to catch. While I was surfing the Net for a transcript, I was certain that somewhere out there an executive from Summit Entertainment was letting out a deep sigh of relief. If the attendance of the panel was any indication, Summit had a potential blockbuster film on their hands.

For weeks after Comic-Con, television networks, magazines, and the Internet were saturated with talk about, and footage from, the event. People commented on the actors, the vivacity of the crowd, their eager anticipation for the film, and the screened footage.

Web resource

www.comic-con.org

A San Diego Comic-Con Press Conference: Stephenie Meyer

Stephenie Meyer's first exposure to the overwhelming phenomenon known as the San Diego Comic-Con proved to be an eye-opener. With a record attendance of over 125,000, popular culture fans, mostly males, found themselves in new company: thousands of female fans whose sole interest in attending was the Twilight *programming.*

Summit wisely realized that being at Comic-Con, which helped build buzz on the Web, was instrumental in getting the early world out four months before the movie release. Summit then brought Stephenie Meyer, the film's director, and the principal cast to give interviews, pose for pictures, and sign autographed pictures. A film clip would also be shown. The result was that the movie got a lot of attention from Twilighters and entertainment-based magazines, which proved instrumental to its eventual success.

The following, which I've edited for clarity, is Meyer's unique take on her book, the film adaptation, and the fandom that has made Twilight *a worldwide phenomenon. This was at a press conference at which reporters identified themselves by name and affiliation, and posed questions.*

✳

What do you think is the reason for the incredible popularity of your Twilight *series?*

Stephenie Meyer: I don't know. It's hard for me to answer that because it's an absolute mystery. I read a lot of books and some of them that I love are really popular, and there are just others that I just think, "Why isn't everybody in the world reading this book? It's so amazing." Why does it ever happen? I don't know why people respond to these books the way they do, but I know why I do; it's because I wrote it for me. It's exactly what I wanted to read, so of course I'm really hooked on it.

Did you write it with the idea that it was going to be skewed to preteens or young teenage girls? Was that intended to be your audience?

No, I had a very specific audience: a 29-year-old mother of three. No one was ever supposed to read this except for me; and if I'd had any idea that anyone else would ever see what I was doing, I would have never been able to finish it because that's way too much pressure.

How much input did you have with the script, and how much did they listen to you insofar as events or lines you wanted to keep in.

It was a really pleasant exchange from the beginning, which is not very typical. They were really interested in my ideas. I really didn't want to step on anyone's toes. I didn't want to get in the way and make it worse or somehow screw it up. I don't know how to make a movie. They came to me and they kept me in the loop. They let me see the script and said, "What are your thoughts?" They really opened themselves up. I sent them back the script with red marks: "Wouldn't Bella say this more like this? Wouldn't this sound more like her voice?" Not "this whole scene needs to go," because the script was in really good shape from the beginning. But they let me have input on it. I think they incorporated ninety percent of what I said into the script.

There was a key line about the lion and the lamb that you insisted they keep: "And so the lion fell in love with the lamb."

I actually think the way the screenwriter wrote it sounded better for the movie: "And so the lion fell for the lamb." It really did; it was just a little bit more relaxed. The problem is that the line is actually tattooed on peoples' bodies. I said, "If you take that one line and change it, that's a potential backlash situation." And if there's a place in the movie where we can give a little shout-out to the fans and do something for them, that was what I was thinking.

Is it true that you didn't want to commit to the film until they promised you there would be no fangs?

Yes. Before Summit, I actually sold the rights to a different company. I got a look at a script that, objectively, was probably a decent vampire movie, but it had nothing at all to do with *Twilight*. That was a horrifying experience. I had realized it could go wrong and that they could do it badly, but when they did something that had *nothing* at all to do with the story, it was shocking to me because I'm really naïve. So when Summit said, "We really want to do this," I was weary and said, "I'm just not sure." Summit said, "What can we do for you?" I said, "What if I give you a list of things that absolutely can't be changed?" I'm talking about very fundamental things, the foundation of the story: the vampires have to live within the basic rules of the vampire world I've created, which means no fangs, no coffins, and they sparkle in the sunlight. The characters have to exist by their present names and in their present forms, and they can't kill off anyone who doesn't die in the book.

And you got that in writing?

Yes. I got it in writing. That's the best thing about working with a new company—they're really open to working with you. You don't get that with a big group.

How did you get the rights back?

The option period was up, and that's actually where Summit came in and said, "Can we roll over your option? Can we have it?"

You were approached before you were actually published, so did that change the way you wrote the next few books? Did you write them more cinematically, thinking they might be turned into films?

No. What's funny about that is when I was writing *Twilight* just for myself, I was not thinking of it as a book. I was not thinking about publishing; yet at the same time I was casting it in my head because when I read books, I see them very visually. I pretty much cast every book I read. I'm thinking, "Who could play this? Who would do this?" I did exactly the same thing when I was writing *Twilight*.

Did you have any direct interaction with the actors, and what did you think of Catherine Hardwicke? She's an interesting person as well as a director.

Catherine's fantastic. The first time we started talking to each other, I was surprised because I knew she was the person whose focus was going to shape this film. And so if she had a different idea from me, it wasn't going to turn out like how I had seen it in my head. But we were on the same page from the very beginning, and she was already on top of the things that I was worried about: "Hey, Catherine, about the wardrobe, I'm a little worried that this is going to go all chokers and leather." And she said, " I've already talked to the wardrobe person and we're thinking ice, and this is what we want it to look like," and it turned out to be exactly what I wanted. So she was great because she got it the same way I got it. I just really loved working with her. We're kind of buddies; she's really cool to hang out with and she's just an awesome person.

Did you have any connection with Robert Pattinson?

A little bit. Before the filming started, I'd just come in and met everyone. With Rob, we sat down and talked about Edward's character. It wasn't an argument, but we actually disagreed on his character. I said, "No, *this* is how it is." He said, "No, it's definitely *this* way." And the funny part about it is that we are arguing about a fictional character, yet in the performance he did what he wanted and it was exactly what I wanted. So that was really cool.

When you saw the finished film, what was your most significant moment where you felt dislocated as opposed to the world you had in your head? And was there also a similar moment where you also felt they had captured the world in your head?

It was a funny experience and it's hard to pull out a moment, because as a whole it was just so overwhelming. I think probably the first scene because I was so braced for it— what if it was really horrid? So I was ready for it to be bad. I was almost watching it through my fingers. So you start hearing Kristen's voice and then it becomes Bella's voice, and it got to where I completely forgot why I was there: I had my little notepad and I was going to give them the notes on what I wanted from the rough cut. There were so many things that were like déjà vu to see them. When the movie was over, the producer turned to me and said, "let's have your notes," and I said, "Give me a minute. I really have to just…" I was so overwhelmed. I had to take a moment to just sit and think, because there was so much to take in, and there were so many scenes just the way I had envisioned them, which was partially creepy and partially wonderful.

Since you wrote Twilight *for yourself, which you've talked about before, what was the day you sat down and said, "I'm going to do this," how did it get published, and how did it all come together?*

I tell this story a lot and I think it starts to sound like I'm making it up, but I'm not. I don't think many authors have as specific an answer to that question as I do. It all started June 2, 2003. I know the exact date because I had other things on my calendar that I had to do that day. I had an awesome dream. It was odd because it was coherent, it was a really complicated conversation, and because I don't ever dream about vampires. I woke up and I just was wrapped up with the idea of what was going to happen next. Was he going to kill her or were they going to be together? It was fifty-fifty at that point. And I wrote it down because there were a lot of nuances to the conversation I didn't want to forget and I knew I would forget everything. But once I got started writing that day, I was completely hooked on it because this was something brand new to me. I had no ambitions for a writing career. I had a full-time career as a mother and I was really busy with it.

Being a mother is about the most full-time job you could have. And I had three little boys, so there was no time to do something else. But I was obsessed with the story from the first day. I'd painted before and I'd done a couple of other little creative endeavors because it felt good to be creative, but they weren't completely fulfilling. But when I found writing, it was like I had just found my favorite flavor of ice cream. All of a sudden, there it is: "*This* is what I should have been doing for the last 30 years. What was I thinking?" So I just keep going with it.

How did you get it published?

Sheer luck or fate. I had the easiest publishing experience in the entire world. I sent out 15 letters to agents and got five "no replies" and nine rejections— and one that said, "I want to see it." A month later, I had an agent. Another month later, I had a three-book deal with Little, Brown and Company. It just doesn't happen that way, and if you expect that going in, get ready for heartbreak.

You listened to Muse a lot when you were writing Twilight. *How important was it to you that they be on the soundtrack?*

I knew that that was out of my hands. I always felt like there was something lacking in the soundtrack if they hadn't been a part of it. Knowing what I know, having seen how Muse brought the "vampire baseball" scene to life–music, action, atmosphere came together so perfectly. It would just not be right if you didn't have "Supermassive Black Hole" playing in that scene. It was so perfect. I knew I was going to enjoy it but not that much. That was cool.

Why this enduring interest in vampires?

My answer here is hypothetical because I am not a vampire fan and I never have been. I don't do horror; I'm an enormous scaredy-cat. Hitchcock is about as much as I can handle, and I love it, but anything more than that and you're not going to see me in the theater. And I have never gotten why people are obsessed with vampires. I know a lot of people who are. I'm actually surprised now that I know how many more people are. And so the fact I would write about them is bizarre and wildly out of character for me. Nobody who knows me believed it for a really long time. But having talked to a lot of people about why people like vampires so much, this is my theory: Everybody really loves to be scared in a controlled environment. Horror movies do really well. It's a big industry. People read a lot of scary books. So I'm missing that gene, but clearly we like to be scared. We look at the monsters we can scare ourselves with. Most of them are disgusting, gruesome and covered with nasty things. They're just there to scare us. And then we've got vampires who are often beautiful, eternally youthful, rich and cultured, and they live in castles. There are so many things that are ideals in our culture that they have, which we want. So there's a double-edged sword: vampires are going to kill us and they're terrifying, and yet maybe we want to be one of them. I personally don't want to be a vampire, but a lot of other people do, and I think it's that duel nature we have: the terrifying and the intriguing.

Also, now that you've had a taste of the Hollywood system, would you think about doing a screenplay rather than writing a book first?

I don't think I could write a screenplay unless Hollywood is ready for a 14-hour movie experience. I tried once to write a short story and it was a horrible thing. I just don't think in short terms; I have to explore every tiny, little detail. I really admire people who can come in, streamline it, and get all the information across so simply, but I can't imagine doing that—it's not my talent.

Have you had any other dreams that have inspired other books?
You don't get a dream like that twice. I got my chance and I feel like I was supposed to be writing, and this dream was my kick in the pants to get going. Once I started it, I didn't need another dream because once I discovered how wonderful writing was for me, I was ready to go with it.

What sets your vampires apart?
In general, my vampires don't have fangs because they don't need them. Because they're as strong as they are, fangs are unnecessary. They're fairly indestructible and wooden stakes and garlic are not going to get you anywhere. They don't sleep at all—they have no periods of unconsciousness. And the sunlight just shows them for what they are, because they sparkle in the sun—it doesn't harm them.

What about reflections?
They totally have reflections and you can take pictures of them. In my world, these are myths that vampires actually spread around since ancient times so that people would say, "Oh, this person can't be a vampire because I can see him in the mirror, so I'm safe."

As the fan base grew for the series and it became more of a phenomenon, did that change in any way how you approached the later books? Also, what was your response to the fan response of Breaking Dawn?
As far as changing things, I couldn't because I actually had the first three books and a rough draft of the fourth one written before *Twilight* ever came out, so the story was there.

I had this conversation with a friend of mine who wrote nonfiction, and she was saying how it must be so hard for me because my editors can't change anything. It's not as if I can just change things. And what she said clicked for me because that's *exactly* how I feel: It's history, and that's just what happened. It's also an awkward position to be in when your editor does want you to change things.

As for fan expectations, as I said, I already knew the story. It did add a little bit of pressure. When I'm writing, I tune that out; I don't think about it at all. But when I'm editing, I get online and I see a blog that says if A and B *don't* happen I'm burning this book; and then on another page, if A and B *do* happen, this is going to be the worst book ever. So I know going in that there is no way I can please everybody. I can't even please half the people, because everybody wants things that are so different; they've written this story in their heads in a way they're happy with.

I read an interview that George Lucas gave about *Indiana Jones* and how all the fans have already written their sequels; and if they don't see that sequel, they're going to be upset. I found myself in that same position with the fourth book, so I was braced going in. The fan response was bigger than I ever would have dared to imagine. It was better in a lot of ways and it was worse in many ways. And there was a lot of overwhelming stuff that I couldn't really take in.

What did you think when you went to the set? How often did you go?

It was actually California and Portland. I was in Portland about four times, in and out, and probably a total of about two weeks altogether.

And what did you think of the filmmaking process?

That was one of the coolest things that agreeing to do a movie gave me. The movie was just fun. I found it fascinating. One time I had my brother Seth with me for a couple of days. I know he was bored stupid. That poor kid. He asked me, "How can they say the same line again for the sixteenth time?" That was with the humans that week, and every time Anna Kendrick said a line she added a new little twist or her eyebrow raised just a little bit differently; those nuances were fascinating to me because it's my story. I don't know if I'd be that way on another film, but I was riveted and looking at the monitor and saying, "Oh I love that." I was just thrilled.

Did the cast embody your vision?

Yes. If someone had pulled me in there and said, "We've got a roomful of your characters. Let's see if you can pin the names on them," it would have been so easy. They were so clearly who they were. I think the acting in this movie is something special. It's amazing. A lot of these kids are new and they're so good. They're just so believable and you feel like you're just sitting there with a bunch of kids from high school, because this is how they sound. It didn't sound like people acting. It sounded like people being people.

So what is the status of Midnight Sun*?*

Midnight Sun is not on my schedule right now. As I was saying before, part of my writing process is that for me to really write a story, I can't think about what other people want and what other people are thinking, and what the editing is going to be and what the expectations are when I'm writing. Because it's paralyzing to do that—I really can't put a word on the page. I have to be very alone with a story. It has to be just me and what's happening.

It's a weird thing and I'm not sure what it's all about, but I think that this is going to die down. People are going to forget about it. It's going to go away and that'll be the time when I sneak back in and give it a try again. But I'm not writing in a fishbowl because I can't work that way.

Which one do you expect to be the most challenging to adapt?

Book four is the hardest thing to do, and there's a really simple reason for that: You have a character [Renesmee] that would have to be a computer-generated image. And while CGI can render dragons and almost anything in the whole world, the one thing that I've never seen is a completely realistic CGI human. So either groundbreaking CGI technology will have to develop in the next couple of years, or it will be impossible.

There's a very critical moment in the film when Bella says, "I'm thinking radioactive plasma and Kryptonite." Did you think it would be tough to switch the teen pop culture away from the superhero and back towards the supernatural, or did it feel like something kids were going to be into?

I never worried about that for a second. I was into it and I am much more drawn to superheroes than I am to vampires. I really think there's a closer connection with my vampires and superheroes than with traditional vampires and who they are. With my writing, what it comes down to is, "Am I getting a kick out of this?" If so, then "Okay, we'll go with it." And if it's not clicking for somebody else, well, that's why there's 40 billion books in the world, because there's something for everybody.

Has your writing process changed since your first dream prompted you into writing?

It has. It's gone through some evolutions as I experiment with different ways to do things. With *Twilight*, I didn't know it was going to happen when I wrote it. I just was writing to find out the answer. With the others, I had to start outlining. I had to be more careful because I knew when I started *New Moon* where it was going to end, so that takes a lot more work to tie up the threads. The biggest change is that when I started writing, I had three kids under the school age all day. All my kids are in school full-time now, so that really has been the biggest change.

How did you find time to write the book?

I lost sleep to write. I had to give something up and I wasn't giving up my time with my kids, and I couldn't give up the things I had to do, so it was sleep.

Was there a certain song on the soundtrack that specifically spoke to you in a really personal way?

Aside from the Muse song, which was already part of what I listen to all the time, these songs were all new for me. And I have to say the Iron & Wine song ("Flightless Bird, American Mouth") was really the one that just made me an instant fan. Probably because the first time I heard it was when I watched the movie, and in that scene it just so perfectly melded in with the feeling. That was when it got me.

Can you talk about shooting your cameo? How many takes?

They talked me into it. It was not my idea to do the cameo. They thought it would be cute for the fans because most of them would recognize me. I was thinking it was going to be more like a "Where's Waldo?" thing where I'd walk by for one second in a crowd and if they could find me, cool. That's the one scene in the movie I would happily cut, and the one that I had to watch with my hands over my eyes and say, "Is it *over* yet?" It was really hard for me. I did however many takes they were doing in that scene, because it wasn't about me, it was about the actors.

For those of us who have no idea, what's your cameo?

Oh, didn't you recognize me? Really? It was in the scene when Bella and Charlie are at the diner and Cora the waitress is asking, "Say, Chief, boys want to know, did you find anything by Queets River today?" There is a woman sitting at the counter, and for some reason the camera focuses on her for a good five seconds, and you're thinking, "Why are we looking at this person?" And that person was me. [*Chapter 15; 1:12:14 into the movie on DVD.*]

Is the series over now for the books? Are you done?

It's done for now. I can't promise that I won't get lonely for the Cullens and come back to them in 10 years. But right now I feel really satisfied with where it is, so I'm not planning on doing anything with it. But no guarantees.

Bella Swan's pick-up truck parked in front of the Visitor Information Center in Forks.

Twilight film director Catherine Hardwicke on location in coastal Oregon.

Twilight: about the Movie

Summit Entertainment. Release date: November 21, 2008. Running time, 121 minutes. (DVD release: March 21, 2009.) Budget: $37 million. Opening weekend: $70 million. Domestic gross (rounded up): $192 million. Foreign gross (rounded up): $192 million. Worldwide gross: $384 million.

Based on the Stephenie Meyer novel, the screenplay was written by Melissa Rosenberg, and the movie was directed by Catherine Hardwicke.

Taglines for movie posters: "When you can live forever, what do you live for?" "Forever. Begins. Now." "Nothing will be the same."

Awards won include: MTV Movie, NAMIC Vision, Teen Choice, Young Artist, and Young Hollywood.

Catherine Hardwicke won a Young Hollywood Award for Director. The film won an MTV Movie Award for "Best Movie," a Vision Award for "Film of Vision," and Teen Choice Awards for "Movie: Drama," and "Movie: Romance."

The soundtrack won a Teen Choice Award for "Music Album: Soundtrack."

✳

Principal Cast

Humans

Kristen Stewart as Bella Swan. Won two MTV Movie Awards for "Best Female Performance" and "Best Kiss." Won Teen Choice Award for "Movie Actress: Drama," and "Movie Liplock."

Billy Burke as Charlie Swan (Bella's father)

Sarah Clarke as Renée Dwyer (Bella's remarried mother)

Matt Bushell as Phil Dwyer (Bella's stepfather)

Ned Bellamy as Waylon Forge (longtime friend of Charlie Swan). *Note: This character does not appear in the book.*

Jose Zuniga as Mr. Molina (biology teacher). *Note: In the book, this character's name is Mr. Banner.*

Anna Kendrick as Jessica Stanley (student, one of Bella's best friends)

Christian Serratos as Angela Webber (student, one of Bella's best friends). Won Young Artist Award for "Best Performance in a Feature Film (Supporting Young Actress)"

Michael Welch as Mike Newton (student)

Gregory Tyree Boyce as Tyler Crowley (student)

Justin Chon as Eric Yorkie (student)

Taylor Lautner as Jacob Black (a Quileute Indian, son of Billy Black). Won Teen Choice Award for "Movie: Fresh Face Male."

Gil Birmingham as Billy Black (Quileute Indian)

Solomon Trimble as Sam Uley (Quileute Indian)

Stephenie Meyer as herself (in a cameo at a diner)

Coven of "Good" Vampires

Peter Facinelli as Dr. Carlisle Cullen ("father")

Elizabeth Reaser as Esme Cullen ("mother")

Robert Pattinson as Edward Cullen (adopted son). Won MTV Movie Awards for "Best Fight," "Best Kiss," and "Breakthrough Performance Male." Won Teen Choice Award for "Movie Actor: Drama," "Movie Liplock," and "Movie Rumble."

Ashley Greene as Alice Cullen (adopted daughter). Won Teen Choice Award for "Movie: Fresh Face Female."

Nikki Reed as Rosalie Hale (adopted daughter)

Jackson Rathbone as Jasper Hale (adopted son)

Kellan Lutz as Emmett Cullen (adopted son)

Coven of Nomadic Vampires

Cam Gigandet as James (hunter/tracker). Won MTV Movie Award (with Pattinson) for Best Fight. Won Teen Choice Award for "Movie Rumble" and "Movie Villain."

Edi Gathegi as Laurent (part of the coven)

Rachelle Lefevre as Victoria (James' lover/mate)

Selected Reviews

Manohla Dargis (*New York Times*, November 21, 2008): "It's love at first look instead of first bite in *Twilight*, a deeply sincere, outright goofy vampire romance for the hot-not-to-trot abstinence set. Based on the foundational book in Stephenie Meyer's best-selling multivolume series, The Twilight Saga (four doorstops and counting), this carefully faithful adaptation traces the sighs and whispers, the shy glances and furious glares of two unlikely teenage lovers who fall into each other's pale, pale arms amid swirling hormones, raging instincts, high school dramas and oh-so-confusing feelings, like, OMG he's SO HOT!! Does he like ME?? Will he KILL me??? I don't CARE!!!)"

Owen Gleiberman (*Entertainment Weekly*, 2008): "And getting Catherine Hardwicke to direct *Twilight* was a shrewd move, because the youthquake specialist of *Thirteen* treats teen confusion without a trace of condescension: She gets their grand passions and prickly defense mechanisms. She has reconjured Meyer's novel as a cloudburst mood piece filled with stormy skies, rippling hormones, and understated visual effects. What Hardwicke can't quite triumph over is the book's lackluster plot. On screen, *Twilight* is repetitive and a tad sodden, too prosaic to really soar. But Hardwicke stirs this teen pulp to a pleasing simmer."

The Washington Times (November 21, 2008): "*Twilight* shares a weakness common to most introductory chapters in a multivolume tale. It takes so long to introduce the characters and create a convincing universe that by the time conflict arises—in this case, an evil vampire from a different clan who threatens to harm Bella in order to spark a confrontation with Edward—the action feels forced, unnecessary and rushed. The last half hour isn't quite a mess, but it isn't terribly interesting either. The first 90 minutes, however, are surprisingly good. Miss Stewart is one of the finest young actresses working today, and she plays off of Mr. Pattinson's brooding intensity with just the right touch of innocence and wariness. Look also for an outstanding turn by Peter Facinelli as the Cullen clan's paterfamilias, Dr. Carlisle Cullen. It's hard not to get sucked in—if one can get past the sometimes hokey, melodramatic teenage dialogue. (Sample laugher: "Your scent is like a drug to me. You're like my own personal brand of heroin.") This is the first in a long string of Twilight movies (a series of sequels have already been green-lit), and intriguing questions remain. A stronger second act is certainly possible, considering this impressive setup."

Fan review from **Jolene Mendez** (www.joreviews.com). "I have heard that the movie does not surpass the novel, but from a one viewing opinion, I loved it. I thought the intensity and the old-time romance feel the film had was just the right touch. Kristen Stewart and Robert Pattinson had amazing chemistry and performances. The mood of the film was played out by the scenery offered, the ominous clouds and forest of trees and fog. A must see and a must for a sequel."

Sukhdev Sandhu (*Telegraph*.uk): "Hardwicke, though, understands that the novels tap into a yearning that a particular kind of adolescent cultivates for a deeper, richer form of romance that seems masochistic and depressing only to outsiders. I watched *Twilight* in a cinema full of young girls who, when they weren't texting friends and guzzling soft drinks, giggled, signed and exhaled with a passion that was not only endearing, but a measure of its emotional truth. ... Still, it's been ages since I've seen such a quiveringly earnest—to say nothing of chaste—film about adolescent desire. Ages since a character told the audience she was 'unconditionally and irrevocably in love' with a boy. True love should wait more often."

Roger Ebert (www.rogerebert.com): "*Twilight* will mesmerize its target audience, 16-year-old girls and their grandmothers. Their mothers know all too much about boys like this. I saw it at a sneak preview. Last time I saw a movie in that same theater, the audience welcomed it as an opportunity to catch up on gossip, texting, and laughing at private jokes. This time the audience was rapt with attention. Sometimes a soft chuckle, as when the principal Indian boy has well-developed incisors. Sometimes a soft sigh. Afterwards, I eavesdropped on some conversations. A few were saying, 'He's so hot!' More floated in a sweet dreaminess. Edward seemed to stir their surrender instincts."

Perspectives:

Stephenie Meyer

On casting Bella in her own mind: "Bella, I'm not so picky about. She should be an "everygirl" and so there are lots of people I think could do a good job. Emily Browning (of "Lemony Snicket" fame) is my first choice at the moment, but that changes often. My big worry with Bella is that they'll pick some horrible 'it' girl actress/musician, and then I will have to kill myself." (William Morris, motleyvision.org, October 26, 2005.)

On adapting the book to a movie: "Obviously certain changes have to be made for the film. Having a book made into a film is a risky process. We all probably see more failures than we see winners on that one. So when they first approached me—it wasn't Summit the first time—and said, 'Do you want to do this? Do you want to make your book into a movie?', I had to really weigh that up. I'm not a risktaker so it was hard. But because I had always seen the book in my head like a movie, it seemed a natural step to me. Basically, there's no way you can take a book this long and make it into a movie without making some changes. I went into the screening terrified. On the days on the set, I had seen maybe about five minutes of actual screen time. I hadn't seen much of it. This was still a rough cut, and I was going to give them everything they needed to change it, and I didn't write a single thing down. At the end, I just sat there and I wanted to watch it again!" (RTE Entertainment, December 12, 2008.)

Summit Entertainment

Patrick Wachsberger (Co-President and Chairman of Summit Entertainment), when asked how the success of *Twilight* changed the company: "There definitely is a change. First, it's fantastic for all our troops. Second, it's fantastic financially. Third, I honestly believe that we made no mistakes. I don't believe any studio could've done a better job. But I do not feel there has been any envy or jealousy—everybody has been looking at it as a piece of good news in a really dark time. Yes, there's hope. There's hope in the banking community, there's hope for independent producers and other studios that it can happen to them on a low-budget movie with no stars. (Matthew Belloni and Stephen Galloway, hollywoodreporter.com, January 13, 2009.)

Screenwriter **Melissa Rosenberg**: "[Summit Entertainment] gave me a call and told me about the book and told me it had quite the fan following. But it was the characters that compelled me to take the job. And actually, more than that, it was what Stephenie did with the vampire genre, which is one of the most well-trodden genres we have. She reinvented the mythology in a fresh way, and that's really quite the feat. I'm a big fan of the genre. Plus, I was really intrigued by Bella, who is really the everygirl brought into this new world. She was something I wanted to see more of and develop." (*Los Angeles Times*: Entertainment section, November 12, 2008).

Media

Moira Macdonald, *Seattle Times*: "Meyer, despite her occasional penchant for purple prose, vividly creates a world of gothic, edge-of-danger romance, the kind in which bookish girls have long loved to lose themselves on rainy afternoons. ... For the movie, it would appear that the *Titanic* audience is already in place: According to a *Movietickets.com* poll of about 2,000 moviegoers, 3 out of 4 females said they planned to attend *Twilight* on its opening weekend, as well as 77 percent of those polled who were under 25. ... But if the film, directed by Catherine Hardwicke, catches enough of Meyer's brooding romance and breathless suspense...there just might be long lines at the multiplexes for a while. Because preteen and teenage girls—and, at times, their grown-up counterparts—like to revisit favorite stories, over and over again."

La Push's First Beach

New Moon movie:
A San Diego Comic-Con Press Conference with Robert Pattinson, Kristen Stewart, and Taylor Lautner

It's fair to say that when Pattinson, Stewart, and Lautner appeared at Comic-Con the previous year, it was a surreal experience, especially for Pattinson who was not expecting the overwhelming fan reaction. A year made all the difference in the world. Of the three, Lautner was obviously the most comfortable in front of a capacity crowd. Open and spontaneous in his comments, engaging them as if one-on-one, Lautner immediately connects with the fans. Stewart engages the fans in a more contemplative yet elliptical manner; she's not so quick to speak her mind but, instead, prefers to string together disparate thoughts and, at the end, pull them together in a summation. Pattinson, like Stewart, holds back a bit; he realizes this is part of what has to be done to market and promote a film, but it's something that puzzles him: the open adoration, the screaming, the fan phenomenon of putting an actor on a pedestal, apart from all other considerations.

How does it feel for all three of you to be back at Comic-Con this year?

Lautner: It's good. It's exciting. I think last year Comic-Con was the big eye-opener for us, so it's awesome to be back and embrace all of our fans again for everything they've done this past year.

In the book, even though you leave Bella, you're very much an integral part of her thoughts. I know that can be a challenge to represent onscreen. How did you and director Chris Weitz try to accomplish this?

Pattinson: It's through a kind of process. Edward's just a voice in the book, and so I guess it would look pretty cheesy if it were just my voice. They've done these hallucinations, these semi-visible apparitions.

Stewart: It's suggestive. It's how she remembers him, not necessarily how he actually is.

The fog rolls into La Push's First Beach.

Taylor, can you talk about Jacob's transformation in this movie and your personal transformation that you had to go through to play the role?

Lautner: When I was filming *Twilight,* I knew that Jacob's character changed a lot; so if I wanted to continue portraying him correctly, I had a lot of work ahead of myself. So as soon as I finished filming *Twilight,* I started hitting the gym. I got a personal trainer. I started eating a lot of food, good food: proteins, good carbs, and I cut the sugars. It was a lot of work, but it was definitely worth it.

Kristen, in the 'Twilight' series, Bella's story arc really starts to develop in New Moon. *She becomes an active protagonist. Was it more difficult to prepare for this role this time around or vice versa?*

Stewart: I wouldn't say that one was more difficult than the other. This is a severely emotional movie. That's the one big difference. This movie is not about discovery or falling in love, which is just an intense emotion, but this is like her low and high points, too. She's basically a manic depressive. But for me, there was no difference. It's a more mature part strictly because she's older and she has more to deal with.

Can you talk a little bit about how your lives have changed since we saw you here last summer?

Pattinson: I'd like to think that I haven't changed that much. I think I look down a lot. There's something wrong with my neck [he laughs]. It's kind of extraordinary. I don't think that any of us expected any of this to happen, or that the magnitude of this franchise seems to keep building and building. Comic-Con 2008 really was the eye-opener and it's just kind of gotten bigger and bigger. It's an interesting thing to deal with.

Lautner: I think that another obvious thing that's changed for me is that the schedule has gotten really busy doing publicity and working on other things. It's crazy. None of us saw it coming and since last year it's definitely been a ride for all of us.

Stewart: I cut my hair off. [For *The Runaways,* a movie about Joan Jett.)

What would you say have been the highs and the lows of this whole experience?

Stewart: Well, this is definitely a high. There's only been a couple of images from the movie that have been released, and they've all been received really well. So I'm really excited for people to see some of it. It's a little overwhelming to have so many people here, but I guess that's a good thing.

Lautner: This is our opportunity to come out and thank our fans for everything that they've done for us and for *Twilight*. We get to embrace them again. We're so thankful for them. So it's awesome that we get to see them all again, waiting for us, a year later with the same, if not definitely more, amount of passion and dedication. So it's really exciting. I'm a little nervous but it's good.

Pattinson: I don't know. I still think it's still so young—to me, anyway. I can't claim anything to be a low. Apart from being recognized, I pretty much live an almost identical life. That's not exactly the worst thing in the world.

How does this massive embracing of Team Edward and Team Jacob plays into your performances?

Lautner: Everything is kind of crazy about this franchise. That's why we and the fans love it so much. But there's definitely a lot of fans who are on the two separate teams. Sometimes it gets me a little nervous because I'm trying to live up to the fans' expectations and trying to represent Team Jacob in the right way. I don't want to disappoint them, so that's why I worked so hard to change, not only mentally and emotionally but physically for this role, because Team Edward is some pretty good competition.

How did you guys address that fact that, unlike Twilight, *Robert's not in this film as much, and might that be disappointing to fans?*

Stewart: Rob's in it a lot.

Pattinson: They won't be disappointed, either. If he doesn't go, you can't miss him and that's what this whole movie is about: that empty, completely dark place where Edward is absent.

Lautner: If Rob was absent, they would miss him very deeply.

Robert, how has it been this time around? The experience of working with a new director and what's the vibe like on set?

Pattinson: It wasn't just the director that made this one different. It was so different because we knew what type of animal that we were dealing with more. In this one, I was much more in a supporting role. I started three weeks after they started shooting and I did a lot of my first scenes doing the apparition scenes. That's a lot of me speaking maybe one word. It was actually one of the most relaxing jobs that I've ever done. Chris has a really peaceful presence. I got on really well with him. I had a pretty much stress-free job for three months. It was great for me, but all the pressure was on Taylor [he laughs].

Taylor, when you see the trailer for the first time and watch yourself morph, what goes through your mind?

Lautner: I thought that they did a pretty good job with the wolf transformation. I'm excited that there are werewolves involved now, because the were-wolves definitely step up the action in the movie. There is double the action in this movie than there was in *Twilight* and there's also a different dynamic. It's not just a romance between a human girl and a vampire, but it's the beginning of a love triangle and so that's exciting.

How much of the final film have you guys seen, and what were your feelings after seeing what you've seen so far?
    Stewart: We saw some clips this morning—the clips that they're going to show today.
    Lautner: We've seen just about as much as the fans have seen.

Are you anxious to see the final movie?
    Stewart: I think it's a different kind of anxious, but yeah, definitely.
    Pattinson: It looks aesthetically very different. The script was very different. It's a completely different mood. So I'm really interested to see how it works out.

Do you have a favorite scene from this film that stands out and why?
    Stewart to Lautner: Well, your favorite scene didn't turn out to be your favorite.
    Lautner: Oh, right. I have a lot of favorite scenes, so that's a really difficult question for me. I like a lot of the cool action scenes I get to do, because I just had a lot of fun with those. Anyway [he laughs], my original favorite scene was a really small scene that I thought was kind of cute.
    Stewart: What was it?
    Lautner: It was the scene where I walk Bella up to her door and say good-bye. I'm going off to fight in the woods and she's worried and scared for me. I thought that it was kind of cute, but I also like the break-up scene.
    Stewart: Yeah, that's my favorite scene in the movie. We call it a break-up scene because Jacob basically tells Bella that they can't be friends anymore and he's transforming. [To Lautner] If you ever, ever treated me like that, you would kill me.
    Lautner: It was also painful to shoot because it was thirty-five degrees and we had cold spring water poured upon us from a rain tower. It was bad.

Rob, do you have a favorite scene or moment?
    Pattinson: I think my break-up scene was my favorite. Hopefully, it'll come off as having quite a few more levels than the relationship in *Twilight*. It was a five-page long dialogue scene. That didn't happen at all in the first one. It's

quite an interesting little moment. It completely bypasses all the supernatural elements of the story as well, which I found quite interesting.

Why do you think people embrace these stories: the themes, the characters, the subject, the darkness, the romance?

Stewart: I don't know. That's the most common question we get asked all the time.

Lautner: I think a lot of the characters are relatable. There are so many different ones, and people can relate to the different characters and their experiences.

Stewart: I always say that it's because it's a first-person narrative and you're so very much inside of her head that it's like being closer to home. You feel like it's not happening to someone else. You feel like it's sort of happening to you.

Can you talk about why teenagers love vampires?

Pattinson: I think we're the worst people to ask about it. The problem is that when I looked at it, right from the beginning, I never looked at it as a vampire story. When I try to play it, I try to eliminate the vampire element as much as I can; I just see it as a tool to make their relationship a little more fraught. Right after the audition I found myself bizarrely invested in the story, and I hadn't even read the books at that point. I've gotten more and more attached to it. I've been talking about the script for *Eclipse* to people over the last few weeks, and I find myself getting very argumentative, which I'm usually not. The books definitely have some kind of power.

Which of the novels resonates the most for you as a reader or as an actor, and which one are you most enthused about working in?

Lautner: My favorite book was actually *Eclipse*. I'm pretty excited that it's got action. The action levels continue to build in this series. So I think that I enjoy that, but also the fact that *Twilight* sets up the romance between Bella and Edward, and then Bella and Jacob's friendship grows in *New Moon*. But in *Eclipse* it's actually the three of them physically together; we have to team up and make a decision to try and be friends to protect her. I think that is the ultimate high point of the series—the love triangle in *Eclipse*. So I'm excited to get going.

Stewart: I liked *New Moon* just in terms of how far I can push myself within the series. I feel like after *New Moon* it's sort of smooth sailing for Bella. She's very, very solid and content and happy. But in the second one she's nothing; she's literally just lost. I got to find her again. But, yeah, the second one for sure.

Pattinson: I think that *New Moon* was my favorite book as well. Edward is such a hyped character; there are so many people looking at him like a romantic hero, but in *New Moon*—the way that I read it—he's just so humbled. He's a character who's looking at Bella and thinking that he loves something too much but he can't be around. He deliberately starts breaking up their relationship, which I think is very kind of painful, and very relatable.

Eclipse is really Edward trying to catch up with Jacob, because he's so out of the loop and he can't speak in superlatives anymore. He's accepted being who he is and he needs to catch up to Jacob. So I've always liked *New Moon*.

Will each of you tell me the one Twilight question that you never want to answer again?
　　Pattinson: What's it like kissing Taylor Lautner.
　　Lautner: To growl. Actually, I get asked that more by fans. They ask me to growl for them and I really don't enjoy doing that [he laughs]. So that's for the fans. Please, don't ask me to growl. Just wait for the movie.
　　Stewart: You can ask me anything you want.

And did you read Midnight Sun, *the book that tells the story through Edward's perspective?*
　　Pattinson: Yes. That was more in relation to *Twilight*. It was more literally what the entire storyline was in *Twilight* just from Edward's perspective. I haven't really looked too much at that for *New Moon* because I could connect a lot more to *New Moon* than to *Twilight*.

Robert, were there any musical contributions from you in New Moon?
　　Pattinson: No.

A San Diego Comic-Con Press Conference with Chris Weitz, Robert Pattinson, Taylor Lautner, and Ashley Greene

Given that Catherine Hardwicke had reluctantly opted out of the director's seat for New Moon, *it made sense that the studio would present the new director to the fans to present his perspectives on the new film. This was also an opportunity for the principal cast to engage in a dialogue with Chris Weitz and show solidarity: one team pulling together to make the movie a success.*

Excited about getting in for this event, the fans simply wouldn't stop talking or, in this case, screaming their approval as the stars came out on stage. In addition to Chris Weitz, the panelists were Kristen Stewart, Robert Pattinson, Taylor Lautner, and Ashley Greene.

Two well-chosen clips were shown, each showing Jacob Black and Edward Cullen removing their shirts. As you may imagine, if you had earplugs, that was a good time to put them in: the women screamed in unison on both occasions—just as Chris Weitz knew they would. He knew exactly how to get this audience's motors revved up.

An open, freestanding microphone was set up in the front on the right side, so fans in the audience could pose specific questions.

✳

How did you become a fan of the Twilight books and why did you want to direct the movie?

Chris Weitz: I've been stalking Rob Pattinson for the last 10 years, so whenever I got a chance to get within touching distance of him, I jumped at the opportunity. Actually, I think an extraordinary cast was assembled for the first film and I was very keen to work with them. Also, like others of my gender, I hadn't read *Twilight* before the possibility of the film came up. But once I read it, I realized that it dealt with all these deep emotions that everyone feels:

first love, heartbreak, and the ecstasy of reunion. Also, having been dumped so many times in my life, I felt like I could also sympathize with Bella's character.

Ashley, because you weren't here last year, you probably heard how excited the fans were with all the cast coming, so I want to know what it's been like for you this past year.

Ashley Greene: It's been incredible to be a part of this franchise. We've got amazing fans. All of you people here are all so supportive and great, so it's been really fun to be a part of it. It's kind of my first job really, so it's an incredibly fun, first job to have.

Taylor, we talked about this a little earlier today, but everybody else out there wants to know about Jacob Black's transformation in the movie. Can you talk a little bit about what you had to do to transform yourself?

Taylor Lautner: Jacob goes through a lot in this movie. He transforms mentally and emotionally, which is extremely important, but the most challenging for me personally was physically. So I had a lot of hard work cut out for me after filming *Twilight*. I worked really hard to try to transform Jacob's body so I could portray him correctly, and I hope you guys are pleased when you see the results.

Kristen, in the Twilight Saga series, Bella's story arc really starts to develop in New Moon. *She's faced with tremendous conflicts and becomes the real protagonist in this film. So I just wanted to know if it was more difficult to prepare for this movie than for* Twilight.

Kristen Stewart: It wasn't about the preparation. It was definitely harder to do this movie just because going through what I had to go through as Bella. I think she's less of a protagonist at the beginning of the story, which makes it more powerful when she finally snaps back. She's literally, completely a non-participant in her own life. She basically dies. So to snap back from that was not that easy.

Rob, we also had a chance to talk about this a little earlier, but in the book, even though you leave Bella, you're very much an integral part of her story because you're constantly in her thoughts. I know this can be challenging to present on screen, so I was just wondering how you went about doing that with Chris Weitz.

I did very little to help the situation. Chris and the special effects team designed everything, which basically allowed me to stand on a green box, and look and stay relatively expressionless, and all these machines did the acting for me. Just the way I like it (he laughs). I hope it looks good.

Chris, to piggyback off that, I think you brought something for us, right?

Weitz: Because we really appreciate all of the energy and devotion that you've brought, and in spite of however glib I may seem, I really do appreciate the tremendous love that the Twilight fans bring to the books. Our fidelity to the books is the key to making the movies work. We have brought this following clip from the movie.

(This first clip shows Bella on her first motorcycle ride. As she rides hell-bent down a country road, she hallucinates and "sees" Edward Cullen standing by the side of the road. Be safe, he had told her previously, but she's not; she's reckless and almost out of control. She, in fact, loses control of the bike and is thrown from it, as Jacob jumps on his bike and rides out to help her. She's got a scalp wound and he removes his shirt to staunch it. In doing so, he reveals a sculpted chest, including a chiseled abdomen. Loud female screaming ensues. When the lights come back up and the screaming dies down, the questions continue.)

To Robert Pattinson: I saw you in How To Be *and I thought it was an excellent movie. I thought that your mannerisms and facial expressions lent themselves really well to comedy, so I was wondering if you're thinking of doing anymore comedic roles in the future?*

Pattinson: Why not? But I don't know if I'm particularly funny. One of my legs is shorter than the other one, so it makes everything look very awkward, and I can just pretty much look like an idiot, so I don't know whether I can be witty. It could be a problem.

What aspects of yourself did you bring to your respective characters?

Greene: I had a lot of fun playing Alice because she's very optimistic and positive, and I definitely try and be positive and generally be a very happy person. There's a really intense bond that Alice has with her family, and I have the same bond with my personal family, so I definitely use that.

Stewart: I think Bella is intent on doing what she needs to do for herself and not being ashamed of it. And even when she changes her mind, it's okay; she's sort of everywhere. Talk about mood swings.... But she's not ashamed of it. She doesn't have to explain herself. She just feels what she feels, and that's it—especially him [*She points at Taylor Lautner*].

Lautner: I would hope that most of my close friends and family or people that know me would say that I'm more like Jacob's pretransformation side. Because that's before he goes wacko. So I hope I'm more friendly and outgoing than this dark, disturbed person, this monster. Actually, I don't think he's a monster.

Stewart: You're not a monster.

Lautner: Yeah, you're right [he laughs].

Pattinson: Chris, do you think that I'm similar to my character?

Weitz: I've noticed that you're very cold to the touch and have skin like marble and that you glow like a diamond when the sun hits you.

Pattinson: [he laughs] Yeah, I kind of look a bit like him.

To Kristen Stewart: Did you actually ride the motorcycle or do any of your stunts?

Stewart: No. I got in the back of this really dorky rigged thing, and it wasn't cool.

To Robert Pattinson: I'm in love with your music and your style. Would you ever be interested in doing open microphone nights ever again, even with your fame?

Pattinson: I'd love to.

Have any of you seen the fan reaction videos to the New Moon *trailer? If you have seen them, what do you think and are you afraid?*

Weitz: I and everybody in the editing room and the people working on visual effects have seen the fan reaction videos. We could not be more pleased and tickled by them. Some of them are very intense in their reactions, so I wouldn't want to get them mad at me by getting anything wrong in the movie. But to be honest, Peter Lambert [the film's editor] and I were talking about how we should do a fan reaction video to the fan reaction videos, because it's just incredibly amusing and inspiring in these very dark and long days when we work at the rather tedious job of putting together the little bits of film. We love the fan reaction videos.

How has it been different to film in Vancouver as opposed to Portland? And how has the fan response to your location shooting been different from the first filming?

Greene: To start with, I think Portland has a lot more of an "edge" to it. For me, there's definitely a bigger following in Vancouver. There are a lot more people there that are aware of who we are. There's a ton of fans there versus just a couple here and there in Portland.

Taylor: But both places are cold and wet. Don't get me wrong; they're beautiful, but it's just not fun not wearing any clothes there. [audience screams in unison]

To Chris Weitz: What did you find to be the biggest challenge? Was there a scene or moment or technical aspect that was the biggest challenge in this film?

Weitz: There are a lot of challenges to this film because of the werewolves and because of the trip to Italy. There are a lot of logistical challenges, which are rather boring, so I won't even enumerate them, I'll just say that the wolves are going to be great.

Filming in Italy was a tremendous challenge because everybody knew that we were going to be in Montepulciano. And I mean *everybody*. Everywhere that the camera wasn't pointed, there were hundreds of fans standing there. And it wasn't so much that we minded them being there. It was just the sheer logistics of getting through all the fans to get to where we had to stand by the camera. As a matter of fact, people applauded after every take, which is unheard of, as if we were doing live theater.

There was one moment where I really had to go to the bathroom, but there was not a single café that I could walk into where I wouldn't be mobbed. And by the way, that's not because I'm me; it's just because people were interested to see if I could set up a meeting with Rob or with another member of the cast. So that was quite difficult, actually, but it was also quite intriguing and funny in its own way.

To Taylor Lautner: What is it like filming half-naked with the random weather conditions in Vancouver? And for fans who want to see it, can you do a back flip for us?

Weitz: Please don't—we don't want you to hurt yourself.

Lautner: Alright, let me answer the first half of that. It was quite cold. We did a scene where we used a rain tower. All I was wearing was jean shorts. It was a long scene, and we did that scene all day long, for twelve hours. It was really cold, so it was hard, but I'm doing it all for you guys.

My question is for the whole cast. When you were filming New Moon, *what were your funniest memories on set?*

Weitz: I think it was seeing me on set every day, pretending to be the director.

Taylor: With your walking stick?

Weitz: I grew attached to it because we shot a lot of scenes in the forest. Like Gandalf the wizard [*The Lord of the Rings*] I felt having a stick on hand would give me an air of authority, which it absolutely didn't. I suppose that would be the most unintentionally funny moment.

Stewart: I like the way your clothes fit you. It was freezing cold and he would wear at least six different shirts when he could have worn one big sweater.

I happened to be traveling over Italy with my mom and got picked to be an extra in the film. What was your favorite memory of filming in Italy?

Stewart: Definitely finishing. I felt like I might not be able to stand up anymore. It was such a charged moment when the movie was finished that I didn't want to believe it was done. No, we can't go home because then we won't get a chance to get everything else. It just didn't feel right, but at the same time it felt so great for having a sense of accomplishment.

Pattinson: It's the town square set. The first sight of that was so bizarrely and eerily similar to how I pictured it from the book and from the script. It was kind of astonishing as well. That was a good moment.

To all of you: What are you most looking forward to in the upcoming films?

Greene: I for one am very excited to be able to work with David Slade. I think he's going to be really fun to work with. I'm really excited about the whole intense fight scene we're supposed to have.

Taylor: I'm excited for the height of the love triangle and Edward Cullen and I have to try and become friends to protect Bella. And the sleeping bag scene!

Stewart: I can't wait to actually get pregnant.

Pattinson: I actually think being involved in the cesarean would be ... I just can't wait! [he laughs]

What it's like working with a different director with the same character, and what are the differences between the directors.

Weitz: Feel free to just say anything you like. Don't worry about my big ears.

Pattinson: I had a supporting role in this one, so I liked it because it was relaxed to begin with. Chris is a seemingly peaceful person, so it was just very smooth sailing; everybody knew what they were doing. It was a good experience.

Lautner: Chris is so calm. He keeps the set so relaxed and we're just having a blast doing what we love to do. We're looking at the results and just having a great time on set and not stressing at all because that's how he keeps the set.

Stewart: Chris is sort of the perfect guy to have done this. In the first one, Catherine was very impulsive and natural and like fast. *Impulsive* is the best word to describe it. It just felt like we didn't have to think of anything, we just went for it. And in this case, we had more time to think. It was a bit more cerebral. Considering what I had to go through in the movie, Chris is one of the most considerate guys I've ever met in my life.

Greene: I think it's pretty much unanimous that we all absolutely *hate* him. No. We all *love* him; he was so great. He was really considerate of us and it was really great. And, again, in the first one, Catherine was good as well, but there was a lot more increasing, nervous energy.

Stewart: Which is why I liked the first one so much, but this is a different storyline.

I'm assuming you guys got a lot of action in this movie, so I'm just wondering were there any difficulties performing certain stunts or did anybody got injured?

Weitz: [he laughs] There were several injuries. Kristen went down with a sprained ankle at one point. No deaths—I'm very proud of that. I'm maintaining a longstanding record of not killing anyone on my films. There's a CGI element to this film and an action element to this film that are more intense than in the first movie. It was stuff that I had done before and, frankly, it's really about hiring the best people who know more than I do about it. So it's not like I'm an impresario of action or CG. I just happen to know people who are good at it. I wish I could tell you more exciting stories of horrible injuries. I will tell you that Taylor did every single stunt that he could possibly get his hands on—every stunt except the ones the insurance company said he wasn't allowed to do. So, if Jacob is doing something dangerous or impressive in the film, it's pretty much Taylor doing it and Rob just stood there looking good.

For Ashley Greene: How was it working with the rest of the cast?

Greene: It was so much fun. The cast in the original *Twilight* movie was great and we all get along. So it's really fun to go to work every day. There were a couple of new kids that came in, all of whom are very talented actors, and all of us really got along, which I think is kind of unheard of for such a huge, young cast. I've learned a lot from working with a lot of different people.

For Taylor Lautner: I want to get buff for my girl, and these love handles ain't working, bro, so can you tell me how you worked out?

Lautner: Obviously, getting into the gym and finding a personal trainer to help me. I put on some weight and then randomly started losing weight, and I started freaking out. "Where is all this weight I'm supposed to be putting on going?" What I found was that I was actually overworking myself. I was in the gym six to seven days a week, and I was actually burning more calories than I was taking in. So that was my biggest problem. I actually had to cut things back. Whenever I would break a sweat, my trainer would have me stop and relax. Kristen teased me about that on set a lot.

Stewart: Don't freak out. You might burn a few too many calories!

Taylor: But the hardest thing for me was eating. Eating constantly, good food, but always eating.

Weitz: It helps to eat constantly. You should give a shout-out to your trainer Jordan.

Lautner: Yeah, my trainer, Jordan Young, is really talented. He helped me a lot with this process. He's always on set, shoving food in my mouth. I'll be talking to somebody, and he comes up with a plate! And he wakes me up in the morning, and he says, "take this protein shake", and I'd say, "Dude, I'm sleeping!" I have a lot of people to thank.

How much have you guys benefited from everything? Does it make you stronger, being Edward Cullen?

Pattinson: No, not really. At the end of the day, it's just a part.

Weitz: I'd actually like to add—though I'm sure you much rather hear from the actors—that the last film that I made was recut by the studio, and my experience with it ended up being quite a terrible one. And this experience has been entirely different for both dealing with Summit and dealing with this young cast. As you know, they've said some very kind things about me, which I told them to [audience laughs]. But it's been a tremendously rejuvenating process for me. I now remember how much fun it can be to make a film, and that really comes from the people that you work with.

For Taylor Lautner. I'm one-eighth Quileute, and one-eighth Cherokee Indian. Have you learned anything about the Native Americans' cultures or traditions?

Lautner: Yes. For *Twilight*, I actually had the opportunity to meet Quileute Indians who came to Portland. I had the opportunity to have dinner and talk with them. The main thing I was focusing on is that I wanted to learn more about the Quileute kids my own age and what they liked to do in their free time. I was expecting something really different and expecting to have to change myself.

I asked this kid who looked around my age, "So what do you do in your free time? What do you do for fun?" He said, "I play basketball. I go to the beach." I said, "And what do you do at the beach? Throw the football around?" And he said, "No, I check out girls." He was really funny! So, the interesting thing that I learned is that they're *just* like me. They do the same things I do. So that's that.

It was awesome to have the opportunity to meet with them and learn more about their legends and stuff. It was really great. I'm really thankful that they came down to Portland from Forks.

Weitz: Taylor actually speaks some Quileute in *New Moon*. It's true.

Lautner: It's true. I do get to say a Quileute line. I'm excited for you guys to hear it!

Could each of you touch upon the increase in the size and scope over the first movie of New Moon.

Weitz: One thing that I think was really important in approaching this movie was to notice that its strengths lay in the intimate details, the emotional relationships between the characters. Even if they are vampires or werewolves, they're still people. The book expands massively from Bella's small world in Forks to Italy and the world of the Volturi, and to the world of the werewolves in the forest. The key thing was to keep all that coherent and faithful to the book, and to really try to make something grand and beautiful out of this book.

Pattinson: It was different doing this because of the aesthetic, which Chris shows. I have always found with Edward that his whole character is obviously about restraint, so I always found it quite difficult to incorporate movement as the character. In *New Moon*, it felt as if a lot of the shots seemed to be set up so I can have as little movement as possible, which really helped. It is, I didn't have to drive the scenes. It was always camera movements that drove them. So I just look like a machine and the cameras did everything.

Weitz: You just wanted to expend as little energy as possible, which is how it's supposed to look.

Pattinson: Taylor can do all the energy of moving around. I can just stand there in literally every scene.

Weitz: But you had a good fight scene. It was a very good fight scene.

Pattinson: Catherine used a lot of zoom. There was a lot more handheld shots and it's quite difficult to look graceful when you're doing that. With Chris, there was a lot more flowing camera movements, so you can see it's kind of a dance with the cameras, so even that the fight scene at the end, its almost balletic. It felt more, right, I think.

Lautner: When we were making *Twilight*, we really knew what we were making, but we didn't know the reaction we were going to get from the fans. So we were really thankful over the past year for what you guys have done.

Going into *New Moon*, we know what we're doing, and we know you guys are all behind us. So I think we were more confident because we know we have you supporting us. I'd be lying if I say I've never gotten nervous, because we all want to please you and make sure that we live up to your expectations. Thank you.

We had a great time during *New Moon*, and it was awesome to reunite with the team, to be back with the cast. Chris was phenomenal, too so I'm really pleased with the experience.

Stewart: I don't think you really get to know yourself unless you get to a point that is as low as Bella gets in this film. In terms of what she wants, she's so righteous. I feel you actually believe that she knows what she wants. In the third one she's actually content and happy and she can rest a little bit more easy, but in this one I played an insane person.

Greene: In *New Moon*, I was a lot more comfortable in my skin. It was nice to be able to go into it and not be thinking about trying to make myself not be nervous the whole time. In this one, the relationship between Bella and Alice shows itself more, so it was a lot of fun. The other thing is that we really have the fans behind us. For the first one, we were so nervous because we didn't know what to expect, what you guys wanted, and if you were going to accept us. In the second one, I had a lot more confidence because the fans really embraced us, which has been so great and so gracious. It was just a really great experience.

For Chris Weitz: Do you have anything else you want to tell the audience?

Weitz: There is another scene about three-quarters of the way through the book, where Alice and Bella are racing to save Edward [*New Moon*, chapter 19, "Race."]. This is actually the first time this footage has been seen by anyone outside of the editing room.

The film clip shows Bella in the Porsche with Alice as they frantically race time to reach Edward Cullen who, thinking that Bella is dead, wants to take his own life by forcing the Volturi to take action. He will reveal himself to be a sparkling vampire, which will force the Volturi to kill him. Unless, of course, Bella reaches him in time and changes his mind.

The Twilight Saga, *New Moon*: about the movie

Summit Entertainment. Release date: November 20, 2009. DVD Release: Spring 2010. Stated budget: $50 million; actual budget, unknown.

Based on the Stephenie Meyer novel of the same name, the screenplay was written by Melissa Rosenberg. The movie was directed by Chris Weitz.

Humans:
Kristen Stewart as Bella Swan
Billy Burke as Charlie Swan (Bella's father)
Anna Kendrick as Jessica Stanley (student, a best friend of Bella's)
Christian Serratos as Angela Webber (student, a best friend of Bella's)
Michael Welch as Mike Newton (student)
Justin Chon as Eric Yorkie (student)
Justine Wachsberger as Gianna (attached to the Volturi vampires)

Quileute tribe:
Gil Birmingham as Billy Black
Graham Greene as Harry Clearwater (Elder tribesman)
Tinsel Korey as Emily Young (fiancée of Sam Uley)

Quileute werewolves:
Taylor Lautner as Jacob Black (son of Billy Black)
Chaske Spencer as Sam Uley (Solomon Trimble played this role in *Twilight*)
Bronson Peletier as Jared
Tyson Houseman as Quil Ateara

The Cullen Coven of Vampires:
Peter Facinelli as Dr. Carlisle Cullen ("father")
Elizabeth Reaser as Esme Cullen ("mother")
Robert Pattinson as Edward Cullen (adopted son)

Actress Ashley Greene signs autographs at the U.K. premiere of *Twilight* in London's
Leicester Square on December 4, 2008.

Ashley Greene as Alice Cullen (adopted daughter)
Nikki Reed as Rosalie Hale (adopted daughter)
Jackson Rathbone as Jasper Hale (adopted son)
Kellan Lutz as Emmett Cullen (adopted son)

Coven of Nomadic Vampires:
Edi Gathegi as Laurent (part of the coven)
Rachelle Lefevre as Victoria (mate to the deceased James)

Coven of Italian Vampires:
Michael Sheen as Aro
Christopher Heyerdahl as Marcus
Charles Bewley as Demetri
Daniel Cudmore as Felix
Dakota Fanning as Jane
Noot Seear as Heidi
Cameron Bright as Alec
Jamie Campbell as Caius

Comments regarding trailers

When the first trailer was posted online, some fans loved it and others did not. Posting on www.ew.com, they voiced their concerns. "The wolf CGI: Oh dear. First Harry Potter [*Prisoner of Azkaban*], now this. They can't get werewolves right! This looked like a cuddly toy!" Another reader chimed in: "Seeing the wolf was an incredible surprise. Now that I've seen it again, I see why Catherine Hardwicke thought the budget was too low for this movie."

Mindful of the constructive criticism, Weitz went back to the drawing board and consulted with his CGI director. For their third trailer, which premiered at the 2009 MTV Video Music Awards, Weitz beefed up the CGI for the werewolves to make them truly menacing: They are massive, slathering beasts that positively bristle with power and fury, which is exactly what Meyer had envisioned.

In an interview reprinted on numerous fan websites, Chris Weitz was asked, "I'm wondering since you're so good with CGI, how's the design for the werewolves coming?"

Weitz responds: "I think it's going to be good. We're taking Stephenie's lead—they're supposed to be wolves the size of horses. We've avoided any temptation to go Lon Chaney [*The Wolfman*, 1941] with it, or to make it kind of humanoid. The werewolves are very much creatures of nature. ... Phil Tippet, who is a multi-Oscared guy from ILM, worked on *Star Wars* and he's doing the wolves: They're going to be great. They're going to be fantastic."

I believe Weitz is correct in saying so. The short sequence in the third trailer is proof positive that the horse-sized wolves are *exactly* what Meyer envisioned.

Weitz also has an advantage that Hardwicke did not have when she helmed *Twilight*: She had to do all the groundwork to establish the setting, populate the scene with the right actors, show us the characters and tell us their history, and also get the story underway. Weitz built on that, which allowed him to concentrate on character development, action sequences, and introducing of new characters, notably the Volturi, in an exotic new setting, Italy.

We also see Jacob evolve from being a relatively minor character in the first film to a central character in the sequel when he becomes part of the love triangle that eventually forces Bella to chose between Jacob and Edward: Jacob stays by her side, but Edward abandons her for what he erroneously feels is her own good. This dramatic tension is what gives the second book its emotional power. It's really the time for Jacob to shine, to show his stuff.

Happily, judging from the film clips, Weitz has avoided the temptation to color the film with a sickly green hue that, to my mind, visually marred *Twilight*.

My educated guess is that *New Moon* will eclipse *Twilight* in box office ticket receipts. If you saw *Twilight*, you will be irresistibly drawn back to the theater to see the second film in the series. It's a film that promises, in many ways, to be a dramatic improvement. And, in the interim, the Twilight phenomenon has gathered new momentum, so there will be newcomers—new blood, as it were—who have been bitten by Twilight.

Perspectives

Stephenie Meyer: "I've had a chance to talk to Chris, and I can tell you he is excited by the story and eager to keep the movie as close to the book as possible. He is also very aware of you, the fans, and wants to keep you all extremely happy. Torches and pitchforks are not going to be necessary." (Quoted by Peter Gicas on www.eonline.com, December 15, 2008.)

Chris Weitz: When asked "how weird was it, stepping into somebody else's franchise?", Weitz responded, "It was a bit odd at first. But then again it's pretty amazing to have a huge fan base just dropped in your lap. And it was a pleasure to be able to deliver faithfully on a book. With *Golden Compass* I felt that by being faithful to the book I was working at odds with the studio. But Summit understands that it's Stephenie Meyer's world, and really it's about recreating the experience the reader has, in some kind of faithful manner. Creating a picture that doesn't violate too badly the picture they have in their minds." (Lev Grossman, *Time* magazine, July 28, 2009.)

Screenwriter Melissa Rosenberg: "*New Moon* becomes bigger in scope. The first film was really a small romance in a way. There was the battle with James (Cam Gigandet) at the end. That was as big as it got. With *New Moon*, we have the werewolf clan, we have the Volturi—and in *Eclipse*, there is an epic battle, so with every book, with every episode of the movie, it gets grander in scope, which is fun to write. So, going into *New Moon* and *Eclipse*, I knew who I was writing for. I knew who the characters were and what their voices were." (Nikki Katz, *Entertainment Tonight*, August 7, 2009.)

Robert Pattinson on *New Moon* being his favorite of the series: " "Mainly because I like the juxtaposition. Edward is such a hyped character, and there are so many people looking at him like a romantic hero. In *New Moon*, the way that I read it anyway, he's just so humbled. It's a character who's looking at Bella and thinking that he loves something too much, but he can't be around. He deliberately starts breaking up their relationship, which I think is a very relatable thing that is very painful. And, in the fight sequence at the end, Bella ends up saving Edward, as she does in every single one of the books. It's really funny how everyone looks at Edward as the hero, and he's continuously saved by the damsel in distress. I think he really realizes that in *New Moon*. *Eclipse* is really him trying to catch up with Jacob because he's so out of the loop and he can't speak in superlatives anymore. He's accepted being alive and he needs to catch up to Jacob." (Quoted by Fred Topel for www.canmag.com, August 20, 2009.)

Taylor Lautner: "*New Moon* is very complicated. There's a lot of heartbreak, there's a lot of things going on. Edward leaves at the beginning, she goes into this depression, I come to try and bring her out of it. Then I go through my own issues, and then she leaves me." (Interviewed by MTV.)

Kristen Stewart on preparing for her role: "[Making *Twilight*] was much more of a fight. Everyone was a little more scared. We needed to make something commercial but stay true to the book. We didn't have enough money. It was all very impulsive, and that's what I love about that movie. But I think *New Moon* is gonna be even better." (Quoted by Issie Lapowsky, *New York Daily News*, August 13, 2009).

Ashley Greene: It was fun for me because it was a little more in-depth for Alice's character. It's more about the angst part of it than the love story as far as Edward and Bella. Edward leaves Bella, so she kind of falls into a depression and gets close to Jacob, and discovers a couple more crazy things about the town. We had a blast filming. We got to go to Italy, which was amazing. A couple of us got to go to Italy, and I was included. It was coming back to the people we got really close to in the movie before, so it was like a little reunion. And Chris Weitz directed it, and he was incredible. I feel like the set was so chill and really comfortable, and it seemed like it was all very planned out and very put together so we weren't going crazy and stressing out. I'm excited to see it all put together. I'm really confident that it will be good. (*Saturday Night Magazine*, October 2009).

Hayley Williams of Paramore, when asked if she knew "*Twilight* would be the huge deal that it was?" "No! I knew our fans were obsessed with [us doing] it. I would go on the message boards—I'm such a nerd, I hang out on my own band's message board—so I knew they liked it. Or they liked it until it made us famous, and then they were like, 'This sucks.' It's weird to go from that [small] world to one where you're everyone's game, you know? It's like you're not special anymore." Paramore turned down an offer to have a song appear on the *New Moon* soundtrack. (*Entertainment Weekly*, October 2, 2009.)

The Twilight Saga, Eclipse:
about the Movie

Summit Entertainment. Release date: June 30, 2010. DVD Release: Fall 2010. Budget: not known.

Based on the Stephenie Meyer novel of the same name, the screenplay was written by Melissa Rosenberg. The movie was directed by David Slade.

Humans:

Kristen Stewart as Bella Swan
Robert Pattinson as Edward Cullen
Bill Black as Charlie Swan
Sarah Clarke as Renee Dwyer
Anna Kendrick as Jessica
Michael Welch as Mike Newton
Christian Serratos as Angela
Justin Chon as Eric
Jack Huston as Royce King
Sarah Clarke as Renee Dwyer

Quileute tribe:

Gil Birmingham as Billy Black
Tinsel Korey as Emily

Quileute werewolves:

Taylor Lautner as Jacob Black
Chaske Spencer as Sam Uley
Bronson Pelletier as Jared
Alex Meraz as Paul
Kiowa Gordon as Emby Call
Tyson Houseman as Quil Ateara
Julia Jones as Leah Clearwater
BooBoo Stewart as Seth Clearwater

A clock tower in Montepulciano, Italy, is prominent in the pivotal scene of *New Moon*.

Coven of "Good" Vampires:
Peter Facinelli as Dr. Carlisle Cullen
Elizabeth Reaser as Esme Cullen
Ashley Greene as Alice Cullen
Nikki Reed as Rosalie Hale
Jackson Rathbone as Jasper Hale
Kellan Lutz as Emmett Cullen

Nomadic Vampires:
Bryce Dallas Howard as Victoria

Vampires controlled by Victoria:
Xaiver Samuel as Riley
Jodelle Ferland as Bree

Volturi:
Dakota Fanning as Jane
Cameron Bright as Alec
Charlie Bewley as Demetri
Daniel Cudmore as Felix

Other vampires:
Catalins Sandino Moreno as Maria

Robert Pattinson: Team Edward

"About three things I was absolutely positive. First, Edward was a vampire. Second, there was a part of him—and I didn't know how potent that part might be—that thirsted for my blood. And third, I was unconditionally and irrevocably in love with him."

—Bella Swan's observation about Edward Cullen
in *Twilight* (chapter 9, "Theory").

✳

As with Daniel Radcliffe who will forever be known as Harry Potter, Robert Pattinson will forever be known for his role as Edward Cullen in the film adaptations of the Twilight Saga. The fictional worlds of Harry, the boy who lived, and Edward, the boy who will live forever, intersected in the film adaptation of *Harry Potter and the Goblet of Fire*, in which Pattinson played the key role of an upperclassman, a student named Cedric Diggory who met his foul fate at the hands of Lord Voldemort's "faithful servant" Peter Pettigrew, nicknamed Wormtail.

In the beginning of that movie, Pattinson literally drops out of a tree in front of Harry, Hermione, and members of the Weasley family. Instantly smitten by his undeniable good looks and boyish charm, Hermione (actress Emma Watson) and Ginny Weasley (Bonnie Wright) exchange knowing glances. To Harry and Ron Weasley, Cedric's just another bloke, but to Hermione and Ginny, he's someone they could fancy —their hearts just melted.

Though Pattinson had previously appeared in other productions for the theatre and the big screen, it's *Harry Potter and the Goblet of Fire* that brought him to the rapt attention of a worldwide audience—females of all ages who were smitten by his obviously good looks and undeniable charm.

Judging from the female Harry Potter fans, Robert Pattinson had already begun building his fan base, largely female and passionate.

Pattinson wasn't the first leading vampire actor to be called on the carpet for what was prematurely perceived as a miscast choice: Tom Cruise, as the vampire Lestat in *Interview with the Vampire*, had been roundly lambasted by

Laurie Matthews

Robert Pattinson at the *New Moon* panel at the San Diego Comic-Con in 2009.

one particular critic who famously remarked to the *Los Angeles Times*, "I was particularly stunned by the casting of Cruise, who is no more my Vampire Lestat than Edward G. Robinson is Rhett Butler."

That famous critic was none other than *Interview with the Vampire* author herself: Anne Rice, who later supped on crow when she recanted and gushingly wrote, "From the moment he appeared, Tom was Lestat for me....The sheer beauty of Tom was dazzling, but the polish of his acting, his flawless plunge into the Lestat persona, his ability to speak rather boldly poetic lines, and speak them with seeming ease and conviction were exhilarating and uplifting. The guy is great."

Likewise, the vocal fans' call to arms regarding the casting of Pattinson as Edward dimmed and became white noise when, after the film adaptation came out, women of all ages swooned: Robert Pattinson slayed them all. Though some felt his acting was a tad forced, most had no complaint. In fact, the general consensus was that Pattinson was *perfectly* cast. Twilighters—the most passionate of fans—were now in unison, some even proclaiming that when God made Pattinson, He was just showing off.

Today, Pattinson is a hunted man. Armed with cell phones and Twitter, fans—especially in Los Angeles or New York—broadcast real-time information on his whereabouts. By Pattinson's calculations, he can only stay in any given place for approximately twenty minutes, because someone will inevitably spot him, even if he's wearing a knit cap and sunglasses, and a Rob Mob will then converge on him.

As RPattz (as he's known) explained to *People* magazine, "It's pretty nuts. It doesn't seem very real at all. I just go to these different cities and people start screaming."

To Pattinson, he's just an ordinary mate, an actor who plays the role of a fictional character in a bestselling book series. But to his ardent fans who, on countless web sites, follow his every move and movie, Pattinson is the embodiment of star power, of Hollywood, in an archetypal role irresistible to women who see in him an idealized, perfect man: They have fallen in love with an iconic image, not the flawed human being.

Women, of course, are willing to overlook Edward Cullen's minor flaws: He sparkles in sunlight and is ice cold to the touch; he can accidentally kill them if he's too hasty, and has a taste for drinking human blood, but as they like to point out, no one's perfect—except maybe Pattinson, who is understandably bewildered by all the fuss and attention.

When Pattinson signed on to *Twilight*, he had no idea how his life would change in terms of his public visibility. He hadn't counted on the mass appeal of his character, Edward Cullen. In the book and in the film adaptation, it's

Edward Cullen who stands at the center of the franchise; he's a babe magnet that irresistibly draws women. Like female baby boomers in the sixties who screamed so loudly at Beatles concerts that their music simply couldn't be heard, Pattinson's vocal fans shout their approval of him at every public gathering: a twitch, a smile, an offhand gesture, an innocuous remark—they all produce an instant and sustained shriek from leather-lunged fans who simply can't believe they are in the same room with Robert *freaking* Pattinson!

It's a phenomenon that leaves most men completely baffled. As one female friend of mine explained: "They just don't *get* it. Edward's our *hero*."

✳

A scene from the *Twilight* movie may help to explain Pattinson's enormous appeal. As Bella Swan, in her prom dress, encumbered by a leg cast, clunks downstairs, Edward Cullen is appreciatively looking on. Actress Kristen Stewart is heartbreakingly lovely; Pattinson, in turn, is the handsome knight in a custom-tailored business suit.

Later, under a sprinkling of Christmas-like lights decorating a gazebo—beautifully filmed at the View Point Inn in Corbett, Oregon—the two began to dance as the other partners on the floor leave and give them the privacy they need. The haunting, romantic music of Iron and Wine, "Flightless Bird, American Mouth," can be heard in the background.

Bella says, "I dream of being with you forever." The look on her face tells us she means it. She doesn't want a half-hearted commitment with a man; she wants an all-consuming love for all time, a fusion with a soulmate that makes life worth living. It is a poignant moment as her eyes shine with love, as he looks deeply into hers, and they realize that against all odds and reason, they were fated to meet in a small town called Forks and fall in love: an extraordinary vampire boy and an ordinary mortal girl.

If Bella can find her Edward in Forks, it gives hope to women of all ages that they, too, may be able to find that kind of combustible and all-consuming love in their lives as well.

That is what Pattinson represents and that's why he will be forever remembered in his role as Edward Cullen; like Harry Potter, he *will* be the boy who will live forever.

Film Quips: Quotes

Robert Pattinson

"I spent a long time trying to figure out how to play [Edward's part] without making a fool out of myself. The whole book is written from Bella's perspective and she's in love with him. I mean, the guy could be anybody—he could be an alien—and you see past everything if you're in love with someone." (RPattz on his role in *Twilight*, from http://robertpattinson.org.)

"I had no idea how to play the part when I went in, and it was a good thing to find during the audition. I really wanted it after that, but I didn't really even know what it was. I hadn't really read any of the books. And just from that, 'I want this job.' It was pretty much because of Kristen." (RPattz quoted in an interview with MSN Movies on www.filmschoolrejects.com.)

"I read the book like five months before casting. I read the first 50 pages, up until when he gets introduced and I was just like, 'No.' Because I was really fat last year as well. So it was just like embarrassing. I thought the whole thing was embarrassing, even turning up to the audition. I hadn't read the whole book before the audition, but from its four-line synopsis ("Edward is the perfect being. He's so witty and beautiful. He's crazy and funny. He'll open doors for you. He'll drive you in his Volvo."), I thought even turning up would be embarrassing. (Laremy Legel, www.film.com, November 17, 2008.)

Twilight **author Stephenie Meyer:** "When I found out that Robert Pattinson was given Edward's role, it was a terrible moment for me. Edward existed in my head; he had a face, a smile. I was really skeptical. But when I saw him, I was immediately conquered. I can understand why girls are so attracted by him. Robert Pattinson has done a terrific and impressive job. He is exactly how I imagined Edward." (Benjamin Locogne, *Paris Match*, translated to English by Maddalena.)

Twilight **Film director Catherine Hardwicke:** "I remember when we first cast him. We put it on the Internet, and people were sending emails, 'He's revolting! He's disgusting! He can't be Edward!' And of course, the fans, after we started putting out some photographs of him looking like Edward, they turned around. Now he's pretty much on the cover of every magazine! It's pretty crazy." (From MTV.com, quoted on http://en.twilightpoison.com.)

New Moon **film director Chris Weitz on the Pattinson Effect:** "It was this crazy thing, which everybody was warning us about: 7,000 *Twilight* fans in a room screaming for Rob. That high, keening noise. The only thing I can think of is the Beatles. You see old footage of that type of thing. It happened in Montepulciano, Italy, when we were shooting there. It was like *The Birds*, but with young girls. You'd turn a corner and there would be one or two or three. And the next time you looked, there would be 10, 20, 50, 100." (From *Time* magazine, Lev Grossman, July 28, 2009.)

Actress Kristen Stewart: "Rob and I are great friends. But I understand why you would assume that when we lean on each other for support, there must be something more. And I'm not criticizing anyone for thinking it, either. If anything, they're really perceptive because they can see a closeness." (Stewart dispelling rumors that she and RPattz are a couple, in an interview by Marc Malkin on www.eonline.com.)

Robert Pattinson nicknames: Online, R-PATTZ from the fans. The nickname he came up with for himself: Spunk Ransom.

Bands he performs in: Bad Girls. When solo, he performs under the stage name of Bobby Dupeau.

Web Resources

http://robertpattinson.org • www.robert-pattinson.co.uk
www.robertpattinsononline.com • http://robert-pattinson.net
http://robert-pattinson.info

Books: unofficial

The Robert Pattinson Album by Paul Stenning (very readable in a large format and excellent color photos); *Robert Pattinson: True Love Never Dies* and *Robert Pattinson Annual 2010: Beyond Twilight*, both by Josie Rusher; *Robert Pattinson: Eternally Yours* by Isabelle Adams; *Robert Pattinson: Fated for Fame* by Mel Williams. (Several calendars are also available.)

Contacting Pattinson

Robert Pattinson
c/o Endeavor Agency
9601 Wilshire Blvd, Floor 3
Beverly Hills, CA 90210

Robert Pattinson
c/o Curtis Brown Group Ltd.
Haymarket House, 5th Floor
28-29 Haymarket
London SW1Y 4SP
UNITED KINGDOM

Kristen Stewart:
Team Switzerland

All the news fit to print. *So* not.

OK! Weekly's September 2009 cover story, with a photo of Kristen Stewart and Robert Pattinson, promises to spill the beans: "Twilight Wedding: Rob & Kristen ENGAGED! Weeks after moving in together, Rob proposes to Kristen on set in Vancouver. Why they're moving so fast."

As fans eagerly snatched up copies to get the dirt, they are inevitably crestfallen to learn that the story is purely speculative. "Life *might* just imitate art," the story suggests.

Welcome to the world of tabloid "journalism."

For some fans, the notion that an on-screen romance would blossom off-camera between Stewart and Pattinson is too irresistible to resist. So the scuttlebutt is endlessly discussed online, on message boards, on websites, on blogs, in emails, in text messages, and on social networks online: MySpace, Facebook, and Twitter. There's no escape: Big Brother has nothing on fandom. The problem is that it just ain't so.

In an interview with E!Online's Malkin, Twilight Saga screenwriter Melissa Rosenberg diplomatically told fans that they need to move on and put speculations permanently behind them. "The chemistry on film is so extraordinary. They were beautifully cast for those roles and their chemistry is amazing. I think people often confuse chemistry on-screen with chemistry off-screen. I think people should just enjoy what's on-screen and leave their private lives wherever they are. I don't actually know what they are."

A California Valley Girl born on April 9, 1990, Stewart showed up on Hollywood's radar when she was only eight years old. She was performing in an elementary school Christmas play when a talent scout "discovered" her.

Like most actresses, she has a long list of credits, small and large, and at 19 is poised to become the Jodie Foster of her generation: a versatile actress from whom we can expect great things. Stewart slips seamlessly into a role, loses herself in it, and convinces us that she *is* that character.

Stewart's breakthrough came at age twelve when she played the role of Jodie Foster's daughter in *Panic Room* (2002). After that, Stewart's star rose rapidly; she appeared in several films, including Sean Penn's *Into the Wild*. While shooting *Adventureland*, she gave an impromptu screen test for Catherine Hardwicke, who at a New Jersey Twilight convention in 2009 said that "She has depth deeper than any actress I've ever known."

That's why I stand firmly by my statement that Stewart is, simply, one of the best actresses of her generation, and the one from whom we can expect stellar performances in the future.

Film critic Roger Ebert, in his review of *Twilight*, wrote that "I checked Pattinson out on Google Images and found he almost always glowers at the camera 'neath shadowed brow. Kristen Stewart's Bella, on the other hand, is a fresh-faced innocent who is totally undefended against his voltage."

In the movie posters for *Twilight*, Stewart does indeed come across as a 'fresh-faced innocent" with aching vulnerabilities, and does so with such artlessness that we are convinced she's a 17-year-old girl who is experiencing a tsunami-sized, irresistible force of teen love.

On set, when the lights turn on and the cameras are rolling, she's suddenly in a world where she feels truly comfortable. It's when we see her at her personal best.

Freely admitting that on-the-spot interviews are not her strong suit, and ever mindful that every faux pas is duly noted, chronicled, recorded, and speculated upon by fans, Stewart's interviews highlight honesty over glibness, thoughtfulness over the memorized sound byte, all linked together by a train of thought that finally pulls it all together in the end. In short, she's deliberately contemplative in her responses.

What really interests me are the kind of roles she'll play in the future: The *Twilight* films are well within her comfort range of acting, but like Hardwicke, I'm waiting to see her draw from her deeper depths and give us even more.

"She's really the best actress of her generation," Robert Pattinson remarked to *Premiere* magazine. Stewart, in fact, is one of the primary reasons Pattinson signed on to *Twilight*: he wanted to have an opportunity to work with her.

Websites
- www.kristenstewart.com
- www.kstewartfan.org
- http://k-stewart.net
- www.kristenstewart.net
- www.kris-stewart.org
- www.kstewart.org

Books
- *Kristen Stewart: Bella of the Ball!* by Jo Hurley.
- *Kristen Stewart* (Blue Banner Biographies) by Tamra Orr

Contact Information
Kristen Stewart
c/o The Gersh Agency
232 North Canon Drive, #201
Beverly Hills CA 90210

Taylor Lautner:
Team Jacob

When the word began circulating that Taylor Lautner might not reprise his role as Jacob Black for *New Moon* (and, by extension, *Eclipse* and *Breaking Dawn*), Twilighters howled their disapproval. Not surprisingly, a "Keep Taylor Lautner" petition, created by one Evelyn Brown, went up and soon collected 14,258 signatures. "The movie is for the fans," wrote Brown, "and if we are OK with Taylor being Jacob, even though he doesn't fit the description, then why shouldn't they be OK with it? More importantly, Stephenie Meyer has approved of Taylor. So let us get our voice heard, and keep Taylor Lautner."

Taylor, who then lacked the physical bulk to be the ideal Jacob, immediately began a regimen that would transform him into a bulkier, more muscled, and obviously buff Jacob Black. A martial artist with several major awards under his belt, Lautner knew that no matter how much the fans implored, the final decision to be made by Summit—regardless of how Stephenie Meyer felt—had to address the burning question: Would Taylor Lautner be physically up to the task?

Fans, already smarting from the loss of Catherine Hardwicke from *New Moon*, didn't want to be disappointed twice: They *really* wanted Taylor Lautner and no one else.

The debacle ended when Summit Entertainment issued a press release on January 7, 2009, when *New Moon* director Chris Weitz explained, "I'm very happy that Taylor will be playing Jacob Black in *New Moon* and that he's doing so with the enthusiastic support of Summit, the producers and Stephenie Meyer. The characters in Stephenie's books go through extraordinary changes of circumstance and also appearance; so it is not surprising that there has been speculation about whether the same actor would portray a character who changes in so many surprising ways throughout the series. But it was my first instinct that Taylor was, is, and should be Jacob, and that the books would be best served by the actor who is emotionally right for the part."

In the same press release, Taylor Lautner added: ""My experience on *Twi-

light was wonderful and I am looking forward to continuing on with the team for *New Moon*," said Lautner. "I have been working hard preparing for the physicality that this role will require and can't wait to get started with the filming of *New Moon*."

The Twilighters' howls of initial disapproval were turned into deafening roars of approval, especially when pictures began appearing of Lautner displaying his megawatt smile, his perfect white teeth, and his tight abdomen displaying his toned six-pack.

Make no mistake: Team Jacob is back in business for the duration of the franchise.

✳

Born on February 11, 1992, Lautner's early years as a child actor were instrumental in bringing him, at age thirteen, to the attention of the producers of *The Adventures of Sharkboy and Lavagirl in 3-D*, which took full advantage of his martial arts skills: Wikipedia noted that at age twelve, he ranked #1 at NASKA's Black Belt Open Forms, Musical Weapons, Traditional Weapons, and Traditional Forms; and that one year later, he won the Junior World Championships.

No question, Lautner can *really* kick butt. Now, beefed up and bulked out, at 17, he's ready to take on the challenging role of Jacob Black, a role that becomes increasingly more demanding in *Eclipse* and *Breaking Dawn*.

Jacob's role in the Twilight Saga is a demanding one emotionally as well. The third leg of a love triangle, he's Bella's BFF (Best Friend Forever), which is how Bella sees him. Jacob, however, wants more; he wants but cannot have what Edward already has—her heart. Consequently, in *New Moon*, when Edward leaves her shattered, it's Jacob who comes along and picks up the broken shards and helps put her back together again. The friendship deepens as Bella realizes he's very special. She loves him deeply as a friend, but not romantically.

Even knowing that, Jacob wants to keep what he has instead of what he risks losing: her abiding friendship and her presence in his life. Edward, of course, sees things quite differently. To him, Jacob is direct competition. Moreover, Edward is concerned about her safety when Jacob and the others are in their wolf state because of their reactionary nature.

It's the classic romantic triangle, a plot that has fueled countless books and movies, updated with a supernatural twist by Stephenie Meyer for tweens, teens, and young-at-heart women of all ages. They have traveled rocky roads to find love where they can: love found, love lost, and love unrequited. As Shakespeare, one of Meyer's favorite writers, observed: "The courses of true love never did run smooth" (Lysander in *A Midsummer Night's Dream*: Act 1, scene 1, line 134).

A fan favorite at public events, it's Taylor Lautner—more than Robert Pattinson or Kristen Stewart—who loves engaging the audience, talking it up, smiling broadly, and giving the fans the warm feeling that he's connected with them. Pattinson, with the touch of British reserve, is friendly and polite but self-effacing and somewhat distant by nature. Kristen Stewart, on the other hand, shows her discomfort when dealing with the media and fans—she puts on her game face and does her best, but it isn't one of her strengths. The world of public appearances, interviews, press conferences, fan encounters is much more Taylor Lautner's native environment.

Considering that his biggest role before the Twilight series was as Sharkboy in *Sharkboy and Lava Girl-3D* (1995), followed by a role in *Cheaper by the Dozen 2*, his being tapped to play Jacob Black is a big leap forward: a role that, with each installment of the Twilight Saga, becomes measurably more demanding. No doubt he'll be able to make the transition to bigger roles to come later.

Unofficial websites
  www.taylor-lautner.com, http://taylorlautnerfan.net, http://taylor-lautner.org

Unofficial books
  • *Taylor Lautner: Breaking Star, an Unauthorized Biography* by Lexi Ryals
  • *The Taylor Lautner Album* by Amy Carpenter
  • *Taylor Lautner: Overnight Sizzlin' Sensation* by Mel Williams
  • *I [heart symbol] Taylor Lautner* by Harlee Harte
  • *Taylor Lautner: The Star of TWILIGHT and NEW MOON* by Josie Rusher
  • *Blood Rivals: The Biographies of TWILIGHT Stars Robert Pattinson and Taylor Lautner* by Martin Howden

Contact information
  Taylor Lautner,
  c/o Management 360
  9111 Wilshire Blvd,
  Beverly Hills CA 90210

Taylor Lautner at the *New Moon* panel at San Diego Comic-Con 2009.

Insider's Tip:
Where to Buy Signed Twilight
Film Star Photos

Unfortunately, online auctioneers are not the best place to get a signed photo because there is absolutely no assurance that the signature you are getting is authentic.

There is, however, one source where stars' photos can be found, and at a reasonable prices. As the seller, Creation Entertainment, points out: "Collecting autographs is a great hobby that we personally also love doing, but one that is hazardous if not done properly. Estimates are that 90% or more of autographs offered at on-line auction sites are not legitimate, and certificates of authenticity are only as good as the entity issuing them. Buyers must know the company you are purchasing from and how the signatures are gotten. Creation Entertainment has been proud to offer signed autographed photos for over 25 years. Our autographs are received directly from the guests as part of their contracts when they appear at our conventions."

Unfortunately, the two most coveted signatures are not available because Robert Pattinson (as Edward Cullen) and Kristen Stewart (as Bella Swan) have not attended any of the Creation conventions. As to future availability: it's possible they may eventually make a convention appearance where they will have an opportunity to sign photos but, for now, it's unlikely; they've been overwhelmed by their public interaction with fans and choose to preserve what little privacy they enjoy.

The secondary characters and supporting cast, however, do make the rounds at the Creation convention circuit and, as such, sign stock photos provided by Summit Entertainment:

Burke, Billy (as Charlie Swan): $30
Facinelli, Peter (as Dr. Carlisle Cullen): $40
Gathegi, Edi (as Laurent): $30
Greene, Ashley (as Alice Cullen): $40

Hardwicke, Catherine (film director): $30
Lutz, Kellan (as Emmett Cullen): $40
Pelletier, Bronson (as Jared): $30
Serratos, Christian (as Angela Weber): $30
Spencer, Chaske (as Sam Uley): $30
Welch, Michael (as Mike Newton): $30

Web Resource
http://www.creationent.com/autographs/index.htm

Insider's Tip: How to Get Cast

Many are called but few are chosen.

That, in a nutshell, is the problem with a casting call for any motion picture. The other problem is that, for newbies, the process itself is fraught with mystery, so they are suckers for online ads that promise to give you the inside information on whom to contact, when in fact the information is posted online and freely available.

When Rene Haynes, a casting director, was tasked to handle the casting for two key roles for *New Moon* (Seth Clearwater and his sister Leah), she held multiple open casting calls, including an online call exclusive to actorcastblog.com.

That online call drew over 3,000 hopefuls who saw this as their chance to become movie stars. In an interview she gave to actorcastblog.com, she shed a lot of light on what she was specifically looking for, which is useful for any aspiring actor or actress.

When asked what she looked for, she responded: "I always look for something in the eyes. There's an indefinable 'it factor' that makes someone 'watchable.' This is usually a perfect combination of intelligence, charisma and skill. Whether it's looking at photos or watching taped auditions, I want to see something going on in the eyes. If there's a spark, there's 'potential.'"

She also shared some advice, pointing out the most common mistakes newbies make, which hurt their chances for selection. (1) They want to see your face—not a profile, not a long shot, but close enough where you are clearly recognizable. (2) Show reactions. When the reader is delivering lines, engage the viewer by reacting in appropriate fashion. (3) Don't ever apologize, especially at the preface of a tape or audition. Be prepared and be camera-ready, not unprepared and apologetic.

As Hayes pointed out, "We were looking for the right young man and young woman to bring these important characters to life. Talent that had range and worked with our director's vision of the picture."

She also stressed that just because someone's unknown is no reason to not try out in an audition. "We genuinely were interested in finding new faces."

Web resource

http://actorcastblog.com/blog/?p=106#more-106

Forks High School

A Documentary
Twilight in Forks:
The Saga of a Real Town

Residents of Forks, Washington, are used to seeing tourists taking pictures and film crews from TV stations, but they usually come and go in a couple of days.

York Baur and Jason Brown of Heckelsville Media, however, stuck around and came back repeatedly, interviewing locals, shooting scenic shots, and attending a Twilight symposium held in June 2009. As the symposium's website explained, its purpose was to "investigate, deconstruct, discuss, debate and celebrate these novels in the company of fellow enthusiasts."

Baur and Brown shot a lot of footage that weekend in and around Forks.

In August, they finally spilled the beans: They were in town to make a film. "It's a documentary about the town and the impact of the Twilight phenomenon on the town. ... Everybody that's a fan of *Twilight* has a vision of what Forks is like. In the movie, we get a peek at that. But in fact, they didn't shoot the *Twilight* movie in Forks. So we've actually gone out to Forks. And you get a chance to meet some of the real people and see some of the real places that are featured in the story," Bauer told MTV's Larry Carroll. Baur added, "The project was the instigation of us saying that we wanted to expose this really cool and unique area to the world through the lens of the Twilight phenomenon."

It seemed altogether appropriate that an extended look at the documentary be shown in Forks first, which is what happened; on Saturday afternoon during Stephenie Meyer Day (September 12 and 13, 2009), parts of the documentary were shown at the local high school. The audience consisted of curious locals wanting to see how their town was portrayed and Twilighters as well. They'd have an opportunity to see the finished documentary on October 15, 2009, when it was scheduled for release.

Or so everyone thought.

The big news, announced that afternoon, was that after months of negotiations with Summit Entertainment, Heckelsville Media had struck a distribution deal. Recognizing how inextricably linked the documentary about Forks is to the Twilight universe, Summit plans on distributing it in March 2010, in conjunction with the DVD release of *New Moon*.

Originally, the plan was to incorporate part of the documentary in the special features section on the supplementary disc, but Summit realized it simply made more sense to distribute the documentary itself. For that reason, the dedicated website for the film has deleted all the information it had previously posted, since that's now Summit Entertainment responsibility.

Look for this documentary to be released in March 2010.

Web resource

www.twilightinforks.com

PART 5:
RESOURCES

JT's
Sweet Stuffs

The Sweetest Place in Forks!

FRESH FUDGE
CHOCOLATES
SALTWATER TAFFY
JELLY BELLYS

SANDWICHES & SOUP
ESPRESSO

ICE CREAM
MILKSHAKES
SUNDAES
CONES

PARTY
ROOM

FREE
WI-FI

REST ROOMS

Official Books

1. Books: the Twilight Saga

Note: All prices provided are suggested manufacturer's price at presstime.

With the series completed, the four Twilight books, termed the "Twilight Saga" by its publisher, collectively and individually, are available in a wide selection of formats: print, e-book, audiobook, and audio download.

The Twilight Saga: $83.

The best value for new fans is the boxed set of four books in hardback. Each book is protected with a dust jacket and the set comes with "four collectible prints" (the jacket art sans text), each measuring 5x7 inches.

Unfortunately, the publisher has yet to issue a matching set of collector's editions. Consequently, fans who want a more elegant package than the trade edition will have to buy them individually as issued. At press time, *New Moon* is getting the "Collector's Edition" treatment, so I'm confident the publisher will, in time, have all four available in this elegant and affordable format.

Even more puzzling, the publisher has not issued a signed, limited edition of the entire set, nor of its individual books. Given that *Twilight* fans would want signed copies, especially now that Meyer has cut back her public appearances to insure more time for writing, signed editions are a no-brainer.

Twilight: Collector's Edition ($30)

This is a handsome book designed for gift-giving ($30). Though it lacks a dust jacket, it does come with a slipcase with a decorative design and the cover photo of the hands cupping the red apple. The book's front cover repeats the photo design and sports an elegant silver stamping. The interior page is an upgrade from the paper used for the trade edition; the pages are untrimmed. Printed in two-color ink (black and red), the chapter heads are distinctive with their scroll design. Stephenie Meyer's artistic signature is reproduced in facsimile in red ink on the title page. (In other words, this is *not* an actual signature; it's a *printed* signature.) The publisher has also added a red silk ribbon.

New Moon: Collector's Edition ($30)

Though not available for review at press time, the specifications appear to be identical to that of the Collector's Edition of *Twilight*: i.e., slipcase, facsimile signature in red ink, upgraded paper stock, two-color ink throughout, newly designed chapter heads, and a red silk ribbon.

To be released in conjunction with the *New Moon* movie release, this edition will be share the same production values as *Twilight*'s Collector book.

Eclipse ($19.99)

No Collector's Edition has been announced, but it will likely be published in 2010. No "deluxe edition" is available, either. For now, the best available edition is the trade hardback.

Breaking Dawn: **Deluxe Edition ($24.99)**

Given that the trade edition is $22.99, the deluxe edition gives more bang for only two more bucks. Additional textual material includes an interview conducted by Tami Heide (Royce Hall, University of California, on August 7, 2008), and lyrics for the songs sung at the *Breaking Dawn* concert series at which Justin Furstenfeld (Blue October) and Stephenie Meyer were present. In the back of the book, in a protective plastic sleeve, is a facsimile reproduction of the handwritten lyrics to "My Never" by Furstenfeld and a DVD that includes footage of the concert they gave in New York at the Nokia Theater in Times Square (August 2008). As a special bonus, the reverse of the dust jacket serves as a mini-poster with manga-style art by Young Kim, which will be used for the graphic novel adaptation of *Twilight: The Graphic Novel*. (Kim is also one of the contributing illustrators for *The Twilight Saga: The Official Guide*.)

2. Audiobooks: the Twilight Saga

All four books are available on CD as unabridged audiobooks. Though an audio download is available from www.audible.com and iTunes, my recommendation is to buy the CD because you can rip it to your iPod and, when in your car, listen to the discs if you have the appropriate input jack. (It saves storing a thick stack of CDs in the car.)

Twilight (11 CDs; 12 hours, 55 minutes) is read by Ilyana Kadushin.

New Moon (12 CDs; 14 hours, 51 minutes) is read by Ilyana Kadushin.

Eclipse (13 CDs; 16 hours, 23 minutes) is read by Ilyana Kadushin.

Breaking Dawn (16 CDs; 20 hours, 29 minutes) is read by Ilyana Kadushin and Matt Walters.

Ilyana Kadushin is a singer, songwriter, and actress known for her stage and film work. Her website is at www.ilyanakadushin.com.

Matt Walters is known for his stage and film work.

3. Official Tie-in Books from Little, Brown

The Twilight Saga: The Official Guide ($21.99) by Stephenie Meyer. A long-awaited reference book to the series written by Meyer with illustrative work by contributing artists, this book (at press time) has no firm publication date. Quite naturally, fans are disappointed because they want to know more about the characters and the Twilight universe from the definitive source, billed as "the only *official* guide—the definitive encyclopedic reference to the Twilight Saga. ... It will include "exclusive new material, character profiles, genealogical charts, maps, and extensive cross-references."

Some of this material has already appeared on Meyer's own website, in the *Twilight* and *New Moon* section, with outtakes, extras, and remixes. There's also detailed correspondence ("Correspondence with Stephenie") that contains information about the Twilight world. The remainder has to be written from scratch from her extensive notes, and to some extent, from her contributions to the fan website, www.Twilightlexicon.com.

Given that she'd probably rather write fiction and that promotion for *Twilight* and visits to the film sets for *Twilight*, *New Moon*, and now *Eclipse* are essential for consulting purposes, the book has been understandably delayed time and again.

A "must" buy for fans no matter when it is published, it will be eagerly snatched up by fans who only wish it would come out sooner rather than later.

Twilight: The Complete Illustrated Movie Companion ($16.99) by Mark Cotta Vaz. An official movie guide that takes the reader behind the scenes to the filming of *Twilight*, this full color, 8.5x11-inch book is very well done. For fans, the color pictures are the big draw, since the text is heavily oriented toward the actual production of the movie—something more of interest to film fans or budding filmmakers than to a general audience. The author has published dozens of other books, focusing on film/TV-related titles.

New Moon: The Complete Illustrated Movie Companion ($18.99) by Mark Cotta Vaz. Like its predecessor, this is a full color, 8.5x11-inch book with a similar scope: exclusive pictures prior to the actual film's release, interviews, personal stories and anecdotes, and other proprietary material. In the mold of the earlier film companion, expect to see a blow-by-blow explication of how the movie was made, peppered with brief snippets of interviews from the cast and crew.

Twilight: Director's Notebook: The Story of How We Made the Movie Based on the Novel by Stephenie Meyer ($17.99). More a personal scrapbook of the filming of *Twilight* through the lens of its director, this book offers a lot of information but presents it in a small format that makes reading difficult. As the title states, it's a "notebook" more than anything else: random thoughts, some directed shots, and a lot of notes. For an overview, get Mark Cotta Vaz's book, but if you want a small-sized, intimate book that is suffused with Hardwicke's obvious enthusiasm for *Twilight*, this is a worthwhile addition to your shelf.

Lots of color photos, stills from the movie, storyboards, and conceptual art makes this book a keeper.

4. Movie DVDs

I wish I could be more charitable when talking about the marketing of the various DVDs of *Twilight*, but I cannot. Confusing in the extreme, it's also costly for fans who are forced to decide what they can live with and what they can live without in terms of goodies offered because of the many editions offered for sale.

As the *Chicago Sun-Times* put it, shopping for the *Twilight* DVD is enough to make your head spin.

Target's three-disc set (the two-disc set plus supplemental disc) is the best buy and the *only* one that offers a downloadable version for your computer/iPod—that alone made it my first pick.

Borders offers its "Exclusive Edition" with "dazzling" photo cards supplementary material not available elsewhere, all packaged in an imaginative fold-out casing.

Costco offers an "Ultimate Gift Set" that includes a keepsake box containing a bookmarker, a certificate of authenticity, the standard two-disc Special Edition DVD, the soundtrack on a CD, six collector cards, a watch, and a charm bracelet.

And there's the standard two-disc set that most retailers carry.

Unfortunately, when the DVD of *New Moon* in released in the spring of 2010, we'll see variant versions of *New Moon*, plus *Twilight* packaged with *New Moon* as well. In other words, there will be far too many to choose from, each with its unique selling points. Die-hard fans will be forced to buy them all—a lamentable practice among virtually all the studios that shows no signs of diminution. My advice is to check the fan websites to see comparison charts on what each offers and make your buying choices accordingly.

5. Music CDs

All the soundtracks and scores available in CD are excellent buys. Younger listeners will be more likely to recognize the name of the bands—they skew heavily to listeners in their teens and twenties—but there's enough varied work to interest anyone whose tastes are sufficiently eclectic.

The *Twilight* soundtrack includes Muse, Paramore, The Black Ghosts,

Linkin Park, Mutemath, Perry Farrell, Collective Soul, Blue Foundation, Iron & Wine, Carter Burwell, and, amazingly, Rob Pattinson who turns out to be a pretty good singer and pianist. Stephenie Meyer fans will instantly recognize some of the bands, notably Muse, which has always been her musical muse, and Linkin Park.

Twilight: The Score is, like the soundtrack, a good value and a "must" buy. Burwell, who has scored numerous soundtracks, delivers a tonal scale from dark to light, from moody to romantic, encompassing the atmospheric geography of the Pacific Northwest and the range of the human (and inhuman) heart, as well.

The best soundtrack value for the money is the *Twilight: Special Edition*, which includes two discs: 17 tracks on the music CD; and on the second disc, interviews and four music videos: Paramore, The Black Ghosts, and Iron & Wine (a standout piece that builds slowly, beginning with vocals, as instruments are slowly introduced and layered in, building to a satisfying whole).

The New Moon soundtrack includes 15 tracks by Death Cab for Cutie, Band of Skulls, Thom Yorke, Lykke Li, The Killers, Anya Marina, Muse, Bon Iver & St. Vincent, Black Rebel Motorcycle Club, Hurricane Bells, Sea Wolf, OK Go, Grizzly Bear, Editors, and Alexandre Desplat.

6. Unofficial books

I make a distinction herein between a traditionally printed book and a *print-on-demand* book (POD) because of the significant differences in production values and (usually) their higher cost of the latter.

A traditionally bound and printed book reproduces text, photos, and artwork with fidelity; the paper stock is more varied and of better quality; the book itself may have sewn (instead of glued) signatures; and the typesetting and design are typically more professional. They are also available in most bookstores and usually more reasonably priced because they can achieve an economy of scale that printing single copies cannot. Finally, the text has usually been carefully read and (one is hopeful) corrected for content, grammar, and typographical errors.

A print-on-demand book means that when the publisher gets an order, he prints out one copy just for you. Using a photocopying process (toner that consists of electrostatically charged particles), it's the least attractive printing because text can look gray and photos/art appear significantly degraded. Bound with glue and printed on stock white paper, the book's typesetting and design is understandably problematic: self-published authors are seldom graphic designers. Moreover, the text may or may not have gone through any kind of fact-checking; it may not have been proofread thoroughly; and it may have typographical errors.

For some readers, these are not important considerations, but all should at least know of the potential differences between a print-on-demand book and one produced lithographically.

A book is assumed to be professionally printed, unless it's noted to be a print-on-demand book, which I've indicated with a dingbat [✍]. Also, none of these books are official; i.e., they exist without the assistance or endorsement of Stephenie Meyer, her publisher, Summit Entertainment, or any other affiliated company.

Note: No Kindle-only books are reviewed since most readers don't have Kindles (Amazon's proprietary e-book reader).

✳

Twilight Tours: An Illustrated Guide to the REAL Forks, by George Beahm. Underwood Books. Trade hardback ($19.95), trade paperback ($11.95), in full color; 112 pages, oblong format (10x8 inches), written in collaboration with the Forks Chamber of Commerce. Numerous photos were taken by Mike Gurling of the Forks Chamber of Commerce.

Since it's not appropriate to review one's own book, let me simply say that this is a photo tour of Forks, Washington, with all the key *Twilight* destinations in town highlighted, along with addresses and contact information.

Principally photo essay, the text is supplementary; some of the photos were taken especially for this book by Beahm; others were drawn from Mike Gurling's considerable photo files. Tim Kirk, a veteran Disney artist, contributed a whimsical map of Forks, which is sufficiently detailed to use for navigational purposes.

Twilight Territory: A Fan's Guide to Forks & La Push ($10.99), by Chris Cook. Olympic View Publishing LLC/Forks Forum. Trade paperback, black-and-white; 90 pages, 5.5 x 8.5 inches. ✍

Cook is the editor of the local newspaper and affiliated website, *Forks Forum*. An insider's view of the Twilight phenomenon, this covers a lot of ground. From its introduction: "*Twilight Territory* tells what there is to do and see here, with the basic information needed to find your way around ... These include listings of Twilight-focused shopping, dining, and accommodations available in Forks and La Push." A Twilight-centric travel guide, this book's text is authoritative and there's lots of photos that are only available from a locally produced book. You also can't beat the local angle: He knows Forks and its environs as only an insider can.

Experience Twilight: The Ultimate Twilight Fan Travel Guide ($14.95), by Katherine Kidd. Create Space. Trade paperback, 40 pages, 6.5 x 9.7 inches. ✍

This covers book locations of interest (Forks, Port Angeles, and La Push) and movie locations, as well. In Oregon: Portland, Oregon City, Silver Falls Park, Columbia Gorge, Carver, Coastal Oregon, Vernonia, and Saint Helens. In Washington: Kalama, Longview, and Vancouver. In short, it covers only the *Twilight* movie destinations. It does not cover any of the Canadian movie sites associated with *New Moon*, shot in Vancouver, Canada and the Tuscany region of Italy.

This is an impressive little book. If you want to rent a car and drive through Oregon and Washington, you will be able to use this to navigate to all the known movie sites. A lot of research went into this tome, written by fans *for* fans.

7. Critical Texts

A New Dawn: Your Favorite Authors on Stephenie Meyer's Twilight Series, edited by Ellen Hopkins with Leah Wilson. Borders, Inc., packaged by BenBella Books. Trade paperback ($14.99), black-and-white; 174 pages, 6x9 inches.

An anthology of critical essays from thirteen writers—all female except one male (James Owen).

Academia has lend its voice to the proceedings: papers are presented at Twilight conferences, some of which will subsequently be published in anthologies like this.

Students writing on *Twilight*-themed subjects will find this book especially useful as a model of how to write essays—critical and informal.

Parables from Twilight: A Bible Study, by Diane Schantin. AuthorSolutions. Trade paperback, 80 pages, 5 x 7.9 inches. From the publisher: "Ten lesson guaranteed to spark great discussions among Twilight fans about their favorite characters and great Biblical themes." ✍

Twilight and Philosophy: Vampires, Vegetarians, and the Pursuit of Immortality, edited by Rebecca Housel and J. Jeremy Wisnewski (William Irwin, series editor of The Blackwell Philosophy and Pop Culture Series). Trade paperback ($17.95). From the publisher: "*Twilight and Philosophy* gives you a new perspective on *Twilight* characters, storylines, and themes; and helps you gain fresh insights into the *Twilight* novels and movies."

From the introduction: "Perhaps, surprisingly, we have a lot to learn from the undead, as well as from the way they relate to the living—about ourselves, our experiences, and our relationships with other people. This book aims to help you with just that, asking such questions as: What is the nature of love? Is death something to be feared? How should feminists react to Bella Swan? Is there a moral obligation to be vegetarian? What is it like to experience the world as a vampire? What does it mean to be a person? How free are we?"

8. Biography

Stephenie Meyer, by Lisa Rondinelli Albert. Enslow Publishers, Inc. Paper-on-board hardback with a reinforced library binding ($31.93), full color; 112 pages, 7 x 9.5 inches.

Part of the "Authors Teen Love" series, this is intended for library sales, not individual sales to readers, which is reflected in its high price and reinforced binding.

Intended for young readers, it's a quick overview of Meyer's life and the Twilight phenomenon.

Stephenie Meyer: Who Wrote That?, by Tracey Baptiste. Chelsea House Publications. Library binding ($30). Intended for library sales, not individual sales to readers, which is reflected in its high price. As presstime, no other information was available.

9. Miscellaneous Books

Bite at Twilight Cookbook: Vampires, Forks, & Knives, by Gina Meyers. Serendipity Press. Trade paperback $11.95, black-and-white; 94 pages, 8.25x11 inches. ✍

This was published in May 2009. Confusingly, a previous edition, *Love at First Bite: The Unofficial Twilight Cookbook*, is still available but essentially covers the same material.

The layout and design are perfunctory, as is the format, but the recipes are good. That's not surprising, since the author also published a similar cookbook themed to the television show, *Bewitched*.

Themed food includes breakfast dishes, sandwiches, salads, main meals, Italian dishes (a great touch), desserts (another inspired choice), and beverages (alcoholic and non-alcoholic).

With a more focused title, color photos of the dishes a more imaginative layout and design, and comb-binding so it'd lay flat, this book could corner the Twilight cookbook market. (I'd drop its trivia quiz and Prom Primer—they're just filler. Better to use the space for more recipes.)

The Twilight Companion: Completely Updated, "the unauthorized guide to the series" by Lois H. Gresh. St. Martin's Griffin. Trade paperback ($12.95); 252 pages, 5.5 x 8.5 inches.

Because I have provided a blurb for one of her previous books and consider her a professional acquaintance, and because *Bedazzled* is a competitive title to hers, I am recusing myself from a review. If you'd like to read what others have written, however, go check out the reviews online at www.bn.com and www.amazon.com.

This second edition corrects errors from a previous edition and adds one chapter, "The Twilight Movies."

The book is current through spring 2009.

Defining Twilight: Vocabulary Workbook for Unlocking the SAT, ACT, GED, and SSAT, by Brian Leaf. Cliff Notes. Trade paperback ($9.99); 192 pages, 5.5x8.5 inches.

A tangential book, this instructional text uses vocabulary from *Twilight* to increase a student's word power using repetition, memorization, exercises, and quizzes to enhance comprehension and retention. A unique twist to an old problem: how to get students to willingly up their vocabulary skills. Impressive!

10. Forthcoming books

Defining New Moon: Vocabulary Workbook for Unlocking the SAT, ACT, GED, and SSAT, by Brian Leaf. Cliffs Notes. Trade paperback ($9.99), 192 pages. Second in the series. Expect similarly themed books in the future to include *Defining Eclipse* and *Defining Breaking Dawn*. See my earlier comments about *Defining Twilight*.

Stephenie Meyer. Bluewater Productions (November 2009). A comic book billed as an illustrated biography, the text is by Ryan Burton and the art is by Dave MacNiel. The cover art is by Vinnie Tartamella. Trade paperback, 32 pages. Three editions will be available: the trade edition ($3.99), a "bonus" edition with additional pages about Forks, Washington ($6.99), and a limited edition ($10.99) exclusively available from Dazzled by Twilight. This is part of Bluewater Productions' line of female-inspired comic book bios, which include Hillary Clinton, Michelle Obama, Oprah Winfrey, Sarah Palin, Princess Diana, and (forthcoming) J.K. Rowling.

Touched by a Vampire: Discovering the Hidden Messages in the Twilight Saga, by Beth Felker Jones. Multnomah Books. Trade paperback ($13.99), 192 pages. An assistant professor of Theology at Wheaton College—which, by the way, has a large repository of C.S. Lewis and J.R.R. Tolkien material—Ms. Jones is a pastor's wife who examines the *Twilight* books through a Christian perspective. "Can vampires teach us about God's plan for love?"

11. Websites: Official, unofficial, and fan

There's a wealth of material available online about Stephenie Meyer, the Twilight book series, the film adaptations, the licensed products, and tie-in products. Much of it is repetitive, as fan websites essentially repeat what's been posted elsewhere, since all necessarily draw on original sources: the official websites.

Stephenie Meyer

www.stepheniemeyer.com. This is the exclusive source of official news about Stephenie Meyer. In a posting on June 4, 2009, she wrote, "I am taking down my bloated MySpace page. It was a lot of fun while it lasted, and I really miss the early days when I could hang out with people online. Many of you are hilarious and insightful, and I wish it was easier for me to talk to everyone the way I used to.

"With the MySpace no longer in existence, I can now clearly state that—besides this website—there is no other outlet where I communicate with people online. I do not have a Facebook page, and I have never had one. I don't do Twitter. So if you're communicating with someone online that you think is me, it's not."

The webmaster is Seth Morgan, Stephenie's youngest brother, a student in optometry school. For that reason, postings are infrequent and usually limited to official tie-ins (e.g., *New Moon: The Complete Illustrated Movie Companion*, updates from Stephenie (e.g., the Book Babe auction) shout-outs to readers, and personal recommendations on books and pop music.

Incorporating a file folder "tab" design for easy navigation, the site also includes an abbreviated biography, extensive background information on each book in the Twilight saga, information on *The Host* (reportedly, the first in a series).

Two tabs ("Other Projects" and "Calendar") tend to be sparse with information, which suggests Meyer is concentrating on writing fiction and cutting back on non-essential public appearances.

The "movies" tab simply links to the official movie websites. Similarly, the "Books and Gear" links to online booksellers for books and audio adaptations, with a tab for "shirts" that links to Summit Entertainment's website, HotTopic. com (a licensee), and a vendor in Arizona that was the first to offer tee-shirts online to Twilighters, TwilightTeez.com.

For fans wanting to know as much as possible about Meyer and the Twilight saga, the "Twilight Series" tab is a goldmine of information. Much of what's herein has been repeated online elsewhere, but it's all consolidated here, including "outtakes" and "extras" of excised or revised scenes.

Of special interest: a partial manuscript of a work-in-progress, *Midnight Sun* (a retelling of *Twilight* from Edward Cullen's point of view), is posted in a menu on the "Twilight Series" tab. Naïve to a fault, Meyer gave the manuscript in PDF form to a friend, who passed it around online. The result is that *Midnight Sun*, which would likely have been published by now, is on the back burner and simmering until she decides to heat things up and bring it to a boil on the front burner.

This site, obviously, is the first place you should go for authoritative information on the author and her work. As fan websites are typically strong on news and post frequent updates on everything under the midnight sun regarding Meyer, this site's main strength is its wealth of back story information found in the extended discussions of the Twilight series.

Stephenie Meyer makes an occasional posting, but usually no more than a paragraph of two—enough to make her point and then turn the website back over to her brother.

Book Websites

www.thetwilightsaga.com. Billed as "the official online destination for all Twilight fans," this is an interactive site with 185,848 members as of September 2009. This site is where Meyer's book publisher, posts information about new releases, tie-in editions, and official movie tie-in books.

New fans will find especially useful the reading guides, the excerpts, and the ability to browse all of Meyer's books.

www.hatchettebookgroup.com. Type "Stephenie Meyer" in the search engine. The page links to a bibliography that offers excerpts of each book and video interviews and trailers.

Movie website

www.twilightthemovie.com. A major film franchise, the Twilight saga gets the five-star treatment on this thoroughly professional website that will have Meyer's readers and moviegoers salivating uncontrollably with teasers (judiciously edited film trailers), videos, a gallery of stills from the movies, wallpaper, and much more. Affiliated links include: MySpace.com, Facebook. com, YouTube.com.

MySpace.com/twilightthemovie has 723,003 friends as of September 2009.

The "official Twilight Series fan page," which can be found at **Facebook.com/TwilightMovie**, has nearly three million fans.

YouTube.com features film and fan trailers. The official *New Moon* trailer has been viewed over nine million times.

On Twitter, at **http://tweetpml.org/Twilight-stars**, subscribe to the tweets of Peter Facinelli, Ashley Greene, Anna Kendrick, Christian Serratos, Jackson Rathbone (100 Monkeys), Edi Gathegi, Rachelle Lefevre, Justin Chon, Billy Burke, Gil Birmingham, Jamie Campbell-Bower, Michael Sheen, BooBoo Stewart, and film director David Slade.

Forks, Washington

www.forkswa.com. This is the official Forks Chamber of Commerce site and is the best place to start online for information about this small-sized town with their big-hearted people who live and work in one of the rainiest places in the continental United States. The site is especially useful for fans traveling to Forks, with linked entries to lodging, dining, and retail businesses. The information directory is detailed, with information available from nowhere else.

Note: When in Forks, if Wi-Fi access is important to you, check *before* you book. (Pacific Inn, for one, does have wireless web access in every room. Be sure to check with the front desk and get the password.) If your motel doesn't have Wi-Fi, you can go to the Chamber of Commerce that runs their Wi-Fi 24/7 for the benefit of fans.

When in town, your first stop should be the Forks Chamber of Commerce Visitor Center at 1141 South Forks Avenue, Forks, WA 98331. Say "howdy" to Mike Gurling (the Visitor Center manager) and Marcia Bingham (Chamber Director), both of whom are acknowledged Twilight experts. (They also coach staffers on everything under the midnight sun.)

www.forksforum.com. This is the online version of the print newspaper that serves the local community. Edited by Chris Cook, this weekly newspaper is published every Thursday. Its circulation is 5,000 copies. Twilight fans should go to its menu and click on "Twilight" for all the news about Twilight-related events, activities, and news stories.

www.forks-web.com. If you're planning a trip to Forks, be sure to check out the weather *before* you go. (Traveler's tip: If you want to blend in, leave the umbrella at home. If it starts raining really hard, slip into the drugstore that carries a wide selection just for tourists caught by surprise.)

www.dazzledbytwilight.com. No question, this is *the* place to shop for Twilight-related merchandise in town, with two stores on the same block. (A satellite store is located in Port Angeles, an hour east on highway 101.)

Fan Websites

There are hundreds of fan websites. These are the ones I bookmark because I find them most useful. I usually check these daily, especially in the half year preceding a film release because of the previews, sneak peeks, and excerpts in mainstream magazines.

www.newmoonmovie.org. Consistently ranked #1, this is updated several times daily, which is how often I check in. All the Twilight news that's fit to print online shows up on this site. It doesn't get any better than this. Webmaster Will Wright is one of this planet's most knowledgeable Twilight fans—and a great guy, too. His related sites include:
www. NewMoonMovie.org,
www.EclipseMovie.org,
www.Breaking DawnMovie.org.

www.twilightsource.com. Some of the staffers from the J.K. Rowling fan website (www.mugglenet.com) have spun off and created a site with a similar look, feel, and scope. News is reported several times daily. Navigation is especially easy, with all the key information on the left hand side of the page.

www.twilightlexicon.com, one of the earliest sites, is endorsed by Meyer. For that reason, you'll find postings of illuminating correspondence from Meyer, who unfortunately hasn't had time to update any entries. (She's so busy these days that it's everything she can do to occasionally add a comment on her own official website.)

www.twilight.top21sites.com is a good place to go to find the other top-ranking websites.

Other websites of interest
www.borders.com, **www.amazon.com**, **www.booksamillion.com** and **www.bn.com**. All four carry proprietary Twilight-related books/merchandise.

www.ebay is one of the best places to pick up new and used Twilight-related memorabilia.

www.tonnerdoll.com is the manufacturer of the high-end collectible figurines of Bella Swan and Edward Cullen.

www.dazzledbytwilight.com has the most complete line of locally produced (i.e., Forks and the Pacific Northwest) inspired Twilight-related product, and a full line of licensed product from Twilight's various licensees. It's your one-stop shop for all things Twilight.

www.hottopic.com is a major Twilight licensee, especially with its line of apparel.

12. Travel books

The major travel book publishers update their books on a regular basis, so make sure you've got the most recent edition. Here's some that I've found especially useful .

Arizona & The Grand Canyon from DK (www.dk.com). Well known for its innovative approach to integrating text with photos and art, this full color compact-sized, illustrated guidebook is 176 pages. Color-coded to help you locate the various sections within the book, this is a superb book.

Moon Handbooks: Arizona (www.moon.com) by Bill Weir. Now in its ninth edition, this thick but compact book of 647 pages is printed in black and white, except for a color signature in the front, which includes maps. Exceptionally detailed, this covers the whole state in exquisite detail.

Olympic National Park: A Natural History from the University of Washington Press. For an in-depth explanation of Washington's Olympic Peninsula, which encompasses 1,400 square miles, this is especially useful for Twilighters who want to get off the beaten track and explore the beauty of nature in all its pristine glory. This book, written by a local who lives in the foothills of the Olympic Mountains, does a thorough job explaining the flora and the fauna.

Olympic National Park: Impressions, by James Randklev, from Farcountry Press. No text but 80 pages of magnificent photography taken with a large format camera, which gives a crispness of detail that's unsurpassed: The view camera's larger image area yields image quality markedly superior to that of most other cameras, which is obvious when leafing through this impressive book. Randklev is well known for his work for the conservation group, the Sierra Club. If you buy one book about the Olympic National Park, get this one.

Olympic Peninsula: A Timeless Refuge by Nicky Leach, from Sierra Press. Not to be confused with Sierra Club books, this Press's 32-page offering is a compact-sized overview of the Olympic Peninsula with gorgeous photos and explanatory text. Leach's informal, first-hand impressions of the Olympic Peninsula are useful; you'll get a feel for the terrain, the sites, and the sights that make a trip here essential. Like Randlkev, Leach uses a large format camera that captures images of unparalleled quality: a picture of seastars and green sea anemones is amazing for its details and beauty; the seastars of varying colors contrast sharply with the advocado-green anemones.

The Pacific Northwest (www.insightguides.com). My personal favorite, the

Insight Guide books are uniformly excellent, printed on glossy stock, packed with information, and beautifully illustrated with color photos. With front and back cover flaps designed to facilitate access to the book's interior pages, the front flap has a location finder, and the back cover flap offers travel tips. Each flap, on its reverse side, sports a color map. Within its 380 pages is a cornucopia of information. Perfect for the armchair traveler and indispensable for the real-world traveler, this particular Insight Guide is a worthy addition to your list of things to pack when you head out to Washington and Oregon.

13. Travel Tips for Twilighters

In my *Twilight Tours*, I provide detailed information about the specific Twilight sites and sights of principal interest in Forks. The following material supplements the information in that book with information about professional guided trips, my personal pick of the most romantic places to stay in the Pacific Northeast, general information about Twilight-themed dining, and recommended romantic activities that can be shared in Forks itself.

✳

Touring Twilight and New Moon:
Professional Tours

Given the enormous interest in all things Twilight, it's understandable as to why amateur and pro tour guides take groups to the book and movie locations.

Forks: Self-Directed Tour

If you have a car and prefer to get around on your own for a leisurely tour of the small town that Stephenie Meyer put on the literary map, stop off first at the Forks Chamber of Commerce, which has a wealth of information about Forks and the surrounding area. In fact, it's the first place you should visit when in town.

Do-it-yourselfers may want to pick up *Twilight Tours* (Underwood Books), written and photographed in collaboration with the Forks Chamber of Commerce, which provides detailed information about each Twilight site of interest, along with its tie-in to the Twilight saga.

Dazzled by Twilight Tours: based in Forks

For those who wish to take the guided tour, which covers Forks and La Push, it's up to three hours on a bus that hits all the high points. A great way to see the major points of interest in the company of friends, the tours start at 8:00 a.m. and run until 6:00 p.m. The cost is $39. The tour guides are real Twilight experts who live locally. From its website:

> Experience Forks and La Push Washington the way Bella Swan did. Step onto our spacious Twilight Tour Shuttle and be whisked away to the world of Twilight in Forks, Washington. Along the way, you will stop at locations described so eloquently by Stephenie Meyer in *Twilight*, *New Moon*, *Eclipse* and *Breaking Dawn*. You will see the Swan House, the Cullen House, the Forks Community Hospital where Dr. Cullen works and the Forks Police Station where Chief Swan spends his work days. You will see Forks High School where Bella first met Edward and the rest of the Cullen Family. Then be transported beyond the treaty line to La Push for lunch or a snack at the Three Rivers Resort. You will continue your journey with a visit to First Beach where you will experience the wild Washington coastline and see where Bella first heard the legend of the "Cold Ones." You will hear the history of the Quileute people and see where Jacob went to school and currently lives. You will then head back across the treaty line to Forks. ... The tour lasts two to three hours (depending on size and participation), and Tour Guides Travis and Rianilee Belles keep the tour jam-packed with insider information and offer plenty of stops and photo opportunities for even the biggest Twilight Fan.

Portland Movie Tours

www.portlandmovietours.com/twilight.php

For $25, a mini-bus personally transports you to movie sites of interest where *Twilight* was filmed. The tour comes in two packages: Twilight East and Twilight West.

Twilight East takes you to "the beautiful inn where the prom scene was filmed, and you get to stand in the same room as the stars of the movie. While watching film clips from this popular film, you'll also journey to other locations such as Bella and Charlie's café and the mossy rocks where 'the lion fell in love with the lamb.' You'll get insider information, visit beautiful Oregon sites, and have opportunities to purchase *Twilight* souvenirs."

Twilight West "takes you to the town of St. Helens, Oregon, where you'll see Petite Jolie's, the Thunderbird and Whale book store, the location where Edward saves Bella from thugs, the Swan house, and the Bloated Toad. ... We'll take you to the high school that was used for the exterior shots, where Edward saves Bella from the van."

The Twilight Tour

www.thetwilighttour.com

You get two choices: the book tour or the movie tour, each running three days.

The book tour includes Washington destinations: Seattle, Port Angeles, Forks, La Push, and the Hoh Rain Forest.

The movie tour includes Oregon destinations: Portland, Saint Helens, Vernonina, Cannon Beach, Pacific City, Salem, Carver, Clackamas, Multnomah Falls, View Point Inn, and the Columbia River Gorge.

Forks Adventures

www.forksaventures.com

A five-day tour designed for Twilight fans who are 12 years of age and older, "it's a comprehensive trip: a Lake Quinault wilderness cruise, a tour of Forks, La Push, and the Hoh Rain Forest, a trip to Neah Bay an Cape Flattery, to Port Angeles, and other scenic locations.

Twilight Fan Trips (http://fantrips.travel/twilightfantrips)

Affiliated with Fan Trips, which has taken Harry Potter fans to England and Scotland, Jane Austen fans to England, and other literary destinations, this pro tour group has put on a prom party at the View Point Inn, combined with a tour of Forks, La Push, the Hoh Rain forest, and Port Angeles.

They also hosted Vampire Baseball at PGE Park in Portland, Oregon, on July 4, 2009. (See page 315.)

Let's hope to see more interactive events like this, where fans are not merely spectators but active participants, mixing it up with the pros in an informal setting where everyone can have fun. Kudos to tour organizer Jeannie Barresti for coming up with such a novel idea—a home run!

Novel Journeys International (www.noveljourneys.com) is a new tour group that specializes in tours in Italy, France, England, and Corsica. In Italy, they offer a tour of Tuscany, where *New Moon* was filmed: Six days that cover Montelpulciano, Montalcino, Monte Ollveto, Siena, Volterra, and Florence.

"Twilight Convention at Sea" Cruise (August 8-15, 2010)

www.twilightfanscruise.com

The first ever Twilight Cruise sets sail out of Seattle for Alaska and, by bus, a trip to Seattle and Forks. A convention at sea, the movie stars who have tentatively signed up include Ashley Greene (Alice Cullen), Alex Meraz (Paul, a wolf pack member), and Michael Welch (Mike Newton, Forks High School student). (Kellan Lutz, who plays Emmett Cullen, dropped out due to other commitments, hence the substitution of Meraz.)

For Twilighters who want to take in a convention and enjoy a cruise, this trip looks like a lot of fun, because when you tire of con activities (as if!), you can enjoy the cruise ship's pools, spa, gym, restaurants, lounges, and open deck. The ship is Holland America's Oosterdam, which has a 135-year history of circumnavigating the globe.

The tour group organizer is expecting approximately 900 fans to sign up for this nautical event.

Twilight Saga Vancouver Set Tours (www.twilightsettours.com)

For movie fans who want to see the sights connected to the *New Moon* movie, this tour group offers packages vary in cost and scope: customized packages, hourly tours, the "Twilight Set Blast" (a four-hour tour), "Total Twilight" (eight hours), and the "Twi-Vancouver" (Twilight and Vancouver; ten hours).

Moon River:
Romantic Nights in the Pacific Northwest

Before Edward Cullen arrived on the scene, Forks was not appreciated for its romantic ambience: fishermen geared up for the salmon season in October and November; and from November to April, they geared up for steelhead. Tourism, mostly in the summer, headed to the nearby beaches at La Push or the Hoh Rain Forest.

A vampire changed all that forever.

Now, moony-eyed girls talk excitedly as they walk the streets of Forks, a landscape they know all too well because of Stephenie Meyer's Twilight saga. They wear tee-shirts that say "Team Edward because Jacob doesn't sparkle" and "Team Jacob because I can take the heat."

Each one dreams of walking, hand in hand, during twilight in Forks with her Edward or Jacob. (Insert a teenage girl's deep sigh here.)

For those fortunate enough to be in Forks and the environs with a significant other and can afford to splurge a bit on lodging, here's a few places to check out:

The Kalaloch Lodge (www.visitkalaloch.com)

Located 35 miles south of Forks, by the ocean and in the Olympic National Park, this resort sits high on a bluff overlooking the beach. Their rustic rooms and cabins incorporate light wood throughout and cabins have an open, airy feel with light-colored wood as a design motif. The restaurant offers an excellent selection of seafood, including grilled King Salmon, Olympic Style Crab Cakes, Pan-seared Halibut, and Pacific Northwest Wild Mushroom Strudel.

What could be more romantic than watching the sun set far out as sea from such a vantage point?

Twilight fans can take advantage of the "New Moon-Twilight package" that includes one night's stay, a map of Forks with Twilight sites marked, a Twilight water bottle, a Twilight trivia quiz, and a special Twilight dessert.

Another romantic place, closer to Forks, is the Quileute Nation's luxury ocean view cabins; these are studio, one, and two-bedroom units with kitchens, a propane fireplace, and a Jacuzzi tub. Take a long walk on First Beach or Sec-

Travis Belles, a former Hollywood tour guide, prepares to load up his passenger van for a tour of the scenic sights and sites in Forks and nearby La Push.

Twilight Tours: an illustrated guide to the REAL Forks, published by Underwood Books.

Britton McDaniel Edwards displays the map she colored of Forks, drawn by Tim Kirk, that appears in *Twilight Tours*.

ond Beach as the sun sets; the next morning, wake up to the relaxing sound of waves crashing on the nearby shoreline.

The Shadynook Cottage (www.shadynookcottage.com)

In Forks itself, these are quaint cottages named after key characters from *Twilight*. I've stayed in the Jacob and the Bella and look forward to staying in the Edward on my next trip to Forks. The Jacob may be too small for some people, but the Bella is roomy and lovely, and the Edward is the roomiest.

If you like to get away from civilization, this place is a good choice. Located on a residential street off the main drag, these cottages eschew the usual electronic fixtures in motels: no wireless capability, no telephone, and no television programming (except for satellite TV in the Edward cottage). In other words, if you absolutely must be wired all the time to the rest of the world, this place won't be your cup of tea. But if you're a book reader, this place offers the peace and quiet that the motels often lack.

Veteran Disney Imagineer Tim Kirk, who has traveled worldwide, toured the Bella and gave his approval. Noting that it was cozy and quaint, he felt it was a change of pace for someone who comes to Forks and normally stays in a motel.

Colette's Bed and Breakfast (www.colettes.com)

In Port Angeles, which is famed for its many bed-and-breakfast inns, one of the most romantic ones I've seen (alas, only online!) is Colette's Bed & Breakfast inn set on 10 acres of oceanfront property. All of its suites offer waterfront window views and a private patio as well; and at night, when the sun goes down, you can cuddle up on the loveseat in front of the fireplace or snuggle up in the Jacuzzi spa tub that seats two.

The décor is very Californian—light and airy—and, outside, the garden invites walking, lingering, and intimate conversations on the wooden benches.

The multi-course breakfast offers a varied menu with locally grown food for even the most discriminating diner, including Northwest Eggs Benedict with rosemary-infused hollandaise and smoked wild salmon, Spinach Quiche with caramelized Walla Walla onions, Hashed Dungeness Crab, Cilantro Omelet with cheddar and salsa fresca, Raspberry Almond Croissant French Toast, and Flower Waffles with orange ginger sauce, to name but a few of their mouthwatering selections.

The perfect getaway for a local Twilighter who wants to get away from the nearby big cities—a lot of folks from Seattle find their way to Port Angeles for the weekend—this is a bed and breakfast worth the time and attention that you and someone special will always remember and cherish. For many, a bed and breakfast is a welcome alternative to motels and hotels that may offer a more generic travel experience.

Miller Tree Inn (www.millertreeinn.com)

For a romantic getaway in Forks, this is the place to check into for a Twilight-suffused stay. Informally known as the "Cullen House," this renovated, three-story home has rooms named after the characters in the *Twilight* novel. At night, the outdoor lights and string of light bulbs decorating the house turn on and impart an almost festive, holiday air.

A home away from home with its eight guest rooms, if you've left your favorite feline behind, don't worry: a friendly white-furred house cat named Tunny, who prefers to be the only cat on the premises, can be seen in his favorite place on top of the sofa near the picture window. The feline presence is a reminder that you, too, should stretch out and enjoy yourself, enjoy the scenes of nature from the house, and as the evening winds down, let nature take its course: sit in front of the crackling fire, open up a bottle of wine, and enjoy the magnificent view from the oversized picture window.

The View Point Inn (www.theviewpointinn.com)

Take it as a recommendation: When Catherine Hardwicke scouted locations for a romantic locale to film the finale of *Twilight*, when Edward takes Bella to the prom, she finally chose this inn, and for good reason. An old-fashioned inn with a breathtaking view—in this case, the Columbia River Gorge, is enough to get anyone in the mood for love.

The Inn's restaurant is also conductive to setting the proper mood in terms of its menu; all the settings allow unobstructed views of the grounds. "Romantic, charming, and elegant" is how the Inn bills itself. Once you walk its grounds or dine in the restaurant, you'll agree that it more than fits that bill.

Romancing in Forks:
What would Bella and Edward do?

Guys who want to make a good impression with their sweethearts in Forks can do so by keeping romance on the front burner:

At First Beach or Second Beach, go for a long hand-in-hand or arm-around-waist walk as the sun sets. Then get a fire permit and buy wood from the nearby store. Bring a blanket big enough for two as you find a comfortable place and watch twilight turn into night. Take a picnic basket and fill it with desserts and a thermos of your favorite hot beverage to keep the chill off.

Buy her a single, significant red rose.

Take a long stroll down Forks Avenue and stop off at J.T.'s Sweet Stuffs and buy your sweetie something for her sweet tooth.

Stop off at Dazzled by Twilight and give her a gift certificate so she can buy what *she* wants.

On a rainy evening, buy an umbrella, huddle under it together, and take a walk past the storefronts on Forks Avenue.

Talk a long walk together through the Hoh Rain Forest.

Hire a pianist to play "Bella's Lullaby" at the Smoke House Restaurant.

Make reservations at the Miller Tree Inn for the weekend celebrating Stephenie Meyer Day.

Buy her the collector's editions of *Twilight* and *New Moon*.

Buy her the Special Edition of the *Twilight* soundtrack and *Twilight: The Score*.

If ever there's a formal ball in Forks, take her there, dressed to the nines.

Finally, tell her she's your Bella forever.

The Bella Cottage in Forks (Shadynook Cottage).

A handheld sparkler spells out a favorite theme of the View Point Inn.

The Chanticleer Room at the View Point Inn.

The Roosevelt Suite at the View Point Inn.

The Miller Tree Inn stands in for the Cullen home in Forks.

Cullenary Delights:
In the Mood for Food

When Bella and Edward go on an impromptu dinner date in *Twilight*, Bella orders a Coke and a dish of mushroom ravioli. And when the waitress turns her rapt attention to Edward to see what he wants to order, he replies: "Nothing for me."

Given that Edward can, with the exception of Bella's, read minds, he knows full well what the comely waitress wants to dish out, but he's not interested: Always the gentleman, he only has eyes for Bella. (That's one reason why women love him: He's a one-woman man—er, I mean vampire!)

Thirsty and hungry, Bella bites into the breadstick, wolfs down the ravioli, and sucks down the Coke, but Edward only hungers for (what else?) Bella's company.

✳

Unlike mortals, vampires don't need to eat or drink for sustenance. In the film adaptation of *Twilight*, the Cullens' kitchen is merely show, a prop, though with Bella on the scene, the kitchen finally bustles with activity. Esme Cullen tells Bella, "I hope you're hungry" and Carlisle Cullen says, "It gives us an excuse to use the kitchen for the first time." (Putting salt in Bella's wound, so to speak, Rosalie mutters, "Here comes the *human*" as the other members of her family take note of her snarky tone of voice.)

As it turns out, Bella had already eaten and was obviously wasn't hungry. No matter: It would have been an odd sight with the entire Cullen family sitting around the dinner table with only Bella eating while the others play with their food and Jasper eyes Bella hungrily.

✳

Twilight is peppered with references to food and cooking. To name just a few: Charlie Swan's bachelor cooking (he eats a lot of bacon and eggs), Bella's requesting that she "be assigned kitchen detail for the duration of my stay," Bella's trips to the local Safeway (the only large grocery store in town), Bella's wrapping "potatoes in foil" and covering "a steak in marinade" for a classic lumberjack dinner of steak and potatoes, and chicken enchiladas for a dinner.

If you're in the mood for food, several real-world places suggest themselves. In Port Angeles, Bella Italia is the first choice for any Twilighter. Fictionalized as La Bella Italia in *Twilight* ("Port Angeles," chapter 8), Bella Italia is open for dinner only. Diehard fans will only order Bella's meal (mushroom ravioli and Coke), but in the true spirit of things, any Italian food fits the bill.

Your Twilight-themed choices in Forks, Washington, are more varied, with food named after key characters from the *Twilight* novel: at Subway, the Twilight Submarine Sandwich: roast chicken, ham, and bacon smothered with marinara sauce). At the Forks Coffee Shop, Jacob's Blackberry Pie. At Gathering Grounds, Bella Selva Coffees. At Pacific Pizza, Bellasagna served with Ed-bread, Swan Salad, and mushroom ravioli. At the Smokehouse Restaurant, Bella Berry Pie. And at Sully's Drive-in, the now-famous Twilight Bella Burger: Swiss cheese, lettuce, tomato, pineapple, and special sauce served up with a pair of plastic, white vampire teeth.

No stop in town is complete unless you satisfy your sweet tooth at JT's Sweet Stuff. Stephenie Meyer, who visited the store, stated that "the sweetest spot in Forks will satisfy even a vampire's sweet tooth." In fact, they have her proclamation emblazoned on its picture window. Having consumed with no help nearly a pound of their peanut clusters dipped in dark chocolate, I can second Meyer's observation.

Those who can't get to Port Angeles or Forks may want to try some Twilight-inspired recipes of their own from Gina Meyers' *Bite at Twilight Cookbook: Vampires, Forks, & Knives.*

Throughout the book, she ties her recipes to *Twilight* by quoting (within the limits of fair use) text that explains the connection. For instance, the first page is titled "Bite at Dawn (Breakfast)" and offers several egg dishes: "Charlie's Fried Eggs," "Eggs Benedict," and "Eggs Bellentine."

There's recipes for cold-cut sandwiches, main meal, Italian meals, desserts, nonalcoholic beverages, and adult beverages (i.e., booze).

An experienced cook who knows her way around the kitchen, Meyers has served up an outstanding themed cookbook that every Twilight fan will want to sample at least a few recipes.

In the window of Sully's Drive-in, a *Twilight* movie poster greets hungry customers wanting a Bella burger.

Food & Wine's Recommendations:
Recipes for Twilight Fans

Want a succulent taste of Twilight-inspired food? Check out the mouth-watering recipes at www.foodandwine.com, which serves up ten dishes, each spiced with narrative that explains just why the dish in particular is appropriate for a hungry Twilight fan; e.g., "Charlie's a meat-and-potatoes kind of man, so Bella prepares a fast steak and potato meal like the one in this recipe."

Here's a few of their mouth-watering Twilight-themed recipes. Go ahead and try one out. You know you can't resist a bite!

- Grilled strip steaks with sweet potato hash browns
- Chicken and cheese enchiladas Verdes
- Three-Cheese grilled cheese sandwiches
- Fettuccine with mushrooms, tarragon, and goat-cheese sauce
- Spinach and pepper-jack pizza
- Lasagna-style baked pennette with meat sauce
- Fried catfish sandwiches with spicy mayonnaise
- Cod-and-clam avgolemono stew
- 10-minute tomato sauce
- Salted fudge brownies

Coda:
Stephenie Meyer's Brave Girls

"Because I know, I like to tell people that amongst all my readers I have a lot of writers. Some of them are very brave. Some of them will come up to me and say, 'I'm writing a book. I'm halfway through it now. I've written 80,000 words already and this is what it's about.'

"They're very excited about what they're doing.

"But then there's the other girls in the audience, and sometimes I can spot them. Their eyes shine a little bit when I talk about writing, and they never come up and tell me that because they're shy— maybe even shyer than I was when I first started writing. But I can see them sometimes and I know that they are going to keep writing whether anyone reads them or not, and that's what the measure of a true writer is to me."

—Stephenie Meyer, from her talk at the Library of Congress's National Book Festival (September 29, 2006).

✳

When the seventh and final *Harry Potter and the Deathly Hallows* was published on July 21, 2007, the book industry lamented that there would never be another literary phenomenon like J.K. Rowling.

They were wrong.

Undead wrong.

With *Eclipse* (Stephenie Meyer's third book), the Twilight phenomenon had reached critical mass: Its first printing of one million copies made it crystal clear to everyone in the book trade that here was a new, major franchise. With *Breaking Dawn*, the climatic fourth (and final) book still on the horizon, and a major motion picture of the first book in the series waiting in the wings, the Twilight phenomenon finally took flight and soared.

Breaking Dawn, published on August 2, 2008, went to press with 3.7 million copies. Highly controversial—fans either loved it or hated it—the 754-page novel pushed Stephenie Meyer's literary star high in the celestial vault of the night sky. Sensitive to online criticism, Meyer realized that she couldn't allow the snarky comments to affect her, which in turn would have a diminishing effect on her output.

Her star continued to ascend when the film adaptation of *Twilight* hit screens worldwide on November 21, 2008, transforming her into a nova, a superstar.

It's hard to believe that Stephenie Meyer went from being an unknown housewife to a celebrity writer in only three years.

*

Geographically anchored in a small community northeast of Phoenix, near her parents and some of her siblings, Stephenie Meyer is now dealing with the many horrors of celebrity, including being recognized when she goes out to run errands. The locals, especially teen girls, can't believe they have such a famous person in their midst; she's a local girl who made good. Treated as a rock star—much like veteran fantasy writer Neil Gaiman—Stephenie Meyer is taken aback by the unwanted personal attention. She would prefer not to be recognized in public. She'd also prefer not to be on the cover of a major magazine, because she wants to preserve what little privacy that remains.

Unfortunately, that's no longer possible. She's now a celebrity and people who have never read her books or seen her movies know who she is on sight. It doesn't help her quest for privacy that she's been seen on network and cable TV programs because she's young, telegenic, and articulate; comfortable in front of the camera, she speaks with a warmth that makes her instantly relatable. She's *exactly* the kind of girl whom fans would want at a pajama party—and she's girly enough to attend. In fact, after a formal prom she once sponsored to celebrate *Eclipse* in Tempe, Arizona, on May 5, 2007, she dressed down in pajamas and showed up at a predominantly female-attended pajama party, to their surprise and delight.

That's the secret to Stephenie Meyer's success: At heart, she is one of them: She's a bookworm with her nose always stuck in a book; she's a fan, someone more comfortable being in the audience than being onstage; she's a big sister, a confidante who can relate to new mothers wrestling with familial issues, especially raising children; and she's an adoptive mother to tween and teen girls whom she adores. No matter their age, she serves as an inspiration for them to go out and, like her, realize their dreams.

Her fans, though, want her timeless love story, the proverbial waltz at the end of the high school prom, to last forever. They want to go back somewhere in time and experience anew falling hopelessly in love for the first time with all its heady, intoxicating elements, and get swept up in a maelstrom of romantic feelings.

They want to read *Twilight* from Edward Cullen's perspective. They want more stories about their favorite cold-blooded vampire; and when no more are forthcoming from the author, they write fan fiction and eagerly share the products of their imaginations online with a virtual community. They want to linger for just one more moment in Meyer's Twilight universe. In short, they don't want the enchantment to end; they don't want to see the dazzling glass carriage turn into a pumpkin.

As agonized fans speculate as to when *Midnight Sun* will finally see the light of day, Stephenie Meyer has kept mum.

So, you ask, what *is* she working on?

From the looks of it, she's been working on *The Twilight Saga: The Official Guide*, which promises, according to her publisher, to include "exclusive new material, character profiles, genealogical charts, maps, extensive cross-references, and much more."

Originally scheduled for publication in September of 2008, it's now on temporary hold: no publication date has been announced. Having cried "wolf" at least twice, her publishers are understandably reluctant to announce yet another date until a finished manuscript is in hand.

My guess is that book promotion, movie promotion, and film-related commitments have kept Meyer too busy to concentrate on finishing up *The Official Guide*.

No matter. When it's eventually published, fans will scarf it up like bags of plasma at a Cullen house party on Halloween.

In the meantime, this is a good time to pause and celebrate the salutary fact that, as with J.K. Rowling, Stephenie Meyer has gotten teenagers to go unplugged: they willingly turn off the iPods, the ringing cell phones, the plasma television, the computer, and all the other electronic distractions to immerse themselves into Meyer's world of words.

∗

In "The Ancient and the Ultimate," an essay that appeared in *The Magazine of Fantasy and Science Fiction*, Dr. Isaac Asimov wrote, "When you read a book, you create your own images, you create the sound of various voices, you create gestures, expressions, emotions. You create *everything* but the bare words themselves. And if you take the slightest pleasure in creation, the book has given you something the television program can't."

"What then," asks Dr. Asimov, "can replace the book?"

Nothing can replace the book, because reading is a unique, *participatory* experience between the sender and the receiver: the writer and the reader.

From an impressive first printing of 75,000 copies for her debut novel to the astonishing first printing of nearly *four million* copies three years later, Meyer's books have demonstrably proven, once again, that the story is boss.

For Meyer's millions of fans, Bella is their heroine, Edward is their hero, and her books are their personal brand of heroin.

Let me state it again: In the end, only the *story* matters. Not the klieg lights focused on Meyer as she walks down the red carpet in Hollywood at a major movie premiere based on one of her books; not the countless publicity requests that Meyer's publicist receives daily, most of which are reluctantly turned down; and not the inconceivable fortune in the form of book royalties, which are her just desserts.

Still a young writer who can look forward to a long and productive career, Stephenie Meyer is a born storyteller, a novelist at heart who is most comfortable at telling l-o-n-g stories. Meyer's turbo-charged laptop computer is getting quite a workout: stories about mermaids, sirens, aliens, time travelers—all of these, and more, have been promised by Meyer, who has only hinted about their existence. When they will appear in print, no one really knows, not even her publisher.

In the Twilight world of fandom, her legion of readers are ready to rush to their nearest bookstore to buy whatever she publishes next. They are, in short, bedazzled with whatever she's written.

✳

Somewhere out there are young girls who have followed Meyer's books and career. Like Meyer, these aspiring writers dare to dream. Some will even try to follow in her footsteps and tell stories they feel compelled to share. These young writers, in reaching for the stars, hope one day to become just like Stephenie Meyer: a literary star.

Some of these young girls will persevere and succeed, and make their dreams come true. That could be Stephenie Meyer's greatest accomplishment, her most enduring legacy.

George Beahm
Williamsburg, Virginia

One of Stephenie Meyer's "brave girls," Twilight fan Claire Ruby enjoys *Eclipse*.

Acknowledgments

I owe a big debt of gratitude to a multitude of people, far too many to mention; instead, I'd like to specifically thank those who were instrumental to this book project.

My literary agent and friend, Scott Mendel of Mendel Media Group LLC, who tirelessly shopped the book around and found the perfect home, Underwood Books, which is helmed by my old pal Tim Underwood. I am in good hands with both Scott and Tim, and count my blessings thereby. Thanks, guys. The beers are on me the next time!

For resources and the local angle, I am indebted to Tim and Annette Root of Dazzled by Twilight, and the Forks Chamber of Commerce's Marcia Bingham and Mike Gurling. Y'all are the very best.

For proofreading, I owe thanks to an eagle-eyed trio: Tessa Cox, Jesse Hines, and Rebecca Bowler.

For moral support and advice: my long-suffering wife, Mary; my good friend and artist extraordinaire, Tim Kirk, and his lovely wife Linda Lee; and the loveliest artist I've ever had the pleasure to work with, Britton McDaniel Edwards.

Finally, I am greatly indebted to the contributors who lend their unique voices, photographs, and artwork to this book, including my co-conspirator on *Twilight Tours*, Tim Kirk, again; bookstore manager Tessa Cox; TV producer Sara Gundell; the enthusiastic Rachel Heaton; the talented Megan Irwin, an outstanding journalist; and picture perfect photographers Maggie Parke and Laurie Matthews.

I owe thanks, too, to all the folks who patiently posed for photos, especially Miles Ruby and her enchanting daughters, who really *do* sparkle.

Left: Tim Kirk; right, George Beahm.

About the Contributors

George Beahm is a photographer/author who has published thirty books, mostly on popular culture subjects, several illustrated by Tim Kirk. Beahm has a B.A. degree in English Language and Literature from Christopher Newport University. He lives in southeast Virginia with his wife. His websites include www.georgebeahm.com and www.gotoforks.com.

Tim Kirk is an award-winning artist who has illustrated several of Beahm's books, including *Twilight Tours.* A five-time winner of the prestigious Hugo Award for science fiction illustration, Tim was employed as an Imagineer by the Walt Disney Company, where he contributed significantly to several theme park projects. Currently a partner with his brother and sister-in-law (both Disney veterans) in Kirk Design Incorporated, Tim Kirk's illustrative work has been seen worldwide on a wide variety of books, magazines, fanzines, jigsaw puzzles, costume designs, character concepts for fantasy role playing games, maps, and other product. He lives with his wife, Linda Lee, in Long Beach, California. His company website is at www.kirkdesigninc.com.

Tessa Cox is the Assistant Store Manager for a Borders bookstore in Oxnard, California. A resident of nearby Ventura for 10 years, she has a B.A. in English from California State University. She is, in her own words, "doomed to be single" because of her undying love for Edward Cullen and William Shakespeare. She has been accepted into the Master's Programme for Shakespeare at the University of London.

Sara Gundell is a producer for KPTV/Fox 12 in Portland, Oregon, where she works on the morning newscast. She's also a freelance writer and contributes to Examiner.com. She is a regular staff member at Novel Novice Twilight, the only major education-based fan site for the *Twilight* series.

Rachel Heaton is a teenager who lives in the U.K. and is so Team Edward.

Megan Irwin is a former journalist who currently lives in Portland, Oregon, where she is an education advocate.

Maggie Parke is working on her Ph.D in Film and New Media at the National Institute for Excellence in the Creative Industries at Bangor University, Wales, in the United Kingdom. A co-editor for a forthcoming collection (*Critical Perspectives on The Twilight Saga*), she has also served as the formal programming chair at TwiCon in 2009. In the course of her studies, she has interviewed authors and game designers, spent time on the Twilight set, attended the U.K. premiere of *Twilight*, and served as the official photographer for a game of Vampire Baseball at which some of the Twilight actors were present, sponsored by a professional tour group company. Her travel blog is at www.imstillwandering.blogspot.com. Her website is www.maggieparke.com.

"I'll be back so soon you won't have time to miss me. Look after my heart—I've left it with you."

—A note Edward Cullen gave Bella in *Twilight*